$10

D0741909

THE ART OF
DRAMATIC WRITING

Its Basis
in the Creative
Interpretation
of Human Motives

BY
LAJOS EGRI

WITH AN INTRODUCTION BY
GILBERT MILLER

WILDSIDE PRESS

www.wildsidepress.com

TO

MY WIFE, ILONA

Grateful thanks to Evelyn Cornell, Jeanne Michael, Stanley Ellin, and William Walden —four of my playwriting students—for their splendid co-operation and to all the members of my previous classes who so willingly submitted themselves as subjects for the various experiments I have undertaken.

ACKNOWLEDGMENTS

My thanks are due to: Coward-McCann, Inc., for permission to quote from Moses L. Malevinsky's *The Science of Playwriting*. Covici-Friede, Inc., for permission to quote from *Stevedore* by Paul Peters and George Sklar. Dr. Milisaw Demerec for permission to quote from his speech on *Heredity*, delivered before the American Association for the Advancement of Science, on December 30, 1938. Dodd, Mead & Company, Inc., for permission to quote from William Archer's *Play-Making, A Manual of Craftsmanship*. Farrar & Rinehart, Inc., for permission to quote from DuBose Heyward's *Brass Angle*, copyrighted by the author in 1931. Edna Ferber and George S. Kaufman for permission to quote from their play, *Dinner at Eight*, published by Doubleday Doran & Company, Inc. International Publishers Co., Inc., for their permission to quote from V. Adoratsky's *Dialectics*. Little, Brown & Company for their permission to quote from Percival Wilde's *Craftsmanship*. The Macmillan Company for their permission to quote from Lorande L. Woodruff's *Animal Biology*. The *New York Times* for their permission to quote from Robert van Gelder's interview with Lillian Hellman, April 21, 1941. G. P. Putnam's Sons for permission to quote from John Howard Lawson's *The Theory and Technique of Playwriting*, copyright, 1936; and for their permission and the author's, Albert Maltz, to quote from his play, *The Black Pit*. Eugene O'Neill and his publishers, Random House, Inc., for their permission to quote from his play, *Mourning Becomes Electra*. Random House, Inc., for their permission to quote from Irwin Shaw's play, *Bury the Dead*. Charles Scribner's Sons for their permission to quote from Robert Sherwood's play, *Idiot's Delight*. John C. Wilson for permission to quote from Noel Coward's plays, *Design for Living*, copyright, 1933, and published by Doubleday Doran & Company; and *Hay Fever*, copyright, 1925. Dwight Deere Wiman and the *New York Herald Tribune* for their permission to quote from Mr. Wiman's article, "Advice: Producer to Playwright," April 6, 1941.

NOTE

Readers objected to the previous title of this book, *How to Write a Play*. They claimed that since we cover not only plays, but all forms of creative writing, the title was misleading.

The criticism was justified. The dialectical principles we use here are fundamentals in all creative mediums—as much so as the lungs or heart in man. The present title has consequently been adopted to reflect this wider application and the text itself has been revised and expanded.

Characters in every type of writing must first of all be human beings. The principal aim of all story telling is to expose the inner workings of the human mind through conflict, whether it be told in a short story, novel, radio, movie, or play. This is the principle that this book tries to demonstrate.

If we can be of at least a little help in your creative endeavors, we will feel that our work is not entirely in vain.

INTRODUCTION
TO THE ORIGINAL EDITION

◇◇

I must say at once, in all fairness to both Mr. Egri and to the rules he has helped annihilate in his How to Write a Play, *that his book is far more than a manual on playwrighting.*

It is difficult to catalogue this book in a sentence, just as it must have been difficult to say in a handful of words what, when they first came from the press, Veblen's Theory of the Leisure Class *was to sociology, what* Parrington's Main Currents in American Thought *was to American literature. These books, in addition to casting floodlights into the hitherto dark corners of their respective fields, illuminate so much neighboring terrain, open up windows on so many other provinces of life, that they take some time in the evaluation. Time, I am certain, will deal handsomely with* How to Write a Play.

Being a play producer by profession, I am naturally most keenly interested in what Mr. Egri has to say to me directly, as a professional man. The theater is as studded with rules as is a baked ham with cloves. None is more rigid, none more unfalteringly axiomatic, than the one that says nobody can possibly know what a good play looks like until it has been produced. This is quite obviously a rather expensive procedure. It leaves one with something less than a feeling of satisfaction when, as is all too often true, the ultimate result is so bad. It is no small thing, therefore, to be able to say of a book what I feel I can say of How to Write a Play. *Here is the first book I have come across that can tell why a play is bad long before you have signed contracts with highly paid actors and commissioned various members of seven unions to proceed with the construction of a production that will cost as much as a Long Island mansion.*

I have never met Mr. Egri, but I should imagine he is as much at home in the realms of science as he is in the theater. He writes with the solidity, the authority, the ease that, it seems to me, comes only from knowing more than one profession. He writes with the sort of hard, shining clarity that comes of surefootedness in all the nooks and crannies, all the mountains and valleys of life itself. This man, you feel, has been around a long time and in many places. He has understood much and learned more than most. Mr. Egri writes like a very wise man.

The best of the many things I can say for How to Write a Play *is that from now on the average person, including myself, will have no excuse for inarticulateness. Once you read Mr. Egri's book you will know why any novel, any movie, any play, any short story was boring, or, more important, why it was exciting.*

I feel that this book will greatly influence the American theater and the public as well.

GILBERT MILLER

CONTENTS

FOREWORD

◆◇

The Importance of Being Important

DURING the classic time of Greece a terrible thing happened in one of the temples. One night the statue of Zeus was mysteriously smashed and desecrated.

A tremendous uproar arose among the inhabitants. They feared the vengeance of the gods.

The town criers walked the city streets commanding the criminal to appear without delay before the Elders to receive his just punishment.

The perpetrator naturally had no desire to give himself up. In fact, a week later another statue of a god was destroyed.

Now the people suspected that a madman was loose. Guards were posted and at last their vigilance was rewarded; the culprit was caught.

He was asked,

"Do you know what fate awaits you?"

"Yes," he answered, almost cheerfully. "Death."

"Aren't you afraid to die?"

"Yes, I am."

"Then why did you commit a crime which you knew was punishable by death?"

The man swallowed hard and then answered,

"I am a nobody. All my life I've been a nobody. I've never done anything to distinguish myself and I knew I never would. I wanted to do something to make people notice me . . . and remember me."

After a moment's silence he added, "Only those people die

who are forgotten. I feel death is a small price to pay for immortality!"

*   *   *

Immortality!

Yes, we all crave attention. We want to be important, immortal. We want to do things that will make people exclaim, "Isn't he wonderful?"

If we can't create something useful or beautiful . . . we shall certainly create something else: trouble, for instance.

Just think of your aunt Helen, the family gossip. (We all have one.) She causes hard feelings, suspicion, and subsequent arguments. Why does she do it? She wants to be important, of course, and if she can achieve this only by means of gossip or lying, she will not, for one moment, hesitate to gossip or lie.

The urge to be outstanding is a fundamental necessity in our lives. All of us, at all times, crave attention. Self-consciousness, even reclusiveness, springs from the desire to be important. If failure arouses compassion or pity, then failure might become an end in itself.

Take your brother-in-law Joe. He's always running after women. Why? He's a good provider, a good father, and strangely enough, a good husband. But there is something missing in his life. He is not important enough to himself, to his family, and to the world. His affairs have become the focal point of his existence. Each new conquest makes him feel more important; he feels he has accomplished something. Joe would be surprised to learn that his craving for women is a substitute for the creation of something more significant.

Motherhood is a creation. It is the beginning of immortality. Perhaps this is one of the reasons women are less inclined toward philandering than men.

The greatest injustice imposed upon a mother is when her grown up children, out of sheer love and consideration, keep their troubles from her. They make her feel unimportant.

Without exception everyone was born with creative ability.
It is essential that people be given the opportunity to express
themselves. If Balzac, De Maupassant, O. Henry, hadn't learned
to write, they might have become inveterate liars, instead of
great writers.

Every human being needs an outlet for his inborn creative
talent. If you feel you would like to write, then write. Perhaps you are afraid that lack of a higher education might re-
tard you from real accomplishment? Forget it. Many great
writers, Shakespeare, Ibsen, George Bernard Shaw, to mention
a few, never saw the inside of a college.

Even if you will never be a genius, your enjoyment of life
can still be great.

If writing holds no lure for you, you might learn to sing,
dance, or play an instrument well enough to entertain your
guests. This belongs in the realm of "art" too.

Yes, we want to be noticed. We want to be remembered.
We want to be important! We can achieve a degree of importance by expressing ourselves in the medium which best suits
our particular talents. You never know where your avocation
will lead you.

Even if you fail commercially, you might very well emerge
from your experience an authority on the subject you learned
so much about. You'll be richer in experience—and if you
have been kept out of mischief, that alone will be a great
accomplishment.

So the gnawing hunger to be important will be satisfied at
last without harm to anyone.

PREFACE

◇◇◇

THIS book was written not only for authors and playwrights, but for the general public. If the reading public understands the mechanism of writing, if that public becomes aware of the hardships, the tremendous effort that goes into any and all literary work, appreciation will become more spontaneous.

The reader will find at the end of this book synopses of plays, analyzed according to dialectics. We hope these will add to the reader's understanding of novels and short stories in general, and of plays and movies in particular.

We shall discuss plays in this book without acclaiming or dismissing each one in its entirety. When we quote passages to illustrate a point, we are not necessarily approving the whole play.

We deal with both modern and classical plays. There is an emphasis on the classics because most modern plays are too soon forgotten. Most intelligent people are familiar with the classics and they are always available for study.

We have based our theory on the eternally changing "character" who forever reacts, almost violently, to constantly changing internal and external stimuli.

What is the fundamental make-up of a human being, any human being—perhaps you, who are reading these very lines? This question must be answered before we can settle down to discuss "point of attack," "orchestration," and the rest. We must know more about the biology of the subject that we see later, in movement.

We begin with a dissection of "premise," "character," and

"conflict." This is to give the reader an inkling of that power which will drive a character to greater heights or to his destruction.

A builder who does not know the material he is forced to work with courts disaster. In our case, the materials are "premise," "character," and "conflict." Before knowing all these in their minutest detail, it is useless to speak of how to write a play. We hope the reader will find this approach helpful.

In this book we propose to show a new approach to writing in general, and to playwriting in particular. This approach is based on the natural law of dialectics.

Great plays, written by immortal authors, have come down to us through the ages. Yet even geniuses often wrote very bad plays.

Why? Because they wrote on the basis of instinct, rather than from exact knowledge. Instinct may lead a man once, or several times, to create a masterpiece, but as sheer instinct it may lead him just as often to create a failure.

Authorities have listed the laws governing the science of playwriting. Aristotle, the first and undoubtedly the most important influence on the drama, said 2500 years ago:

Most important of all is the structure of the incidents, not of man, but of action and life.

Aristotle *denied* the importance of character, and his influence persists today. Others have declared character the all-important factor in any type of writing. Lope de Vega, the sixteenth-century Spanish dramatist, gave this outline:

In the first act set forth the case. In the second weave together the events, in such wise that until the middle of the third act one may hardly guess the outcome. Always trick expectancy; and hence it may come to pass that something quite far from what is promised may be left to the understanding.

The German critic and playwright Lessing wrote:

The strictest observation of the rules cannot outweigh the smallest fault in a character.

The French dramatist Corneille wrote:

It is certain that there are laws of the drama, since it is an art; but it is not certain what these laws are.

And so on, all contradicting one another. Some go so far as to claim that there can be no rules whatsoever. This is the strangest view of all. We know there are rules for eating, walking, and breathing; we know there are rules for painting, music, dancing, flying, and bridge building; we know there are rules for every manifestation of life and nature—why, then, should writing be the sole exception? Obviously, it is not.

Some writers who have tried to list rules have told us that a play is made up of different parts: theme, plot, incidents, conflict, complications, obligatory scene, atmosphere, dialogue, and climax. Books have been written on each of these parts, explaining and analyzing them for the student.

These authors have treated their subject matter honestly. They have studied the work of other men in the same field. They have written plays of their own and learned from their own experience. But the reader has never been satisfied. Something was missing. The student still did not understand the relationship between complication, tension, conflict, and mood or what any of these or kindred topics related to playmaking had to do with the good play he wanted to write. He knew what was meant by "theme," but when he tried to apply this knowledge he was lost. After all, William Archer said theme was unnecessary. Percival Wilde said it was necessary at the *beginning*, but must be buried so deeply that no one could detect it. Which was right?

Then consider the so-called obligatory scene. Some authorities said it was vital; others said there was no such thing. And *why* was it vital—if it was? Or why wasn't it—if it wasn't? Each textbook writer explained his own pet theory, but not one of them related it to the whole in such a way as to help the student. The *unifying* force was missing.

We believe that obligatory scene, tension, atmosphere, and the rest are superfluous. *They are the effect of something much more important.* It is useless to tell a playwright that he needs an obligatory scene, or that his play lacks tension or complication, unless you can tell him how to achieve these things. And a definition is not the answer.

There must be something to *generate* tension, something to *create* complication, without any conscious attempt on the playwright's part to do so. There must be a force which will unify all parts, a force out of which they will grow as naturally as limbs grow from the body. We think we know what that force is: human character, in all its infinite ramifications and dialectical contradictions.

Not for a moment do we believe that this book has said the last word on playwriting. On the contrary. Breaking a new road, one makes many mistakes and sometimes becomes inarticulate. Those coming after us will dig deeper and bring this dialectical approach to writing to a more crystallized form than we ever hope to do. This book, using a dialectical approach, is itself subject to the laws of dialectics. The theory advanced here is a *thesis*. Its contradiction will be the *antithesis*. From the two will be formed a *synthesis*, uniting both the thesis and antithesis. This is the road to truth.

THE ART OF
DRAMATIC WRITING

I

PREMISE

◇◇◇

A MAN sits in his workshop, busy with an invention of wheels and springs. You ask him what the gadget is, what it is meant to do. He looks at you confidingly and whispers: "I really don't know."

Another man rushes down the street, panting for breath. You intercept him and ask where he is going. He gasps: "How should I know where I'm going? I am on my way."

Your reaction—and ours, and the world's—is that these two men are a little mad. Every sensible invention must have a purpose, every planned sprint a destination.

Yet, fantastic as it seems, this simple necessity has not made itself felt to any extent in the theater. Reams of paper bear miles of writing—all of it without any point at all. There is much feverish activity, a great deal of get-up-and-go, but no one seems to know where he is going.

Everything has a purpose, or premise. Every second of our life has its own premise, whether or not we are conscious of it at the time. That premise may be as simple as breathing or as complex as a vital emotional decision, but it is always there.

We may not succeed in proving each tiny premise, but that in no way alters the fact that there was one we meant to prove. Our attempt to cross the room may be impeded by an unobserved footstool, but our premise existed nevertheless.

The premise of each second contributes to the premise of the minute of which it is part, just as each minute gives its bit of life to the hour, and the hour to the day. And so, at the end, there is a premise for every life.

Webster's International Dictionary says:

Premise: a proposition antecedently supposed or proved; a basis of argument. A proposition stated or assumed as leading to a conclusion.

Others, especially men of the theater, have had different words for the same thing: theme, thesis, root idea, central idea, goal, aim, driving force, subject, purpose, plan, plot, basic emotion.

For our own use we choose the word "premise" because it contains all the elements the other words try to express and because it is less subject to misinterpretation.

Ferdinand Brunetière demands a "goal" in the play to start with. This is premise.

John Howard Lawson: "The root-idea is the beginning of the process." He means premise.

Professor Brander Matthews: "A play needs to have a theme." It must be the premise.

Professor George Pierce Baker, quoting Dumas the younger: "How can you tell what road to take unless you know where you are going?" The premise will show you the road.

They all mean one thing: you must have a premise for your play.

Let us examine a few plays and see whether they have premises.

Romeo and Juliet

The play starts with a deadly feud between two families, the Capulets and the Montagues. The Montagues have a son, Romeo, and the Capulets a daughter, Juliet. The youngsters' love for each other is so great that they forget the traditional hate between their two families. Juliet's parents try to force her to marry Count Paris, and, unwilling to do this, she goes to the good friar, her friend, for advice. He tells her to take a strong sleeping draught on the eve of her wedding which will make her seemingly dead for forty-two hours. Juliet follows his advice. Everyone thinks her dead. This starts the onrushing tragedy for the two lovers. Romeo, believing Juliet really dead, drinks poison and dies beside her. When Juliet awakens and finds Romeo dead, without hesitation she decides to unite with him in death.

This play obviously deals with love. But there are many kinds of love. No doubt this was a *great* love, since the two lovers not only defied family tradition and hate, but threw away life to unite in death. The premise, then, as we see it is: "*Great love defies even death.*"

King Lear

The King's trust in his two daughters is grievously misplaced. They strip him of all his authority, degrade him, and he dies insane, a broken, humiliated old man.

Lear trusts his oldest daughters implicitly. Because he believes their glittering words, he is destroyed.

A vain man believes flattery and trusts those who flatter him. But those who flatter cannot be trusted, and those who believe the flatterers are courting disaster.

It seems, then, that "*Blind trust leads to destruction*" is the premise of this play.

Macbeth

Macbeth and Lady Macbeth, in their ruthless ambition to achieve their goal, decide to kill King Duncan. Then, to strengthen himself in his position, Macbeth hires assassins to kill Banquo, whom he fears. Later, he is forced to commit still more murders in order to entrench himself more securely in the position he has reached through murder. Finally, the nobles and his own subjects become so aroused that they rise against him, and Macbeth perishes as he lived—by the sword. Lady Macbeth dies of haunting fear.

What can be the premise of this play? The question is, what is the motivating force? No doubt it is ambition. What kind of ambition? Ruthless, since it is drenched in blood. Macbeth's downfall was foreshadowed in the very method by which he achieved his ambition. So, as we see, the premise for *Macbeth* is: *"Ruthless ambition leads to its own destruction."*

Othello

Othello finds Desdemona's handkerchief in Cassio's lodging. It had been taken there by Iago for the very purpose of making him jealous. Othello therefore kills Desdemona and plunges a dagger into his own heart.

Here the leading motivation is jealousy. No matter what caused this green-eyed monster to raise its ugly head, the important thing is that jealousy is the motivating force in this play, and since Othello kills not only Desdemona but himself as well, the premise, as we see it, is: *"Jealousy destroys itself and the object of its love."*

Ghosts, BY IBSEN

The basic idea is heredity. The play grew out of a Biblical quotation which is the premise: *"The sins of the fathers are visited on the children."* Every word uttered, every move made, every conflict in the play, comes about because of this premise.

Dead End, BY SIDNEY KINGSLEY

Here the author obviously wants to show and prove that *"Poverty encourages crime."* He does.

Excursion, BY VICTOR WOLFSON

A few people on an excursion boat, with the help of the captain, want to escape reality. To their sorrow, they find that this is utterly impossible. Reality shatters their dream of escape. For this play, then, the premise is: *"Fear of reality leads to disappointment."*

Juno and the Paycock, BY SEAN O'CASEY

Captain Boyle, a shiftless, boastful drinker, is told that a rich relative died and left him a large sum of money, which will shortly be paid to him. Immediately Boyle and his wife, Juno, prepare themselves for a life of ease: they borrow money from neighbors on the strength of the coming inheritance, buy gaudy furniture, and Boyle spends large sums on drink. It later develops that the inheritance will never come to them, because the will was worded vaguely. The angry creditors descend on them and strip the house. Woe piles on woe: Boyle's daughter, having been seduced, is about to have a baby; his son is killed, and his wife and daughter leave him. At the end, Boyle has nothing left; he has hit bottom.

Premise: *"Shiftlessness leads to ruin."*

Shadow and Substance, BY PAUL VINCENT CARROLL

Thomas Skeritt, canon in a small Irish community, refuses to admit that his servant, Bridget, has really seen visions of Saint Bridget, her patron saint. Thinking her mentally deranged, he tries to send her away on a vacation and, above all, refuses to perform a miracle which, according to the servant, Saint Bridget requests of him. In trying to rescue a schoolmaster from an angry crowd, Bridget is killed, and the canon loses his pride before the girl's pure, simple faith.

Premise: *"Faith conquers pride."*

We are not sure that the author of *Juno and the Paycock* knew that his premise was *"Shiftlessness leads to ruin."* The son's death, for instance, has nothing to do with the main concept of the drama. Sean O'Casey has excellent character studies, but the second act stands still because he had only a nebulous idea to start his play with. That is why he missed writing a truly great play.

Shadow and Substance, on the other hand, has two premises. In the first two acts and the first three quarters of the last act, the premise is: *"Intelligence conquers superstition."* At the end, suddenly and without warning, "intelligence" of the premise changes to "faith," and "superstition" to "pride." The canon—the pivotal character—changes like a chameleon into something he was not a few moments before. The play becomes muddled in consequence.

Every good play must have a well-formulated premise. There may be more than one way to phrase the premise, but, however it is phrased, the thought must be the same.

Playwrights usually get an idea, or are struck by an unusual situation, and decide to write a play around it.

The question is whether that idea, or that situation, provides sufficient basis for a play. Our answer is no, although we are aware that out of a thousand playwrights, nine hundred and ninety-nine start this way.

No idea, and no situation, was ever strong enough to carry you through to its logical conclusion *without a clear-cut premise.*

If you have no such premise, you may modify, elaborate, vary your original idea or situation, or even lead yourself into another situation, but you will not know where you are going. You will flounder, rack your brain to invent further situations to round out your play. You may find these situations—and you will still be without a play.

You must have a premise—a premise which will lead you unmistakably to the goal your play hopes to reach.

Moses L. Malevinsky says in *The Science of Playwrighting:*

Emotion, or the elements in or of an emotion, constitute the basic things in life. Emotion is life. Life is emotion. Therefore emotion is drama. Drama is emotion.

No emotion ever made, or ever will make, a good play if

we do not know *what kind of forces* set emotion going. Emotion, to be sure, is as necessary to a play as barking to a dog.

Mr. Malevinsky's contention is that if you accept his basic principle, emotion, your problem is solved. He gives you a list of basic emotions—desire, fear, pity, love, hate—any one of which, he says, is a sound base for your play. Perhaps. But it will never help you to write a *good* play, because it designates no goal. Love, hate, any basic emotion, is merely an emotion. It may revolve around itself, destroying, building—and getting nowhere.

It may be that an emotion does find itself a goal and surprises even the author. But this is an accident and far too uncertain to offer the young playwright as a method. Our aim is to eliminate chance and accident. Our aim is to point a road on which anyone who can write may travel and eventually find himself with a sure approach to drama. So, the very first thing you must have is a premise. And it must be a premise worded so that anyone can understand it as the author intended it to be understood. An unclear premise is as bad as no premise at all.

The author using a badly worded, false, or badly constructed premise finds himself filling space and time with pointless dialogue—even action—and not getting anywhere near the proof of his premise. Why? Because he has no direction.

Let us suppose that we want to write a play about a frugal character. Shall we make fun of him? Shall we make him ridiculous, or tragic? We don't know, yet. We have only an idea, which is to depict a frugal man. Let us pursue the idea further. Is it wise to be frugal? To a degree, yes. But we do not want to write about a man who is moderate, who is prudent, who wisely saves for a rainy day. Such a man is not frugal; he is farsighted. We are looking for a man who is so frugal he denies himself bare necessities. His insane frugality is such that he loses more in the end than he gains. We now have the premise for our play: *"Frugality leads to waste."*

The above premise—for that matter, every good premise —is composed of three parts, each of which is essential to a good play. Let us examine *"Frugality leads to waste."* The first part of this premise suggests character—a frugal character. The second part, *"leads to,"* suggests conflict, and the third part, *"waste,"* suggests the end of the play.

Let us see if this is so. *"Frugality leads to waste."* The premise suggests a frugal person who, in his eagerness to save his money, refuses to pay his taxes. This act necessarily evokes a counteraction—conflict—from the state, and the frugal person is forced to pay triple the original amount.

"Frugality," then, suggests character; *"leads to"* suggests conflict; *"waste"* suggests the end of the play.

A good premise is a thumbnail synopsis of your play.

Here are a few other premises:

Bitterness leads to false gaiety.
Foolish generosity leads to poverty.
Honesty defeats duplicity.
Heedlessness destroys friendship.
Ill-temper leads to isolation.
Materialism conquers mysticism.
Prudishness leads to frustration.
Bragging leads to humiliation.
Confusion leads to frustration.
Craftiness digs its own grave.
Dishonesty leads to exposure.
Dissipation leads to self-destruction.
Egotism leads to loss of friends.
Extravagance leads to destitution.
Fickleness leads to loss of self-esteem.

Although these are only flat statements, they contain all that is required of a well-constructed premise: character, conflict, and conclusion. What is wrong, then? What is missing? The author's conviction is missing. Until he takes sides, there is no play. Only when he champions one side of the issue does the premise spring to life. *Does* egotism lead to loss of friends? Which side will you take? We, the readers or spectators of your play, do not necessarily agree with your conviction. Through your play you must therefore prove to us the validity of your contention.

QUESTION: I am a bit confused. Do you mean to tell me that without a clear-cut premise I can't start to write a play?

ANSWER: Of course you can. There are many ways to find your premise. Here is one.

If you notice enough peculiarities in your Aunt Clara or Uncle Joshua, for instance, you may feel they possess excellent material for a play, but you will probably not think of a premise immediately. They are exciting characters, so you study their behavior, watch every step they make. You decide that Aunt Clara, though a religious fanatic, is a busybody, a gossip. She butts into everybody's affairs. Perhaps you know of several couples who separated because of Aunt Clara's malicious interference. You still have no premise. You have no idea yet what makes this woman do what she does. Why does Aunt Clara take such devilish joy in making a lot of trouble for innocent people?

Since you intend to write a play about her because her character fascinates you, you'll try to discover as much as possible about her past and present. The moment you start on your fact-finding journey, whether you know it or not, you have taken the first step toward finding a premise. *The premise is the motivating power behind everything we do.* So you will ask questions of your relatives and of your parents about the past conduct of Aunt Clara. You may be shocked to learn that this religious fanatic in her youth was not exactly moral. She sowed her wild oats promiscuously.

A woman committed suicide when Aunt Clara alienated
her husband's affections and later married him. But, as usually happens in such cases, the shadow of the dead woman
haunted them until the man disappeared. She loved this
man madly and saw in this desertion the finger of God. She
became a religious fanatic. She made a resolution to spend
her remaining years doing penance. She started to reform
everyone she came in contact with. She interfered with people's lives. She spied on innocent lovers who hid in dark
corners whispering sweet nothings. She exhorted them for
their sinful thoughts and actions. In short, she became a
menace to the community.

The author who wants to write this play still has no
premise. No matter. The story of Aunt Clara's life slowly
takes shape nevertheless. There are still many loose ends
to which the playwright can return later, when he has found
his premise. The question to ask right now is: what will be
the end of this woman? Can she go on the rest of her life
interfering with and actually crippling people's lives? Of
course not. But since Aunt Clara is still alive and going
strong on her self-appointed crusade, the author has to determine what will be the end of her, *not in reality*, but in
the play.

Actually, Aunt Clara might live to be a hundred and die
in an accident or in bed, peacefully. Will that help the play?
Positively not. Accident would be an outside factor which
is not inherent in the play. Sickness and peaceful death,
ditto. Her death—if death it will be—must spring from
her actions. A man or woman whose life she wrecked might
take vengeance on her and send her back to her Maker. In
her overzealousness she might overstep all bounds, go
against the Church itself, and be excommunicated. Or she
might find herself in such compromising circumstances that
only suicide could extricate her.

Whichever of these three possible ends is chosen, the

premise will suggest itself: *"Extremity* (whichever it is) *leads to destruction."* Now you know the beginning and the end of your play. She was promiscuous to start with, this promiscuity caused a suicide, and she lost the one person she ever really loved. This tragedy brought about her slow but persistent transformation into a religious fanatic. Her fanaticism wrecked lives, and in turn her life was taken.

No, you don't have to start your play with a premise. You can start with a character or an incident, or even a simple thought. This thought or incident grows, and the story slowly unfolds itself. You have time to find your premise in the mass of your material later. The important thing is to find it.

QUESTION: Can I use a premise, let us say, *"Great love defies even death,"* without being accused of plagiarism?

ANSWER: You can use it with safety. Although the seed is the same as that of *Romeo and Juliet,* the play will be different. You never have seen, and never will see, two exactly similar oak trees. The shape of a tree, its height and strength, will be determined by the place and the surroundings where the seeds happen to fall and germinate. No two dramatists think or write alike. Ten thousand playwrights can take the same premise, as they have done since Shakespeare, and not one play will resemble the other except in the premise. Your knowledge, your understanding of human nature, and your imagination will take care of that.

QUESTION: Is it possible to write one play on two premises?

ANSWER: It is possible, but it will not be a good play. Can you go in two different directions at the same time? The dramatist has a big enough job on his hands to prove one premise, let alone two or three. A play with more than one premise is necessarily confused.

The Philadelphia Story, by Philip Barry, is one of this type. The first premise in this play is: *"Sacrifice on both sides is necessary for a successful marriage."* The second premise is: *"Money, or the lack of it, is not solely responsible for a man's character."*

Another play of this kind is *Skylark*, by Samson Raphaelson. The premises are: *"A wealthy woman needs an anchor in life"* and *"A man who loves his wife will make sacrifices for her."*

Not only do these plays have two premises, but the premises are inactive and badly stated.

Good acting, excellent production, and clever dialogue may spell success sometimes, but they alone will never make a good play.

Don't think that every produced play has a clear-cut premise, although there is an idea behind every play. In *Night Music*, by Clifford Odets, for instance, the premise is: *"Young people must face the world with courage."* It has an idea, but not an active premise.

Another play with an idea, but a confused one, is William Saroyan's *The Time of Your Life*. The premise, *"Life is wonderful,"* is a sprawling, formless thing, as good as no premise at all.

QUESTION: It is hard to determine just what is the basic emotion in a play. Take *Romeo and Juliet*, for instance. Without hate of the two families, the lovers could have lived happily. Instead of love, it seems to me that hate is the basic emotion in this play.

ANSWER: Did hate subdue these youngsters' love for each other? It did not. It spurred them to greater effort. Their love deepened with each adversity. They were willing to give up their name, they dared their family's hatred, and, at the end, gave their life for love. Hatred was vanquished at the end, not their love. Love was on trial by hatred, and love won with flying colors. Love did not grow out of hatred, but despite hatred love flourished. As we see it, the basic emotion of *Romeo and Juliet* is still love.

QUESTION: I still don't know how to determine which is the basic trend or emotion in a play.

ANSWER: Let us take another example, then: *Ghosts*, by Ibsen. The premise of this play is: "*The sins of the fathers are visited on the children.*" Let us see if it is so. Captain Alving sowed his wild oats both before and after his marriage. He died of syphilis contracted during his escapades. He left a son, who inherited this disease from him. Oswald, the son, grew to be imbecilic, and was doomed to die with the merciful help of his own mother. All the other issues of the play, including the love affair with the maid, grew out of the above premise. The premise of the play obviously deals with heredity.

Lillian Hellman started work on an idea drawn from one of William Roughead's reports of old Scottish trials. In 1830 or thereabouts, a little Indian girl succeeded in disrupting a British school. Lillian Hellman's first success, *The Children's Hour*, was based on this situation, reports Robert van Gelder in *The New York Times*, April 21st, 1941. The interview goes on:

"The evolution of *Watch on the Rhine*," said Miss Hellman, "is quite involved and, I'm afraid, not very interesting. When I was working on *The Little Foxes* I hit on the idea—well, there's a small Midwestern American town, average or perhaps a little more isolated than average, and into that town Europe walks in the form of a titled couple—a pair of titled Europeans —pausing on their way to the West Coast. I was quite excited, thought of shelving the foxes to work on it. But when I did get to it I couldn't get it moving. It started all right—and then stuck.

"Later I had another idea. What would be the reactions of some sensitive people who had spent much of their lives starving in Europe and found themselves as house guests in the home of some very wealthy Americans? What would they make of all the furious rushing around, the sleeping tablets taken when there is no time to sleep them off, the wonderful dinners ordered and never eaten, and so on and so on. . . . That play didn't work either. I kept worrying at it, and the earlier people, the titled couple, returned continually. It would take all afternoon and probably a lot of tomorrow to trail all the steps that made those two plays into *Watch on the Rhine.* The titled couple are still in, but as minor characters. The Americans are nice people, and so on. All is changed, but the new play grew out of the other two."

A playwright might work on a story for weeks before discovering that he really needs a premise, which will show the destination of his play. Let us trace an idea which will slowly arrive at a premise. Let us assume that you want to write a play about love.

What kind of love? Well, it must be a great love, you decide, one that will overcome prejudice, hatred, adversity, one that cannot be bought or bargained with. The audience should be moved to tears at the sacrifice the lovers make for each other, at the sight of love triumphant. This is the idea, and it is not a bad one. But you have no premise, and until you choose one you cannot write your fine play.

There is a fairly obvious premise implicit in your idea: *"Love defies all."* But this is an ambiguous statement. It says too much and therefore says nothing. What is this "all"? You might answer that it is obstacles, but we can still ask: "What obstacles?" And if you say that "Love can move mountains," we are justified in asking what good will that do?

In your premise you must designate exactly how great this love is, show exactly what its destination is, and how far it will go.

Let us go all the way and show a love so great that it conquers even death. Our premise is clear-cut: "Does love defy even death?" The answer in this case is "Yes." It designates the road the lovers will travel. They will die for love. It is an active premise, so that when you ask what love will defy, it is possible to answer "death," categorically. As a result, you not only know how far your lovers are willing to go; you also have an inkling as to the kind of characters they are, the characters they must be to carry the premise to its logical conclusion.

Can this girl be silly, unemotional, scheming? Hardly. Can the boy, or man, be superficial, flighty? Hardly—unless they are shallow only until they meet. Then the battle would begin, first, against the trivial lives they had been living, then against their families, religions, and all the other motivating factors aligned against them. As they go along they will grow in stature, strength, determination, and, at the end, despite even death—*in* death—they will be united.

If you have a clear-cut premise, almost automatically a synopsis unrolls itself. You elaborate on it, providing the minute details, the personal touches.

We are taking it for granted that if you choose the above premise," *Great love defies even death,"* you believe in it. You should believe in it, since you are to prove it. You must show conclusively that life is worthless without the loved one. And if you do not sincerely believe that this is so, you will have a very hard time trying to provide the emotional intensity of Nora, in *A Doll's House,* or of Juliet, in *Romeo and Juliet.*

Did Shakespeare, Molière, and Ibsen believe in their own premises? Almost certainly. But if they did not, their genius was strong enough to feel what they described, to relive their heroes' lives so intensely that they convinced the audience of their sincerity.

You, however, should not write anything you do not believe. The premise should be a conviction of your own, so that you may prove it wholeheartedly. Perhaps it is a preposterous premise to me—it must not be so to you.

Although you should never mention your premise in the

dialogue of your play, the audience must know what the message is. And whatever it is, you must prove it.

We have seen how an *idea*—the usual preliminary to a
play—may come to you at any time. And we have seen why
it must be turned into a premise. The process of changing
an idea into a premise is not a difficult one. You can start to
write your play any way—even haphazardly—if, at the end, all
the necessary parts are in place.

It may be that the story is complete in your mind, but you
still have no premise. Can you proceed to write your play?
You had better not, however finished it seems to you. If jealousy predicated the sad ending, obviously you might have
written a play about jealousy. But have you considered where
this jealousy sprang from? Was the woman flirtatious? The
man inferior? Did a friend of the family force his attentions
upon the woman? Was she bored with her husband? Did the
husband have mistresses? Did she sell herself to help out her
sick husband? Was it just a misunderstanding? And so forth.

Every one of these possibilities needs a different premise.
For instance: *"Promiscuity during marriage leads to jealousy
and murder."* If you take this as your premise, you'll know
what caused jealousy in this particular instance, and that it
leads the promiscuous person to kill or be killed. The premise will suggest the one and only road that you must take.
Many premises can deal with jealousy, but in your case there
will be *only one* motivating power which will drive your play
to its inevitable conclusion. A promiscuous person will act
differently from one who is not promiscuous, or from a woman
who sells herself to help keep her husband alive. Although
you may have the story set in your mind or even on paper,
you cannot necessarily dispense with a clear-cut premise.

It is idiotic to go about hunting for a premise, since, as we
have pointed out, it should be a conviction of yours. You
know what your own convictions are. Look them over. Per-

haps you are interested in man and his idiosyncrasies. Take just one of those peculiarities, and you have material for several premises.

Remember the fable about the elusive bluebird? A man searched all over the world for the bluebird of happiness, and when he returned home he found it had been there all the time. It is unnecessary to torture your brain, to weary yourself by searching for a premise, when there are so many ready to hand. Anyone who has a few strong convictions is a mine of premises.

Suppose you do find a premise in your wanderings. At best it is alien to you. It did not grow from you; it is not part of you. A good premise represents the author.

We are taking it for granted that you want to write a fine play, something which will endure. The strange thing is that all plays, *including farces,* are better when the author feels he has something important to say.

Does this hold for so light a form as the crime play? Let us see. You have a brilliant idea for a drama in which someone commits the "perfect crime." You work it out in minutest detail, until you are sure it is thrilling and will hold any audience spellbound. You tell it to your friend, and he is—bored. You are shocked. What's wrong? Perhaps you'd better get the opinion of others. You do, and receive polite encouragement. But you feel in your marrow that they do not like it. Are they all morons? You begin to doubt your play. You rework it, fixing a little here, a little there—and go back to your friends. They've heard the darned thing before, so they're honestly bored now. A few go so far as to tell you so. Your heart sinks. You still do not know what is wrong, but you do know that the play is bad. You hate it and try to forget it.

Without seeing your play we can tell you what was wrong with it: it had no clear-cut premise. And if there is no clear-cut, active premise, it is more than possible that the characters were not alive. How could they be? They do not know, for instance, why they should commit a perfect crime. Their only reason is your command, and as a result all their performance and all their dialogue are artificial. No one believes what they do or say.

You may not believe it, but the characters in a play are supposed to be real people. They are supposed to do things for reasons of their own. If a man is going to commit the perfect crime, he must have a deep-rooted motivation for doing so.

Crime is not an end in itself. Even those who commit crime through madness have a reason. Why are they mad? What motivated their sadism, their lust, their hate? The reasons behind the events are what interest us. The daily papers are full of reports of murder, arson, rape. After a while we are honestly nauseated with them. Why should we go to the theater to see them, if not to find out *why* they were done?

A young girl murders her mother. Horrible. But why? What were the steps that led to the murder? The more the dramatist reveals, the better the play. The more you can reveal of the environment, the physiology and the psychology of the murderer, and his or her personal premise, the more successful you will be.

Everything in existence is closely related to everything else. You cannot treat any subject as though it were isolated from the rest of life.

If the reader accepts our reasoning, he will drop the idea of writing a play about *how* someone committed a perfect crime, and turn to *why* someone did.

Let us go through the steps of planning a crime play, seeing how the various elements fit together.

What shall the crime be? Embezzlement, blackmail, theft, murder? Let us choose murder, and get on to the criminal. Why would he kill? For lust? Money? Revenge? Ambition? To right a wrong? There are so many types of murder that we must answer this question at once. Suppose we choose am-

bition as the motive behind the murder and see where it leads
us.

The murderer must reach a position where someone stands
in his way. He will try everything to influence the man who
stands in his path, he will do anything to win his favor. Perhaps the men become friends, and the murder is averted. But
no—the prospective victim must be adamant, else there will
be no murder—and no play. But why should he be adamant?
We don't know, because we don't know our premise.

We might stop here for a moment and see how the play
would turn out if we continued without a premise. But that
is unnecessary. Just a glance at what we have to work with
will indicate how flimsy the structure is. A man is going to
kill another man who thwarts his ambition. That has been
the idea behind hundreds of plays, but it is far too weak to
serve as the basis for a synopsis. Let us look more deeply into
the elements we have here and find an active premise.

The murderer will kill to win his goal. He's not a fine type
of man, certainly. Murder is a high price to pay for one's ambition, and it takes a ruthless man to— That's it! Our killer
is ruthless—blind to everything but his selfish ends.

He's a dangerous man, of no benefit to society. Suppose he
succeeds in escaping the consequences of his crime? Suppose
he attains a position of responsibility? Think of the harm he
might do! Why, he might continue his ruthless path indefinitely, never knowing anything but success! But could he? Is
it possible for a man of ruthless ambition to succeed completely? It is not. Ruthlessness, like hate, carries the seeds of
its own destruction. Splendid! Then we have the premise:
"Ruthless ambition leads to its own destruction."

We know now that our killer will commit a murder as perfect as possible, but that he will be destroyed at the end by
his ambition. It opens up unlimited possibilities.

We know our ruthless killer. There is more to know, of
course. The understanding of a character is not as simple as

this, as we shall show in our chapter on character. But it is our premise which has given us the outstanding traits of our main character.

"Ruthless ambition leads to its own destruction" is the premise of Shakespeare's *Macbeth,* as we pointed out before.

There are as many ways to arrive at a premise as there are playwrights—more, since most playwrights use more than one method.

Let us take another example.

Suppose a dramatist, on his way home one night, sees a group of youngsters attack a passer-by. He is outraged. Boys of sixteen, eighteen, twenty—and hardened criminals! He is so impressed that he decides to write a play on juvenile delinquency. But he realizes that the subject is endless. What exact phase shall he deal with? Holdup, he decides. It was a holdup which so impressed him, and he trusts it will affect an audience the same way.

The kids are stupid, the dramatist reflects. If they are caught their lives are over. They will be sentenced to from twenty years to life imprisonment for robbery. What fools! "I'll bet," he thinks further, "that their victim had very little money on him. They were risking their lives for nothing!"

Yes, yes, it's a good idea for a play, and he starts to work on it. But the story refuses to grow. After all, you can't write three acts about a holdup. The playwright storms, bewildered by his inability to write a play on what he is sure is a fine idea.

A holdup is a holdup. Nothing new. The unusual angle might be the youth of the criminals. But why should such youngsters steal? Perhaps their parents don't give a thought to them. Perhaps their fathers are drunk, wrapped up in their own problems. But why should they be? Why should they turn to drink and neglect their children? There are so many boys like this—not all their fathers can be habitual drunkards, men without any love for their children. Well, they may be men who have lost their authority over their children. They may be very poor, unable to support their children. Why don't they look for work? Oh, yes, the depression. There is no work, and these kids have lived their lives on the street. Poverty, neglect, and dirt are all they have known. These things are powerful motivation toward crime.

And it is not only the boys in this one slum section. Thousands of boys, all over the country, poverty-ridden, turn to crime as a way out. Poverty has pushed them, encouraged them, to become criminals. That's it! *"Poverty encourages crime!"* We have our premise, and the dramatist has his.

He looks around for a locality in which to set his drama. He remembers his own childhood, or something he has seen, or a newspaper clipping. At any rate, he thinks of various localities which might well encourage crime. He studies the people, the houses, the influences, the reason for the poverty abounding. He investigates what the city has done about these conditions.

Then he turns to the boys. Are they really stupid? Or have neglect, illness, near-starvation made them so? He decides to concentrate on one character—the one who will help him write the story. He finds him: a nice kid, sixteen years old, with a sister. The father has disappeared, leaving behind the two kids and a sick wife. He could not find a job, became disgusted with life in general, and left home. His wife died soon after. The girl of eighteen insisted she could look after her brother. She loved him, and it was unthinkable to live without him. She'd work. An orphan asylum could have taken Johnny, of course, but then *"Poverty encourages crime"* would be senseless as a premise. So Johnny prowls the streets while his sister works in a factory.

Johnny has his own philosophy about everything. Other children look to their teachers and parents for guidance. These teach: be obedient, be honest. Johnny knows from his own experience that this is all bunk. If he obeys the law he will go hungry many a day. So he has his own premise: "If you're smart enough you can get away with anything." He has seen it proved time and again. He has stolen things and got away with it. Against Johnny stands the law, whose premise is: "You can't get away with it," or "Crime doesn't pay."

Johnny has his own heroes, too. Guys who got away with it. He is sure they can outsmart any cop. There is Jack Colley, a local boy, for instance. He came from this very neighborhood. All the cops in the nation were chasing him, and he made fools of them. He's tops.

To know Johnny as you should, find out about his background, his education, ambition, hero worship, inspiration, friends. Then the premise will cover him and millions of other kids perfectly.

If you see only that Johnny is a roughneck, and you don't know why, then you will need, and find, another premise, perhaps: *"The lack of a strong police force encourages criminals."* Of course, the question arises as to whether this is true. An ignorant person might say yes. But you will have to explain why millionaires' sons do not go out and steal bread, like Johnny. If there were more police, would poverty and misery diminish in proportion? Experience says no. Then *"Poverty encourages crime"* is a truer, more practical premise.

It is the premise of *Dead End,* by Sidney Kingsley.

You must decide just how you are going to treat your premise. Will you indict society? Will you show poverty and a way out of poverty? Kingsley decided to show poverty only and let the audience draw its own conclusions. If you wish to add anything to what Kingsley said, make a subpremise which will enlarge the original one. Enlarge it again, if necessary, so that it will fit your case perfectly. If in the process you find your premise untenable *because you have changed your mind as to what you wished to say,* formulate a new premise and discard the old.

"Is society responsible for poverty?" Whichever side you

take, you must prove it. Of course, this play will differ from
Kingsley's. You can formulate any number of premises—
"poverty," "love," "hate"—choosing the one that satisfies
you most.

You can arrive at your premise in any one of a great many
ways. You may start with an idea which you at once convert
to a premise, or you may develop a situation first and see that
it has potentialities which need only the right premise to give
them meaning and suggest an end.

Emotion can dictate many premises, but you must elaborate them before they can express the dramatist's idea. Test
this with an emotion: jealousy. Jealousy feeds on the sen-
sations generated by an inferiority complex. Jealousy, as such,
cannot be a premise, because it designates no goal for the
characters. Would it be better if we put it thus: "Jealousy
destroys"? No, although we now know what action it takes.
Let us go further: "Jealousy destroys itself." Now there is a
goal. We know, and the dramatist knows, that the play will
continue until jealousy has destroyed itself. The author may
build on it as he chooses, saying, perhaps, *"Jealousy destroys*
not only itself but the object of its love."

We hope the reader recognizes the difference between the
last two premises. The variations are endless, and with each
new variation the premise of the play is changed. But whenever you change your premise, you will have to go back to
the beginning and rewrite your synopsis in terms of the new
premise. If you start out with one premise and switch to another, the play will suffer. No one can build a play on two
premises, or a house on two foundations.

Tartuffe, by Molière, offers a good example of how a play
grows out of a premise. (See synopsis and analysis on page 274.)

The premise of *Tartuffe* is: *"He who digs a pit for others*
falls into it himself."

The play opens with Mme Pernelle upbraiding her son's

youthful second wife, Elmire, and her grandson and grand-daughter because they are not showing proper respect for Tartuffe. Tartuffe was taken into the house by her son, Orgon. Tartuffe is obviously a scoundrel masquerading as a holy man. Tartuffe's real objective is to have an illicit love affair with Orgon's wife and to take possession of his fortune. His piousness has captured Orgon's heart, and he now believes in Tartuffe as if he were the Saviour incarnate. But let's go back to the very beginning of the play.

The author's objective is to establish the first part of the premise as quickly as possible. Mme Pernelle is speaking:

MME P.: [*To Damis, her grandson*] If Tartuffe thinks anything sinful you can depend upon it that sinful it is. He is seeking to lead you all on the road to heaven, if you would but follow him.

DAMIS: I'll travel no road in his company!

MME P.: That is not only foolish but a wicked thing to say. Your father both loves and trusts him, which should surely dispose you to do likewise.

DAMIS: Neither Father nor anyone else could induce me to love him or trust him! I loathe the fellow and all his ways, and I should lie if I said I did not. And if he tries to domineer over me again, I'll break his head for him.

DORINE: [*The maid*] Truly, Madame, it is not to be borne that an unknown person who came here penniless and in rags should take it on himself to upset everything and rule over the whole house.

MME P.: I did not ask for *your* opinion. [*To the others*] It would be well for this household if he *did* rule over it.

(This is the first hint of what is actually going to happen later, when Orgon entrusts him with his fortune.)

DORINE: *You* may think him a saint, Madame, but to my mind he's a good deal more like a hypocrite.

DAMIS: I'll be sworn he is.

MME P.: Hold your malicious tongues, both of you—! I know you all dislike him—and why? Because he sees your faults and has the courage to tell you of them.

DORINE: He does more than that. He is seeking to prevent Madame from entertaining any company at all. Why should he rave and thunder at her as he does for receiving an ordinary caller? Where's the harm in it? It's my belief that it's all because he's jealous of her!

(Yes, he is jealous, as we'll find out later. Molière takes good care to motivate everything beforehand.)

ELMIRE: Dorine, that is nonsense!

MME P.: It's worse than nonsense. Think what you've dared to hint, girl, and be properly ashamed of yourself! [*To the others*] It is not dear Tartuffe alone who disapproves of your excessive love of company—it's the whole neighborhood.

My son never did a wiser thing in his life than bringing worthy Tartuffe into this house, for if anyone can recall wandering sheep to the fold, it is he. And if you are wise in time you will heed his warnings that all your visiting, your routs, your balls are so many subtle devices of the Evil One for your soul's destruction.

ELMIRE: Why, Mother? For the pleasure we take in such gatherings is innocent enough.

If you reread the premise, you will notice that someone —in this case, Tartuffe—will ensnare innocent, believing persons—Orgon and his mother—with his hypocritical pretension of saintliness. This will enable him later to take possession of Orgon's fortune and make the lovely Elmire his mistress—if he succeeds.

In the very beginning of the play we feel that this happy family is threatened with dire disaster. We didn't get a glimpse of Orgon yet, only of his mother taking up the cudgel for the pseudo saint. Can it be true that a man in his senses, an ex-army officer, believes in another man so implicitly that he may give him a chance to play havoc with his family? If he does believe so much in Tartuffe, the author established the first part of his premise explicitly.

We have witnessed, then, how Tartuffe, with subtle meth-

ods, and with the help of Orgon, his intended victim, is digging a pit for Orgon. Will he fall into it? We don't know yet.
But our interest is aroused. Let us see whether Orgon's faith
in Tartuffe is as firm as his mother wants us to believe.

Orgon has just arrived home from a three-day journey. He
meets his second wife's brother, Cléante.

CLÉANTE: I heard you were expected shortly, and waited in the
hope of seeing you.

ORGON: That was kind. But you must pardon me if, before we
talk, I ask a question or two of Dorine here. [*To Dorine*] Has
all gone well during my absence?

DORINE: Not altogether, Monsieur. Madame was taken with the
fever the day before yesterday and suffered terribly from pains
in her head.

ORGON: Did she so? And Tartuffe?

DORINE: Oh, he's prodigiously well—bursting with health.

ORGON: Poor dear fellow!

DORINE: At supper that evening Madame was so ill that she could
not touch a morsel.

ORGON: Ah—and Tartuffe?

DORINE: He could manage no more than a brace of partridges and
half a hashed leg of mutton.

ORGON: Poor dear fellow!

DORINE: Madame could get no sleep all that night, and we had to
sit up with her till daybreak.

ORGON: Indeed. And Tartuffe?

DORINE: Oh, he went straight from the table to his bed, where, to
judge by the sounds, he slept on sweetly till the morning was
well advanced.

ORGON: Poor dear fellow!

DORINE: But at last we persuaded Madame to let herself be bled,
which gave her relief at once.

ORGON: Good! And Tartuffe?

DORINE: He bore up bravely, and at breakfast next morning drank
four cups of red wine to replace what Madame had lost.

ORGON: Poor dear fellow!

DORINE: So all is now well with both of them, Monsieur, and, with your leave, I will now go and let Madame know you are returned.

ORGON: Do so, Dorine.

DORINE: [As she reaches arch at back] I will not fail to tell her how concerned you were to hear of her illness, Monsieur. [She goes off]

ORGON: [To Cléante] I could almost think she meant some impertinence by that.

CLÉANTE: And if she did, my dear Orgon, is there not some excuse for her? Great heavens, man, how can you be so infatuated with this Tartuffe? What do you see in him that makes you indifferent to all others?

Obviously Orgon can't see the pit Tartuffe is digging for him. Molière unmistakably established his premise in the first third of the play.

Tartuffe has dug a pit; will Orgon fall into it? We don't know—and we're not supposed to know—until the end of the play.

Needless to say, the same principles govern a short story, novel, movie, or radio play.

Let us take Guy de Maupassant's short story, *The Diamond Necklace,* and try to find the premise in it.

Mathilda, a young, daydreaming, vain woman borrowed a diamond necklace from a wealthy schoolmate to wear to a ball. She lost the necklace. Afraid to face the humiliating consequences she and her husband mortgage their inheritance and borrow money to buy a replica of the lost necklace. They work for ten long weary years to repay their debt. They become coarse, work-worn, ugly and old. Then they discover that the original lost necklace had been made of paste.

What is the premise of this immortal story? We think it started with her daydreaming. A daydreamer is not necessarily a bad person. Daydreams are usually an escape from reality;—a reality which the dreamer has no courage to face. Daydreams are a substitute for action. Great minds are dreamers too, but they translate their dreams into reality. Nikola Tesla, for instance, was the greatest electrical wizard who ever lived. He was a great dreamer, but he was a great *doer* too.

Mathilda was a good-natured but idle dreamer. Her dreams led her exactly nowhere, until tragedy befell her.

We must examine her character. She lived in imaginary luxury in a fairy castle where she was a queen. Naturally she had a great deal of pride and couldn't humiliate herself by admitting to her friend that she was unable to afford the price of the lost necklace. Death was preferable to that. She had to buy a new necklace even though she and her husband had to work the rest of their lives for it. They did. She became a drudge because of her vanity and false pride; inherent characteristics which were the result of her daydreaming. Her husband worked along with her because of his love for her. The premise: *"Escape from reality leads to a day of reckoning."*

Let us find the premise in *A Lion Is in the Street,* a novel by Adria Locke Langley.

Even in early youth Hank Martin was determined to be the greatest of men. He peddled pins, ribbons, cosmetics, with the idea of ingratiating himself with people to use them later on. He did use them; so well that he became governor of his state. Then he plundered the people until the multitude rose up against him. He died a violent death.

Obviously the premise of this novel is: *"Ruthless ambition leads to its own destruction."*

Now for *Pride of the Marines,* a motion picture from a story by Albert Maltz.

This is the story of Al Schmid, wounded marine who became blind in the war. At the rehabilitation hospital they cannot induce him to go home to his fiancée. He feels that he is useless to her now. He was brought home by a ruse; his sweetheart convinces him that she still wants him and that, although blind he can still hold a job. He gets a job and they plan to get married. Although the doctors have given up hope of his regaining his eyesight, he does begin to see a little.

Premise: *"Sacrificial love conquers hopelessness."*

The pity of this otherwise promising motion picture is that Al Schmid and, for that matter, the other characters too, never find out what they were fighting for, and why Al lost his eyesight, even at the very end of the picture. Such knowledge would have deepened the story considerably.

Earth and High Heaven, a novel by Gwethalynn Graham, is the story of a wealthy Gentile Canadian girl who falls in love with a Jewish lawyer. Her father refuses to accept the young man and does everything in his power to break up the romance because of the man's religion. Father and daughter had been devoted to each other. The girl must choose between her father or the man she loves. She decides to marry her sweetheart, thereby breaking off relations with her family.

Premise: *"Intolerance leads to isolation."*

Not all of these examples are of high literary value, but they all have a clearly defined premise and this is a necessity in all good writing. Without it, it is impossible to know your characters. A premise has to contain; character, conflict and resolution. It is impossible to know all this without a clear-cut premise.

One more thing should be remembered. No one premise is necessarily a universal truth. Poverty doesn't always lead to crime, but if you've chosen this premise, it does in your case. The same principle governs all premises.

The premise is the conception, the beginning of a play. The premise is a seed and it grows into a plant that was contained in the original seed; nothing more, nothing less. The premise should not stand out like a sore thumb, turning the characters into puppets and the conflicting forces into a mechanical set-up. In a well-constructed play or story, it is impossible to denote just where the premise is and where story or character begins.

Rodin, the great French sculptor, had just finished the statue of Honoré de Balzac. The figure wore a long robe with long loose sleeves. The hands were folded in front.

Rodin stepped back, exhausted but triumphant, and eyed his work with satisfaction. It was a masterpiece!

Like any artist, he needed someone to share his happiness. Although it was four o'clock in the morning, he hastened to wake up one of his students.

The master rushed ahead with mounting excitement and watched the young man's reaction.

The student's eyes slowly focused upon the hands.

"Wonderful!" he cried. "What hands. . . . Master, I've never seen such marvelous hands before!"

Rodin's face darkened. A moment later Rodin swept out of his studio again. A short while later he returned with another student in tow.

The reaction was almost the same. As Rodin watched eagerly, the pupil's gaze fastened on the hands of the statue and stayed there.

"Master," the student said reverently, "only a God could have created such hands. They are alive!"

Apparently Rodin had expected something else, for once more he was off, now in a frenzy. When he returned he was dragging another bewildered student with him.

"Those hands . . . those hands . . ." the new arrival exclaimed, in the same reverent tone as the others, "if you had never done anything else, Master, those hands would make you immortal!"

Something must have snapped in Rodin, for with a dismayed cry he ran to a corner of the studio and grabbed a fearful looking axe. He advanced toward the statue with the apparent intention of smashing it to bits.

Horror stricken, his students threw themselves upon him, but in his madness he shook them off with superhuman strength. He rushed to the statue and with one well aimed blow, chopped off the magnificent hands.

Then he turned to his stupefied pupils, his eyes blazing.

"Fools!" he cried. "I was forced to destroy these hands because they had a life of their own. They didn't belong to the rest of the composition. Remember this, and remember it well: no part is more important than the whole!"

And that's why the statue of Balzac stands in Paris, without hands. The long loose sleeves of the robe appear to cover the hands, but in reality Rodin chopped them off because they seemed to be more important than the whole figure.

Neither the premise nor any other part of a play has a separate life of its own. All must blend into an harmonious whole.

II

CHARACTER

◇◇◇

1. The Bone Structure

IN THE previous chapter we showed why premise is necessary as the first step in writing a good play. In the following chapters we shall discuss the importance of character. We shall vivisect a character and try to find out just what elements go into this being called "man." Character is the fundamental material we are forced to work with, so we must know character as thoroughly as possible.

Henrik Ibsen, speaking of his working methods, has said:

When I am writing I must be alone; if I have eight characters of a drama to do with I have society enough; they keep me busy; I must learn to know them. And this process of making their acquaintance is slow and painful. I make, as a rule, three casts of my dramas, which differ considerably from each other. I mean in characteristics, not in the course of the treatment. When I first settle down to work out my material, I feel as if I have to get to know my characters on a railway journey; the first acquaintance is struck up, and we have chatted about this and that. When I write it down again, I already see everything much more clearly, and I know the people as if I had stayed with them for a month at a watering place. I have grasped the leading points of their characters and their little peculiarities.

What did Ibsen see? What did he mean when he said, "I have grasped the leading points of their characters and their little peculiarities." Let us try to discover the leading points not only in one, but in all characters.

Every object has three dimensions: depth, height, width. Human beings have an additional three dimensions: physiology, sociology, psychology. Without a knowledge of these three dimensions we cannot appraise a human being.

It is not enough, in your study of a man, to know if he is rude, polite, religious, atheistic, moral, degenerate. You must know why. We want to know why man is as he is, why his character is constantly changing, and why it must change whether he wishes it or no.

The first dimension, in the order of simplicity, is the physiological. It would be idle to argue that a hunchback sees the world exactly opposite from a perfect physical specimen. A lame, a blind, a deaf, an ugly, a beautiful, a tall, a short person —each of these sees everything differently from the other. A sick man sees health as the supreme good; a healthy person belittles the importance of health, if he thinks of it at all.

Our physical make-up certainly colors our outlook on life. It influences us endlessly, helping to make us tolerant, defiant, humble, or arrogant. It affects our mental development, serves as a basis for inferiority and superiority complexes. It is the most obvious of man's first set of dimensions.

Sociology is the second dimension to be studied. If you were born in a basement, and your playground was the dirty city street, your reactions would differ from those of the boy who was born in a mansion and played in beautiful and antiseptic surroundings.

But we cannot make an exact analysis of your differences from him, or from the little boy who lived next door in the same tenement, until we know more about both of you. Who was your father, your mother? Were they sick or well? What was their earning power? Who were your friends? How did you influence or affect them? How did they affect you? What kind of clothes do you like? What books do you read? Do you go to church? What do you eat, think, like, dislike? Who are you, sociologically speaking?

The third dimension, psychology, is the product of the other two. Their combined influence gives life to ambition, frustration, temperament, attitudes, complexes. Psychology, then, rounds out the three dimensions.

If we wish to understand the action of any individual, we must look at the motivation which compels him to act as he does. Let us look first at his physical make-up.

Is he sick? He may have a lingering illness that he knows nothing of, but the author must know about it because only in this way can he understand the character. This illness affects the man's attitude toward things about him. We certainly behave differently during illness, convalescence, and perfect health.

Does a man have big ears, bulging eyes, long hairy arms? All these are likely to condition him to an outlook which would affect his every action.

Does he hate to talk about crooked noses, big mouths, thick lips, big feet? Perhaps it is because he has one of these defects. One human being takes such a physical liability with resignation, another makes fun of himself, a third is resentful. One thing is certain, no one escapes the effect of such a shortcoming. Does this character of ours possess a feeling of dissatisfaction with himself? It will color his outlook, quicken his conflict with others, or make him sluggish and resigned. But it will affect him.

Important as this physical dimension is, it is only part of the whole. We must not forget to add the background for this physical picture. These two will round out each other, unite, and give birth to the third dimension, the mental state.

A sex pervert is a sex pervert, as far as the general public is concerned. But to the psychologist he is the product of his background, his physiology, his heredity, his education.

If we understand that these three dimensions can provide the reason for every phase of human conduct, it will be easy for us to write about any character and trace his motivation to its source.

Analyze any work of art which has withstood the ravages of time, and you will find that it has lived, and will live, because it possesses the three dimensions. Leave out one of the three, and although your plot may be exciting and you may make a fortune, your play will still not be a literary success.

When you read drama criticisms in your daily papers you encounter certain terminology time and again: dull, unconvincing, stock characters (badly drawn, that is), familiar situations, boring. They all refer to one flaw—the lack of tridimensional characters.

Don't believe, when your play is condemned as "familiar," that you must hunt for fantastic situations. The moment your characters are rounded, in terms of the three dimensions, you will find that they are not only exciting theater, but novel as well.

Literature has many tridimensional characters—Hamlet, for instance. We not only know his age, his appearance, his state of health; we can easily surmise his idiosyncrasies. His background, his sociology, give impetus to the play. We know the political situation at the time, the relationship between his parents, the events that have gone before and the effect they have had upon him. We know his personal premise, and its motivation. We know his psychology, and we can see clearly how it results from his physical and sociological make-up. In short, we know Hamlet as we can never hope to know ourselves.

Shakespeare's great plays are built on characters: Macbeth, King Lear, Othello, and the rest are striking examples of tridimensionality.

(It is not our intention here to go into a critical analysis of famous plays. Suffice it to say that in every case the author created characters, or intended to. How he succeeded, and why, will be analyzed in another chapter.) Euripides' *Medea* is a classical example of how a play should grow out of character. The author did not need an Aphrodite to cause Medea to fall in love with Jason. It was the custom of those times to show the interference of the gods, but the behavior of the characters is logical without it. Medea, or any woman, will love the man who appeals to her, and will sometimes make sacrifices hard to believe.

Medea had her brother slain for her love. Not long ago, in New York, a woman lured her two children into a forest, cut their throats, poured gasoline over them and burned them —for love. There is no indication of the supernatural in this. It is merely the good old-fashioned mating instinct run riot. If we knew the background and the physical composition of this modern Medea, her terrible deed would become comprehensible to us.

Here is a guide, then, a step-by-step outline of how a tridimensional-character bone structure should look.

PHYSIOLOGY

1. *Sex*
2. *Age*
3. *Height and weight*
4. *Color of hair, eyes, skin*
5. *Posture*
6. *Appearance:* good-looking, over- or underweight, clean, neat, pleasant, untidy. Shape of head, face, limbs.
7. *Defects:* deformities, abnormalities, birthmarks. Diseases.
8. *Heredity*

SOCIOLOGY

1. *Class:* working, ruling, middle, *petite bourgeoisie.*
2. *Occupation:* type of work, hours of work, income, con-

dition of work, union or nonunion, attitude toward
organization, suitability for work.
3. *Education:* amount, kind of schools, marks, favorite subjects, poorest subjects, aptitudes.
4. *Home life:* parents living, earning power, orphan, parents separated or divorced, parents' habits, parents'
mental development, parents' vices, neglect. Character's martial status.
5. *Religion*
6. *Race, nationality*
7. *Place in community:* leader among friends, clubs, sports.
8. *Political affiliations*
9. *Amusements, hobbies:* books, newspapers, magazines he
reads.

PSYCHOLOGY

1. *Sex life, moral standards*
2. *Personal premise, ambition*
3. *Frustrations, chief disappointments*
4. *Temperament:* choleric, easygoing, pessimistic, optimis-
tic.
5. *Attitude toward life:* resigned, militant, defeatist.
6. *Complexes:* obsessions, inhibitions, superstitions, manias,
phobias.
7. *Extrovert, introvert, ambivert*
8. *Abilities:* languages, talents.
9. *Qualities:* imagination, judgment, taste, poise.
10. *I.Q.*

This is the bone structure of a character, which the author
must know thoroughly, and upon which he must build.

QUESTION: How can we fuse these three dimensions into a
unity?
ANSWER: Take the kids in Sidney Kingsley's *Dead End,* for
instance. All but one are physically well. There are no ap-

parently serious complexes resulting from physical deficiencies. In their lives, then, environment will be the deciding factor. Hero worship; lack of education, of clothing,
of supervision; and, above all, the constant presence of
poverty and hunger will shape their views of the world,
and, as a consequence, their attitude and conduct toward
society. The three dimensions have combined to produce
one outstanding trait.

QUESTION: Would the same environment produce the same
reaction on each child, or will it affect them differently as
they differ from each other?

ANSWER: No two individuals react identically, since no two
are the same. One boy may have no mental reservations:
he looks upon his juvenile crimes as preparation for a
glorious career as a gangster; another participates in the
mob activities from a sense of loyalty, or from fear, or to
build up a reputation for courage. Still another is aware
of the danger of his course, but sees no other way out of
poverty. Minute physical differences between the individuals, and their psychological development, will influence
their reactions to the same sociological conditions. Science
will tell you that no two snowflakes have ever been discovered to be identical. The slightest disturbance in the
atmosphere, the direction of the wind, the position of the
falling snowflake, will alter the pattern. Thus there is
endless variety in their design. The same law governs us all.
If one's father is always kind, or only kind periodically, or
kind but once, or never kind at all, he will profoundly
affect one's development. And if the paternal kindness coin-
cided with one's happiest and most contented moments, it
might pass unrecognized. Every move hinges upon the
peculiar circumstances of the given moment.

QUESTION: There are certain human manifestations which
do not appear to fall into the three categories. I've noticed
in myself periods of depression, or excitement, which seem

unmotivated. Being observant, I've tried to track down the source of these mysterious disturbances, without success. I can truthfully say that these periods sometimes occurred when I had no economic stress or mental anxiety. Why are you laughing?

ANSWER: You remind me of a friend of mine—a writer—who told me a strange story about himself. The incident occurred when he was thirty years old. He was apparently healthy; he had won recognition for his work; he earned more money than he knew what to do with; he was married and loved his wife and two children dearly. One day, to his utter astonishment, he realized that he didn't give a hoot about what was going to happen to his family, his career, or his life. He was bored to distraction. Nothing under the sun interested him; he anticipated everything his friends said and did. He couldn't stand the same horrible routine day after day, week after week; the same woman, the same food, the same friends, the same murder stories in the papers day in and day out. They almost drove him mad. It was as mysterious as your case. Perhaps he had ceased to love his wife? He had thought of that, and was desperate enough to experiment. He did but with no success. He found no difference in his love. He was honestly and truly bored with life. He stopped writing, stopped seeing his friends, and finally decided that he'd be better off dead. The thought did not come in a moment of despair. He reasoned it out coolly, without missing a heartbeat. The earth had gone on for billions of years before his birth, he mused, and would go on after his demise. What difference could it make if he left a little before his appointed time?

So he sent his family away to a friend's home and sat down to write his last letter, explaining his course of action to his wife. It was not an easy letter to write. It did not sound convincing, and he sweated over it as he had never done over his plays. Suddenly he felt a sharp, abdominal cramp. There was a stabbing pain, persistent, excruciating. He found himself in an awkward situation. He wanted to kill himself, but it was idiotic to die with an ache in the stomach. Besides, he had to finish his letter. He decided that the sensible thing would be to take a cathartic and ease the pain. He did so. When he went back to his desk again to finish his last epistle, he found it harder to write than ever. The reasons he had marshaled previously sounded fantastic to him—even stupid. He became aware of the brilliant sunshine which played over his desk, of the alternate light and shadow on the houses across the street. The trees had never seemed so green and refreshing; life had never seemed so desirable. He wanted to see, smell, feel, walk. . . .

QUESTION: Do you mean to say that he had entirely lost his desire to die?

ANSWER: Precisely. He found himself minus a clogged-up body and plus a million reasons to live. He really was a new man.

QUESTION: Then physical conditions can really influence the mind so completely as to mean the difference between life and death?

ANSWER: Ask your family doctor.

QUESTION: It seems to me that not every reaction of the mind or body springs from a physical or economic cause. I know cases—

ANSWER: We know cases, too. Let's say X falls in love with a desirable girl. His love is unrequited, so he feels frustrated, becomes despondent, and winds up seriously ill. But how can this be? Love, according to many, is ethereal, outside the pale of economy or mere materialism. Shall we investigate? Love, like all emotions, originates in the brain. Brain, however one looks at it, is composed of tissue, cells, blood vessels. This is purely physical. The slightest physical disturbance registers first on the brain, which reacts instantaneously. A serious disappointment has its effect on the brain—the physical brain—which transmits the message to the body. Remember that love, however ethereal, affects such physical functions as digestion and sleeping.

QUESTION: But suppose the emotion isn't physical at all? Suppose there aren't any factors like desire in it?

ANSWER: All emotion has physical effects. Let us take what is supposed to be the noblest emotion of them all—mother love. This particular mother has no financial difficulties. She has plenty of money, she's healthy, she's happy. Her daughter falls in love with a young man whom the mother considers a liability rather than an asset. He is not dangerous in any way, merely unsuitable from the mother's point of view. But the daughter runs away with him.

The mother's first reaction will be shock, followed by bitter disappointment. Then will come shame, self-pity. All of these might usher in an attack of hysteria. These attacks increase in frequency and kind, weaken the resistance of the body, and culminate in actual illness—even invalidism.

QUESTION: Is all psychological reaction the result of your three dimensions?

ANSWER: Let us see. Why did the mother object so strenuously to the daughter's choice of husband? His appearance? Perhaps, although the average mother hides her disappointment when her son-in-law is not an Adonis. Unless he is actually a monster, his appearance should not cause a violent reaction. But in any case, the mother's disapproval of his appearance would have been conditioned by her own background, by what her father looked like, her brothers, her favorite motion-picture star.

Another source of disappointment—and a more probable one—would be the young man's financial status. If he cannot support her daughter well, or at all, the mother will be a prey to fear for her daughter and for herself. Even if she can afford to keep her daughter from poverty, she cannot keep her friends from sneering at the poor match. She may have to set the boy up in business—only to find him a poor businessman who may lose all her savings. Or perhaps the young man is handsome, and financially stable, and of another race? All of the mother's training will rise up against him. She will have a host of memories springing up from her past: warnings of social ostracism, of mythical differences between the races, of superstitions and chauvinism completely without foundation.

Think of any reason you like, from the young man's physical state through the birthplace of his great-grandfather, and you will find that anything to which the mother objects has a physical or sociological foundation, both in him and in her. Try as you will, you must come back to the three dimensions.

QUESTION: Might not this principle of tridimensionality limit the scope of material for the writer?

ANSWER: On the contrary. It opens up undreamed-of perspectives and an entirely new world for exploration and discovery.

QUESTION: You mentioned height, age, skin coloring, in your outline of a character's bone structure. Must all these be incorporated in our play?

ANSWER: You must know all of these, but they need not be mentioned. They come through in the behavior of the character, not in any expository material about him. The attitude of a man who is six feet in height will differ considerably from that of a man who measures four feet, eight inches. And the reaction of a woman with a pock-marked face will not be the same as that of a girl famed for her lovely complexion. You must know what your character is, in every detail, to know what he will do in a given situation.

Anything that happens in your play must come directly

from the characters you have chosen to prove your premise, and they must be characters strong enough to prove the premise without forcing.

2. *Environment*

When a friend invites you to a party, and after a moment's hesitation you reply, "All right, I'll be there," you are making an unassuming statement. But that statement is the result of a complicated mental process.

Your acceptance of the invitation may have sprung from loneliness, from a desire to avoid a dull evening, from excess physical energy, from desperation. You may have felt that mingling with people would bring forgetfulness of a problem, or new hope, or inspiration. The truth, however, is that even such a simple matter as saying "yes" or "no" is the product of elaborate reviewing, reshifting, revaluating of fancied or real, mental or physical, economic or sociological conditions around us.

Words have a complex structure. We use them glibly, without realizing that they too are compounds of many elements. Let us vivisect the word "happiness," for instance. Let us try to discover what elements go into the making of complete happiness.

Can a person be "happy" if he has everything but health? Obviously not, since we refer to utter happiness, happiness without reservations. So health must be put down as a necessary element for "happiness."

Can a person be "happy" with nothing but health? Hardly. One may feel joy, exuberance, freedom, but not happiness. Remember that we are speaking of happiness in its purest form. When you exclaim, "Boy, how happy I am!" upon receiving a long-desired gift, what you are experiencing is not happiness. It is joy, fulfillment, surprise, but not happiness.

Then we are not daring too much if we say that a man needs, besides health, a job in which he can make a comfortable living. We shall take it for granted that the man is not abused on his job, for that would negate the possibility of his being happy. The ingredients for happiness, so far, are health and a satisfactory position.

But can a man be happy who possesses both of these and no warm, human affection? There need be little argument on this point. A man needs someone whom he can love and who loves him in return. So let us add love to the other requirements.

Would you be happy if your position, although satisfactory, held no chance for advancement? Would a good job, health, and love suffice, if the future held for you no hope of development, of improvement? We don't think so. Perhaps your position will never change, but you can be happy in the hope that it will. Let us therefore add hope to our list of ingredients.

Our recipe now reads: health, a satisfactory position, love, and hope equal happiness. Further subdivisions might be made, but the four main ingredients are enough to prove that a word is the product of many elements. Of course, the meaning of the word "happiness" will go through innumerable metamorphoses, according to the place, climate, conditions, under which it is used.

Protoplasm is one of the simplest of living substances, yet it contains carbon, oxygen, hydrogen, nitrogen, sulphur, phosphorus, chlorine, potassium, sodium, calcium, magnesium, iron. Simple protoplasm, in other words, contains the same elements as complex man.

We referred to protoplasm as "simple," in comparing it with man. Yet protoplasm is complex, compared with inanimate things. It occupies both a high and a low place on the scale of complexity. Contradictory? No more so than anything else in nature. The principle of contradiction and tension makes motion possible, and life is motion, essentially.

What would have happened to the protoplasm at the beginning of time as we know it, if it had not possessed motion? Nothing. It could not have existed and life would have been impossible. Through motion higher forms of life developed, the specific form being determined by the place, climate, type of food, abundance of food, light or lack of light.

Give a person all the elements required for life, but alter one of them—heat, let us say, or light—and you will completely change his life. If you doubt this, you can experiment on yourself. Let us suppose that you are happy, that you have all the four necessary elements. Bandage your eyes for twenty-four hours. Close out all light. You are still healthy, still employed, still loved and loving, still hopeful. Moreover, you know that after twenty-four hours you will remove the bandages. You are not really blind, you are merely refraining from sight at your own will. Yet that experiment will change your entire attitude.

You will find the same thing to be true if you stop hearing for one day, or temporarily deprive yourself of the use of one limb. Eat any one food you like and nothing else, for months —even for a couple of weeks. What do you think your reaction will be? You'll loathe that food the rest of your life.

Would it make a great difference in your life if you were forced to sleep in a bug-infested, foul room, on a dirty floor, with only a few rags for covering or a mattress? Undoubtedly. Even if you lived in foul surroundings for only a day, it would multiply your appreciation of cleanliness and comfort.

It seems that human beings react to environment exactly as the original one-celled creatures did when they changed their shape, color, and species *under the pressure of environment*.

We are forcing this point strenuously because it is of the utmost importance that we understand the principle of change in character. A character is in constant change. The smallest disturbance of his well-ordered life will ruffle his placidity and create a mental upheaval, just as a stone which slides through the surface of a pond will create far-reaching rings of motion.

If it is true that every man is influenced by his environment, health, and economic background, as we have tried to prove, then it is evident that, since everything is in a process of constant change (environment, health, and economic background, naturally, being part of everything), the man too will change. As a matter of fact, he is the center of this constant movement.

Don't forget a fundamental truism: everything is changeable, only change is eternal.

Take, for instance, a prosperous businessman—a drygoods merchant. He is happy. His business is on the upgrade. His wife, his three children are also contented. It is a rare case, in fact, an almost impossible case, but it will illustrate our point. As far as he and his family are concerned, this man is contented. Then a big industrialist somewhere starts a movement to cut wages and destroy unions. It seems to our man that this is a wise thing to do. The worker, he thinks, has become too uppish lately. Why, if things continue at the rate workers wish, they may very well take over industry and ruin the country. Since our man has something to lose, he feels that he and his family are in danger.

A slow but persistently growing uneasiness steals over him. He is profoundly disturbed. He reads more about this grave problem. He may or may not know that his fear is being created by a few rich industrialists who wish to cut wages and are spending fabulous sums to spread panic over the country. Our man is caught in this web of propaganda. He wants to do his share in saving his nation from destruction. He cuts wages, unaware that by this act he has not only antagonized his employees, but has helped a movement which will prove

a boomerang in the end, and may even destroy his own liveli-
hood. With the reduction of purchasing power, which he has
caused, his business may be one of the first to suffer.

Our man will suffer even if he knows what it is all about
and does not cut wages. He will be caught in the reaction to
his fellow employers' wage cutting. Changing conditions will
mold him, whether or not he wants to be molded, and they
will affect his family with him. He can't give them as much
money as he did, because the source of easy money has dried
up. This will precipitate some dissension among the members
of the family and may even cause an eventual split.

The war in Europe and China, a strike in San Francisco,
Hitler's attack on the democracies, will affect us as surely as
if we had been at the scene. Every human event comes home,
at long last, to roost. We find to our sorrow, perhaps, that
even seemingly unrelated things are very much related to
each other—and to us.

There is no escape—for our drygoods merchant or anyone else.

Banks and governments are as subject to change as the rest
of us. We saw this in the 1929 depression. Countless millions
of dollars were lost. After the First World War, government
after government toppled, and new governments or new systems took their places. Your money, your investments, were
swept away overnight, and your security with them. You, as an
individual, are only as secure as the rest of the world is under
prevailing circumstances.

A character, then, is the sum total of his physical make-up
and the influences his environment exerts upon him. Look
at the flowers. It makes a great difference in their development if they receive the morning sun, the midday sun, or the
afternoon sun.

Our minds, no less than our bodies, respond to external
influences. Early memories are so deep-rooted that we are
often unconscious of them. We can make determined efforts

to rid ourselves of past influences, to escape from our instincts, but we remain in their grip. Unconscious recollections color our judgment regardless of how fair we try to be.

Woodruff says, in *Animal Biology:*

It is impossible to consider protoplasm except in connection with its surroundings, whatever they may be, variations in its environment and variations in its activities being reflected directly or indirectly in its appearance.

Watch women walking in the rain under their colored umbrellas, and you'll notice that their faces reflect the color of the umbrellas they carry. Our own childhood recollections, memories, experiences, become an indelible part of us and will reflect upon and color our minds. We cannot see things otherwise than this reflection permits us to see them. We may argue against this coloration, we may put up a conscious fight against it, we may even act against our natural inclinations, but we still reflect all we represent.

Life is change. The smallest disturbance alters the pattern of the whole. The environment changes, and man with it. If a young man meets a young lady under the right circumstances, he may be drawn to her by their common interest in literature, or the arts, or sports. This common interest toward a subject may deepen until they feel fondness and sympathy. The sympathy grows, and before they realize it, it will be attachment, which is deeper than sympathy or fondness. If nothing disturbs this harmony, it will become infatuation. Infatuation is not yet love, but it approaches love as it moves on to the stage of devotion and then to rapture, or adoration which is already love. Love is the last stage. It can be tested by sacrifice. Real love is the capacity to endure any hardship for the beloved.

The emotions of two people might follow this course if everything worked out just right; if nothing interferes with their budding romance, they may marry and live happily ever after. But suppose that when this same young couple reaches the stage of attachment, a malignant gossiper informs the young man that the lady in question had an affair before she knew him. If the young man had a bad experience before, he will shy away from the young woman. From attachment he will change to coolness, from coolness to malice, from malice to antipathy. If the girl is defiant and not sorry for the past, antipathy might ripen into bitterness, and bitterness to detestation. On the other hand, if the mother of the same young man had an experience like this young lady's, and became a better wife and mother in consequence, then the young man's attachment might grow into love much more quickly than otherwise.

This simple love affair is subject to any number of variations. Too much or too little money will influence its course. A steady or insecure job will do the same. Health or sickness may speed up or slow down love's consummation. The financial and social status of either family may affect the courtship for better or worse. Heredity may upset the applecart.

Every human being is in a state of constant fluctuation and change. Nothing is static in nature, least of all man.

As we pointed out before, a character is the sum total of his physical make-up and the influences his environment exerts upon him at that particular moment.

3. The Dialectical Approach

What is dialectics? The word comes to us from the old Greeks who used it to mean a conversation or dialogue. Now, the citizens of Athens regarded conversation as a supreme art—the art of discovering truth—and contested against one another to find the best conversationalist, or dialectician. Above all other Greeks, Socrates stands out as most perfect.

We may read some of his conversations in Plato's *Dialogues,* which yield us, on close study, the secret of his art. Socrates discovers truth by this process: he states a proposition, finds a contradiction to it, and, correcting it in the light of this contradiction, finds a new contradiction. This continues indefinitely.

Let us look further into this method. Movement of the conversation is secured by three steps. First, statement of the proposition, called *thesis.* Then the discovery of a contradiction to this proposition, called *antithesis,* being the opposite of the original proposition. Now, resolution of this contradiction necessitates correction of the original proposition, and formulation of a third proposition, the *synthesis,* being the combination of the original proposition and the contradiction to it.

These three steps—thesis, antithesis, and synthesis—are the law of all movement. Everything that moves constantly negates itself. All things change toward their opposites through movement. The present becomes the past, the future becomes the present. There is nothing which does not move.

Constant change is the very essence of all existence. Everything in time passes into its opposite. Everything within itself contains its own opposite. Change is a force which impels it to move, and this very movement becomes something different from what it was. The past becomes the present and both determine the future. New life arises from the old, and this new life is the combination of the old with the contradiction which has destroyed it. This contradiction that causes the change goes on forever.

A human being is a maze of seeming contradictions. Planning one thing, he at once does another; loving, he believes he hates. Man oppressed, humiliated, beaten, still professes sympathy and understanding for those who have beaten, humiliated, and oppressed him.

How can we explain these contradictions?

Why does the man you befriend turn against you? Why does son turn against father, daughter against mother?

A boy runs away from home because his mother insists that he sweep their dingy, two-room apartment. He hates sweeping. But he is quite content with a job as assistant janitor in a big house—his main function being to sweep the halls and street. Why?

A twelve-year-old girl marries a fifty-year-old man—and is sincerely happy. A thief becomes a worthy citizen, a wealthy gentleman becomes a thief. The daughter of a respectable and religious family crashes into the underworld and prostitution. Why?

On the surface, these examples are part of a riddle, part of the so-called "mystery of life." But they can be explained, dialectically. It is a Herculean task, but not an impossible one if we remember that without contradiction there would be no motion and no life. Without contradiction there would be no universe. Stars, moon, earth would not exist—nor would we. Hegel said: *

It is only because a thing contains a contradiction within itself that it moves and acquires impulse and activity. That is the process of all motion and all development.

Adoratsky, in his *Dialectics,* writes:

The general laws of dialectics are universal: they are to be found in the movement and development of the immeasurable, vast, luminous nebulae from which in the spaces of the universe the stellar systems are formed . . . in the internal structure of molecules and atoms and in the movement of electrons and protons.

Zeno, in the fifth century B.C., was father of dialectics. Adoratsky quotes Zeno's demonstrations:

An arrow, in the course of its flight, is bound to be at some definite point of its path and occupy some definite place. If that be so, then

* *The Science of Logic.*

at each given moment it is at a definite point in a state of rest, that is, motionless; hence, it is not moving at all. We therefore see that motion cannot be expressed without resorting to contradictory statements. The arrow is at a given place, yet at the same time is not in that place. It is only by expressing both these contradictory affirmations coincidentally that we can depict motion.

Let us stop here and freeze a human being into immobility. Let us analyze thoroughly the girl who left a religious home to become a prostitute. It is not enough to say that certain forces caused her degeneration. There were forces, of course, but what were they? Did some supernatural guidance move her? Did she honestly find prostitution alluring? Hardly. She had read about it, heard from her parents, from the pastor of her church, that prostitution is one of the worst evils in society, full of uncertainty, disease, horror. She knew that a prostitute is hunted by the law, fleeced by pimps, taken advantage of by clients and masters alike, and finally left to die a lonely, miserable death.

It is almost impossible that a normal, well-bred girl would wish to become a prostitute. Yet this one did become a prostitute—and others have.

To understand the dialectical reasons for this girl's action we must know her thoroughly. Only then can we perceive the contradictions within and without her, and through these contradictions, the movement which is life.

Let us call this girl Irene; here is the bone structure of Irene's character.

PHYSIOLOGY

Sex: Female.
Age: Nineteen.
Height: Five feet, two inches.
Weight: 110 pounds.
Color of hair: Dark brown.
Color of eyes: Brown.

Skin: Fair.

Posture: Straight.

Appearance: Attractive.

Neat: Yes, very.

Health: She had an appendix operation when she was fifteen. She is susceptible to colds, and the whole family is morbidly afraid that she will become tubercular. She is seemingly unconcerned, but actually she is convinced that she will die young, and wishes to enjoy life while she can.

Birthmarks: None.

Abnormalities: None, if we overlook her hypersensitivity.

Heredity: A weak constitution, from her mother.

SOCIOLOGY

Class: Middle class. Her family lives in comfort. Father has a general store, but of late competition has been making his life miserable. He fears that he will be frozen out by younger people. This fear is eventually proved valid, but he would never burden his family with it.

Occupation: None. Irene is supposed to help around the house, but she prefers to read and let the burden fall on her seventeen-year-old sister, Sylvia.

Education: High school. She wanted to drop out in the second year, but her parents' insistence and outright threats made her finish the course somehow. She never liked school or study. She had no comprehension of mathematics or geography, but she liked history. The bravery, love affairs, betrayals, fascinated her. She read history profusely, but not as nonfiction. Dates and names were unimportant, and only the glamour mattered. Her memory was not retentive, and her sloppy working habits led to constant conflict with her teachers. Her physical neatness was not reflected in her untidy, misspelled compositions. Graduation was the happiest day of her life.

Home life: Both her parents are alive. Her mother is about forty-eight, her father, fifty-two. They married late. Her mother's life was fairly turbulent. She had a love affair lasting two and a half years, at the end of which time the man ran away with another woman. She tried to kill herself. Her brother caught her taking gas in the bathroom. She had a nervous breakdown and was sent to an aunt to recuperate. She stayed there a year, regained her health, and met the man who is now her husband. They became engaged, although she did not love him. Her contempt for men made her indifferent to the identity of the man she married. He, on the other hand, was a plain-looking man, proud that such a pretty girl should consent to marry him. She never told him of her affair with the other man, but did not worry about his finding out. He never did, since he cared nothing about her past. He loved her although she made a very poor wife at first.

After Irene's birth, she changed completely. She took interest in her household, her child, and even in her husband. But now her gall bladder, which has troubled her for years, will never be cured without an operation. She has become nervous and irritable. She no longer reads as she once did—not even a newspaper. She had only an elementary-school education and dreamed that Irene would go to college. But her daughter's abhorrence of learning frustrated this ambition.

Her bringing up was sadly neglected, and she attributes her early misstep to her parents' negligence. As a result, she exercises close supervision over Irene's every step. This leads to constant squabbling between mother and daughter. Irene hates supervision, but her mother insists it is not only her prerogative but her sacred duty.

Irene's father is of Scotch descent. He is frugal, but will go to any length to satisfy his family's needs. Irene is his pet. He worries about her health and often takes her part in her squabbles with her mother. He knows that his wife means well, however, and agrees that Irene should be looked after. He took over his father's store when his parents died, and became sole owner. He, too, went only to elementary school. He reads the local paper, the *Courier*. His parents were Republican, so he too is a Republican. If questioned, he could not give any reason for his beliefs. He believes firmly in God and country. He is a simple man with simple tastes. He makes a modest, annual contribution to the church and is highly respected in the community.

I.Q.: Irene is low normal.

Religion: Presbyterian. Irene is agnostic, when she thinks of religion at all. She's too preoccupied with herself.

Community: She belongs to a singing society and the "Moonlight Sonata Social Club," where young people congregate to dance and play games. Sometimes the games degenerate into outright petting parties. Irene is admired for her grace. She is a good dancer—nothing more. The praises she absorbs here give rise to a desire to go to New York and be a dancer. Of course, when Irene mentions this to her mother, an hysterical scene occurs. Mother's desire to squelch Irene's ambition arises from her fears of what a free life in the city might do to Irene's morals and, to a lesser extent, to Irene's delicate health. The girl never dares mention the matter again.

Irene is not particularly popular with girls, due to a certain delight she takes in malicious gossip.

Political affiliations: None. Irene never could figure out the difference between the Republican and Democratic parties and was not aware that there were any others.

Amusements: Motion pictures, dancing. She is mad about dancing. She smokes secretly.

Reading: Pulp magazines: love stories, romance, screen news.

PSYCHOLOGY

Sex life: She had an affair with Jimmy, a club member. Her fears that some dire fate would overtake her proved groundless. Now she does not go with him, because he flatly refused to marry her when she thought herself in trouble. She was not very much disappointed at his refusal, since her favorite plan is to go to New York and be a chorus girl. Dancing before an admiring public is the apex of her dreams.

Morality: "There is nothing wrong with any sexual relationship if you can take care of yourself."

Ambition: Dancing in New York. For over a year she has been putting aside her pin money. If everything else fails, she will run away. She's glad Jimmy refused to marry her. She can't picture herself as a domesticated wife whose main function is childbearing. She feels that Plainsville would be a terrible place to die in and is unspeakable for living purposes. She was born in the town and knows every stone in it. She feels that even if she fails as a dancer, just being out of Plainsville will make her happy.

Frustration: She has had no dancing lessons. There is no studio in town, and to have sent her to another town would have entailed more expense than her father could meet. She has worn a tragic halo about her head and let the family know that she is sacrificing her life for their good.

Temperament: Quick-tempered. The slightest provocation will send her into a rage. She is vengeful and boasting. But when her mother was ill, she astounded the town by her devotion. She insisted on being with her until she had completely recovered. When Irene was fourteen, her canary died, and she was inconsolable for weeks.

Attitude: Militant.

Complexes: Superiority complex.

Superstitions: Number thirteen. If something unpleasant happens on a Friday, something unpleasant will happen during the week.

Imagination: Good.

The *thesis* in this case will be the desire of the parents to marry off Irene as advantageously as possible.

The *antithesis* will be Irene's intention of not marrying at all, but of being a dancer at any cost.

The *synthesis* will be the resolution: Irene's running away and eventually finding herself on the streets.

SYNOPSIS

Irene, instead of going to the singing society, has been going out with a young man. A girl, meeting Irene's mother on the street, asks, casually, why Irene has dropped out of the group. The mother can barely hide her shock, but explains that Irene has not been well lately. At home, there is a terrible interview. Mother suspects that Irene is no longer a virgin and wishes to marry her off as quickly as possible to a clerk in her father's store. Irene is aware of her mother's determination. She decides to run away and accomplish her ambition. She finds no employment in the theater and, having no profession with which to earn a living, she soon succumbs to pressing necessity and turns to prostitution.

There are thousands of girls who run away from thousands of homes. Naturally, they do not all become prostitutes—because their physical, mental, and sociological make-ups differ in a thousand ways from each other and from Irene. Our synopsis is only one version of how a girl from a respectable home becomes a prostitute.

Suppose a hunchback had been born into the same family. That would never create the type of conflict Irene does. A deformed person would do something else in a pinch. Our character must have a good figure to think of being a dancer. Irene is intolerant; a humble or appreciative person would be

glad to get what Irene got from life. She would never think
of running away; *ergo,* Irene had to be intolerant. Irene is
shallow. Another girl might be intelligent, studious, understanding, sympathetic—she would overlook her mother's obvious shortcomings, would help her, correct her tactfully. She
would not have to run away.

Irene is vain. She receives too much praise, she thinks she
can sing and dance much better than she actually can. She's
not afraid to run away because she believes New York is waiting for her with open arms. Irene must be vain.

Irene is fully developed. She was admired, courted. She had
sexual experience without a dreadful aftermath. Therefore,
it is not unnatural for her to turn to prostitution when no
other course lies open. It was an easier way out of her economic difficulties than suicide. Why didn't she go home? Her
boasting in the past, her intolerance toward those at home,
exclude this solution. That is why she must be intolerant and
why she must boast.

But why should she turn to prostitution? Because you are
forced by your premise to *find a girl* who will turn to prostitution *in lack of other means of support.* Irene is such a girl.

Of course, Irene might get a job as a servant or a salesgirl,
hold it for a while, and then lose it because of her inherent
unfitness for such work. It is even up to you, as the playwright,
to make her try every possible means of avoiding prostitution.
But she *must* fail: not because the dramatist wants her to, *but
because her make-up is such that she cannot make good regardless of the opportunities presented.* If she does succeed
in avoiding her fate, the dramatist must find another girl
whose qualifications are such that she fulfills the original
premise. Remember that the girl has her own standards, and
you cannot judge her with yours. If she had your searching
mind she would never have found herself in such a predicament. But she is vain, superficial, boastful. She's ashamed to
admit defeat. She comes from a small town, where everyone

would know what had happened. She would not be able to face her friends, to tolerate their hidden sarcasm.

It is your task, as the playwright, to exhaust every other possibility and then show, *logically,* how she finds her way into the type of life she would most wish to avoid. It is up to you to prove that nothing else remains for her. *If, for any reason, we feel that prostitution wasn't the only way out for Irene, you have failed as a craftsman and as a dramatist.*

Because all conflict grew from the character's physical and environmental background this approach is dialectical. The inherent contradiction made her do what she did.

Of course, a playwright *can* start with a plot or an idea. *But after that he must formulate a premise which will crystallize his plot or idea.* In this way the plot or idea will not be separate from the play as a whole, but will be an integral part of it.

Frank S. Nugent, formerly motion-picture critic for *The New York Times,* wrote in great astonishment on February 17, 1939, about a picture called *Made for Each Other:* "For that, in fact, is the story of *Made for Each Other,* and it happens to be the story, in one form or another, of every young couple that ever was or will be. Mr. Swerling hasn't said a new thing, taken a stand pro or con, or shed a bit of light on the murky course of human destiny. He simply has found a pleasant young couple, or has let them find each other, and has permitted nature to have its fling. It is an unusual procedure for a script writer. Habitually they toss nature aside and think up the darnedest things for their people to do. It's amazing how interesting normal human behavior can be."

Yes, it is amazing. If only playwrights and producers would permit characters to work out their own destinies!

4. *Character Growth*

The only thing that one really knows about human nature is that it changes. Change is the one quality we can predicate of it. The

systems that fail are those that rely on the permanency of human
nature, and not its growth and development.
                    —OSCAR WILDE, *Soul of Man under Socialism*

Regardless of the medium in which you are working, you
must know your characters thoroughly. And you must know
them not only as they are today, but as they will be tomorrow
or years from now.

Everything in nature changes—human beings along with
the rest. A man who was brave ten years ago may be a coward
now, for any number of reasons: age, physical deterioration,
changed financial status, to name a few.

You may think you know someone who never has changed,
and never will. But no such person has ever existed. A man
may keep his religious and political views apparently intact
through the years, but close scrutiny will show that his convictions have either deepened or become superficial. They
have gone through many stages, many conflicts, and will continue to go through them as long as the man lives. So he does
change, after all.

Even stone changes, although its disintegration is imperceptible; the earth goes through a slow but persistent transformation; the sun, too, the solar system, the universe. Nations are born, pass through adolescence, achieve manhood,
grow old, and then die, either violently or by gradual dissolution.

Why should man, then, be the only thing in nature which
never changes? Preposterous!

There is only one realm in which characters defy natural
laws and remain the same—the realm of bad writing. And it
is the fixed nature of the characters which makes the writing
bad. If a character in a short story, novel, or play occupies the
same position at the end as the one he did at the beginning,
that story, novel, or play is bad.

A character stands revealed through conflict; conflict begins with a decision; a decision is made because of the prem-

ise of your play. The character's decision necessarily sets in motion another decision, from his adversary. And it is these decisions, one resulting from the other, which propel the play to its ultimate destination: the proving of the premise.

No man ever lived who could remain the same through a series of conflicts which affected his way of living. Of necessity he must change, and alter his attitude toward life.

Even a corpse is in a state of change: disintegration. And while a man is arguing with you, attempting to prove his changelessness, he is changing: growing old.

So we can safely say that any character, in any type of literature, which does not undergo a basic change is a badly drawn character. We can go further and say that if a character cannot change, any situation in which he is placed will be an unreal situation.

Nora, from *A Doll's House,* who starts as Helmer's "scatterbrain" and "singing bird," becomes a grown-up woman at the end of the play. She begins as a child, but the terrible awakening catapults her into maturity. First she is bewildered, then shocked, then about to do away with herself, and finally she revolts.

Archer says:

In all modern drama, there is perhaps no character who "develops," in the ordinary sense of the word, so startlingly as Ibsen's *Nora.*

Look at any truly great play, and you will see the same point illustrated. Molière's *Tartuffe,* Shakespeare's *Merchant of Venice,* and *Hamlet,* Lessing's *Nathan the Wise,* Euripides' *Medea,* all build upon the constant change and development of character under the impact of conflict.

Othello starts with love, ends with jealousy, murder, and suicide.

The Bear starts with animosity, ends with love.

Hedda Gabler starts with egotism, ends with suicide.

Macbeth starts with ambition, ends with murder.

The Cherry Orchard starts with irresponsibility, ends with loss of property.

Excursion starts with the longing to fulfill a dream, ends with awakening to reality.

Hamlet starts with suspicion, ends with murder.

Mamba's Daughters starts with violent temper, ends in murder and suicide.

Dead End starts with poverty, ends with crime.

The Silver Cord starts with domination, ends in dissolution.

Craig's Wife starts with overscrupulousness, ends with loneliness.

Waiting for Lefty starts with uncertainty, ends with conviction.

The Big Blow starts with antagonism and hopelessness, ends with unity and hope.

What a Life starts with acceptance of failure, ends with budding self-confidence.

Prologue to Glory starts with aimlessness, ends with direction.

Professor Mamlock starts with isolation, ends with collective struggle.

All these characters move relentlessly from one state of mind toward another; they are forced to change, grow, develop, because the dramatists had a clear-cut premise which it was their function to prove.

When a person makes one mistake, he always follows up with another. Usually the second mistake grows out of the first and the third from the second. Orgon, in *Tartuffe,* made the grievous mistake of taking Tartuffe into his home, believing in his saintliness. The second mistake was entrusting Tartuffe with a small box containing papers "which, if they were brought to light might, for aught I know, cost my friend all his estate, and—if he were caught—his head."

Orgon believed in Tartuffe so far, but now, by putting this box in his care, Orgon jeopardizes a human life. Orgon's growth from trust to admiration is obvious, deepening with every line.

TARTUFFE: It is well hidden. [*The box*] You may feel easy concerning it. As *I* do.

ORGON: My best friend! What you have done is beyond all thanks. It has knit us even closer together than before.

TARTUFFE: Nothing could do that.

ORGON: One thing could, as I have just seen, if it could but be accomplished.

TARTUFFE: A dark saying, brother. Expound it, I pray you.

ORGON: You said a while ago that my daughter needed a husband who could keep her footsteps from straying.

TARTUFFE: I did. And I cannot think that a worldling such as M. Valere—

ORGON: Nor I. And this has lately been borne in upon me—she could have no safer, tenderer guide through the pitfalls of this life than *you*, beloved friend.

TARTUFFE: [*Who is genuinely taken back for the moment*] Than *I*, brother? Oh, no. No!

ORGON: What? Would you refuse to be my son-in-law?

TARTUFFE: It is an honor to which I have never dreamed of aspiring. And—and—I have some cause to think that I have found no favor in the eyes of Mlle Mariane.

ORGON: That matters little if she has found favor in *yours*.

TARTUFFE: Eyes that are fixed on Heaven, brother, have no regard for the beauty that perisheth.

ORGON: True, brother, true—but would you hold that a reason for refusing a bride who is not without comeliness?

TARTUFFE: [*Who is uncertain how a marriage with Mariane would assist his designs on Elmire*] I would not say so. Many saintly men have wedded comely maidens and sinned not. But—to be plain with you—I fear that a marriage with your daughter might not be altogether pleasing to Madame Orgon.

ORGON: What if it be not? She is only her stepmother, and her consent is not needed. I might add that Mariane will bring her husband an ample dowry, but that I know will not weigh with you.

TARTUFFE: How *should* it?

ORGON: But what, I hope, *will* weigh with you is that by declining her hand you would disappoint me grievously.

TARTUFFE: If I thought *that,* brother—

ORGON: More than that, I should feel that you did not think such an alliance worthy of you.

TARTUFFE: It is I who am unworthy. [*He decides to take the risk*] But, rather than you should so misjudge me, I will—yes, I *will* overcome my scruples.

ORGON: Then you consent to be my son-in-law?

TARTUFFE: Since you desire it, who am I that I should say you nay?

ORGON: You have made me a happy man again. [*He rings handbell*] I will send for my daughter and tell her what I have arranged for her.

TARTUFFE: [*Going toward his door right*] Meanwhile I will crave your permission to retire. [*At door*] If I may offer my counsel, it will be better, in laying this matter before her, to dwell less on any poor merits of my own than on your wishes as a father. [*He goes in*]

ORGON: [*To himself*] What humility!

Orgon's third mistake is in trying to force his daughter to marry this scoundrel. His fourth mistake is in deeding his whole estate to Tartuffe to manage. He sincerely believes that Tartuffe will save his wealth from his family, who, he thinks, wants to squander it. This is his most grievous mistake. He has sealed his own doom. But the ridiculousness of this deed is only a natural outgrowth of his first mistake. Yes, Orgon grows perceptibly from blind belief to disillusionment. The author achieved this with step-by-step development in his character.

When you plant a seed, it seems for a while to lie dormant. Actually, moisture attacks it immediately, softening the shell of the seed so that the chemical inherent in the seed, and those which it absorbs from the soil, may cause it to sprout.

The soil above the seed is hard to push through, but this very handicap, this resistance to the soil, forces the young sprout to gather strength for the battle. Where shall it get this additional strength? Instead of fighting ineffectively against the topsoil, the seed sends out delicate roots to gather more nourishment. Thus the sprout at last penetrates the hard soil and wins through to the sun.

According to science, a single thistle needs ten thousand inches of root to support a thirty- or forty-inch stem. You can guess how many thousands of facts a dramatist must unearth to support a single character.

By way of parable, let a man represent the soil; in his mind we shall plant a seed of coming conflict: ambition, perhaps. The seed grows in him, though he may wish to squelch it. But forces within and without the man exert greater and greater pressure, until this seed of conflict is strong enough to burst through his stubborn head. He has made a decision, and now he will act upon it.

The contradictions within a man and the contradictions around him create a decision and a conflict. These in turn force him into a new decision and a new conflict.

Many kinds of pressures are required before a human being can make a single decision, but the three main groups are the physiological, the sociological, and the psychological. From these three forces you can make innumerable combinations.

If you plant an acorn, you reasonably expect an oak sapling, and eventually an oak tree. Human character is the same. A certain type of character will develop on his own line to fruition. Only in bad writing does a man change without regard to his characteristics. When we plant an acorn we would be justified in expecting an oak tree and shocked (at the very least) if it turned out to be an apple tree.

Every character a dramatist presents must have within it the seeds of its future development. There must be the seed, or possibility, of crime in the boy who is going to turn criminal at the end of the play.

Although Nora, in *A Doll's House,* is loving, submissive, and obedient, there is in her the spirit of independence, rebellion, and stubbornness—a sign of possible growth.

Let us examine her character. We know that at the end of the play she is not only going to leave her husband, but her children as well. In 1879 that was an almost unheard-of phenomenon. She had little, if any, precedent to go by. She must have had within her that something, *at the beginning of the play,* which develops into the independent spirit she has at the end. Let us see what this something was.

When the play opens, Nora enters, humming a tune. A porter follows with a Christmas tree and a basket.

PORTER: Sixpence.
NORA: There is a shilling. No, keep the change.

She has been trying to save every penny to pay off her secret debt—yet still she is generous. Meanwhile she is eating macaroons, which she is not supposed to have. They are not good for her, and she has promised Helmer that she will not eat sweets. So the first sentence she says shows us that she is not close with money, and the first thing she does shows her breaking a promise. She is childlike.

Helmer enters:

HELMER: Has my little spendthrift been wasting money again?
NORA: Yes, but Torvald, we may be a wee bit more reckless now, mayn't we?

(Helmer cautions her. It will be a whole quarter before he receives his salary. Nora cries out like an impatient child: "Pooh! We can borrow till then!")

HELMER: Nora! [*He is appalled at her featherheadedness. He resents this "borrow."*] Suppose, now, that I borrowed fifty pounds

today, and you spent it all in the Christmas week, and then on
New Year's Eve a slate fell on my head and killed me, and . . .

(Just like Helmer. He would not be at peace, even in the
grave, with one unpaid debt on his conscience. He is certainly
a stickler for propriety. Can you imagine his reaction if he
were to discover that Nora had forged a name?)

NORA: If that were to happen, I don't suppose I should care
whether I owed money or not. [*She has been kept in perpetual
ignorance of money matters, and her reaction is imperious.
Helmer is tolerant, but not enough so to forgo a lecture.*]
HELMER: . . . There can be no freedom or beauty about a home
life that depends on borrowing and debt. [*At this Nora is very
discouraged. It seems that Helmer will never understand her.*]

The two characters have been sharply drawn. They are facing each other—clashing already. No blood has been drawn
yet, but it inevitably will come.

(Loving her as he does, Helmer now shifts the responsibility
to her father.)

HELMER: You're an odd little soul. Very like your father. You always find some new way of wheedling money out of me, and, as
soon as you have got it, it seems to melt in your hands. . . .
Still, one must take you as you are. It is in the blood; for indeed
it is true that you can inherit these things, Nora.

(With a master stroke Ibsen has sketched in Nora's background. He knows her ancestry better than she does. But she
loves her father, and is not slow to answer: "Oh, I wish I had
inherited many of Papa's qualities."

Right after this she lies shamelessly about having eaten the
macaroons, like a child who feels that the prohibitions set
down by her elders are necessarily senseless. There is no great
harm in this lying, but it shows what material Nora is made
of.)

NORA: I should not think of going against your wishes.

HELMER: No, I am sure of that; besides, you gave me your word.

(Life and Helmer's business have schooled him to think that a given word is sacred. Here again, an insignificant thing shows Helmer's lack of imagination, his complete inability to realize that Nora is anything but what she seems to be on the surface. He is unaware of what goes on behind his back at home. Every penny that Nora wheedles out of him goes to the money-lender, to pay off the debt she has incurred.

Nora is living a double life at the beginning of the play. The forgery was committed long before the play opened, and Nora has been hugging her secret to herself, calm in the knowledge that her deed was a heroic sacrifice to save Helmer's life.)

NORA: [*Talking to her schooltime friend, Mrs. Linde*] But it was absolutely necessary that he should not know! My goodness, can't you understand that? It was necessary he should have no idea what a dangerous condition he was in. It was to me that the doctors came and said his life was in danger and that the only thing to save him was to live in the South. . . . I even hinted that he might raise a loan. That nearly made him angry, Christine. He said I was thoughtless and that it was his duty as my husband not to indulge me in my whims. . . . Very well, I thought, you must be saved—and that was how I came to devise a way out of the difficulty.

(Ibsen takes his time about starting the main conflict. Very precious time is consumed by the scene in which Nora confesses to Mrs. Linde what she did for Helmer. There is something too coincidental about Mrs. Linde's visit at this opportune moment, and also Krogstad's visit. But we are not discussing Ibsen's deficiencies here. We are tracing the completeness of Nora's development. Let us see what else we can learn about her.)

MRS. LINDE: Do you mean never to tell him about it? [*the forgery*]

NORA: [*Meditatively, and with a half-smile*] Yes, someday, perhaps, after many years, when I am no longer as nice-looking as I am now. [*This throws an interesting light on Nora's motive. She expects gratitude for her deed.*] Don't laugh at me! I mean, of course, when Torvald is no longer as devoted to me as he is now, when my dancing and dressing up and reciting have palled on him, then it may be a good thing to have something in reserve.

(Now we can surmise the tremendous shock Nora is in for when Helmer denounces her as a bad wife and mother, instead of praising her. This, then, will be the turning point in her life. Her childhood will die a miserable death, and with a shock she will see, for the first time, the hostile world about her. She has done everything in her power to make Helmer live and be happy, and when she needs him most he will turn against her. Nora has all the necessary ingredients for growth in one direction. Helmer, too, acts in accordance with the character Ibsen has given him. Listen to his storm of impotent rage after learning of the forgery.)

HELMER: What a horrible awakening! All these eight years—she who was my joy and pride—a hypocrite, a liar—worse—worse —a criminal! The unutterable ugliness of it all! For shame! For shame! [*"Nora is silent and looks at him steadily. He stops in front of her."* These are Ibsen's stage directions. *Nora is looking at Helmer with horror, seeing a strange man, a man who forgets her motive and thinks only of himself.*] I ought to have suspected that something of the sort would happen. I ought to have foreseen it, all your father's want of principle—be silent!

(Apparently Nora's sociological background helped Ibsen draw her mind. Her physiological make-up helped, too—she is aware of her beauty, mentions it several times. She knows she has many admirers, but they mean nothing to her until she makes up her mind to leave.)

HELMER: All your father's want of principle has come out in you. No religion, no sense of duty.

All these things are discernible in Nora's character at the beginning of the play. She has brought upon herself everything that happened. These things were in her character and they necessarily directed her actions. Nora's growth is positive. We can watch her irresponsibility change to anxiety, her anxiety to fear, her fear to desperation. The climax leaves her at first numb, then she slowly understands her position. She makes her final, irrevocable decision, a decision as logical as the blooming of a flower, a decision which is the result of steady, persistent evolution. Growth is evolution; climax is revolution.

Let us trace the seed of possible growth in another character—Romeo. We want to know if he possesses the characteristics which will lead him to the inevitable end.

Romeo, in love with Rosalind, is walking around in a daze, when on the street he meets one of his relatives, Benvolio, who accosts him.

BENVOLIO: Good morning, cousin.
ROMEO: Is the day so young?
BENVOLIO: But now struck nine.
ROMEO: Ay me! Sad hours seem long.
    Was that my father that went hence so fast?
BENVOLIO: It was. What sadness lengthens Romeo's hours?
ROMEO: Not having that which, having, makes them short.
BENVOLIO: In love?
ROMEO: Out.
BENVOLIO: Of love?
ROMEO: Out of her favor, where I am in love.

Romeo bitterly complains that his ladylove has "not been hit with Cupid's arrow."

> She is too fair, too wise, wisely too fair,
> To merit bliss by making me despair:
> She hath forsworn to love; and in that vow
> Do I live dead, that live to tell it now.

Benvolio advises him to "examine other beauties," but Romeo cannot be consoled.

> He that is stricken blind cannot forget
> The previous treasure of his eyesight lost:
>
> .   .   .   .
>
> Farewell: thou canst not teach me to forget.

But later, through a queer coincidence, he learns that his beloved Rosalind will be in the house of his family's deadly enemy, the Capulets, where they are entertaining guests. He decides to go, defying death, to steal, if only a glance, at his love. And there, among the guests, he beholds a lady so enchanting that he has no eyes for Rosalind and breathlessly asks a servingman:

What lady's that, which doth enrich the hand of yonder knight?
SERVANT: I know not, sir.
ROMEO: O, she doth teach the torches to burn bright!
It seems she hangs upon the cheek of night
Like a rich jewel in an Ethiop's ear;
Beauty too rich for use, for earth too dear!
So shows a snowy dove trooping with crows,
As yonder lady o'er her fellows shows.
The measure dove, I'll watch her place of stand,
And, touching hers, make blessed my rude hand.
Did my heart love till now? Forswear it, sight!
For I ne'er saw true beauty till this night.

And with this decision his die is cast.

Romeo is haughty, impetuous. Finding that his true love is the daughter of the Capulets, he does not hesitate to storm this citadel of hate where murderous intent is constant against him and his family. He is impatient, brooks no contradiction. His love for the fair Juliet has made him still more high strung. For his love, he is willing even to humble himself. No price is too great for his beloved Juliet.

If we consider his death-defying exploit—jeopardizing his life just to have a glance at Rosalind—then we may surmise what he is capable of doing for Juliet, the true love of his life.

No other type of man could have faced so much danger without flinching. The possible growth was inherent in his character from the very beginning of the play.

It is interesting to note that a certain Mr. Maginn in his *Shakespeare Papers* states that Romeo's hard luck throughout his life was attributable to the fact that he was "unlucky," that had any other passion or pursuit occupied Romeo, he would have been as unlucky as in his love.

Mr. Maginn forgets that Romeo, like everyone else, acts as his character dictates. Yes, Romeo's downfall is inherent; it does not occur because he is "unlucky." His impetuous temperament, which he cannot control, drives him to do what another person could easily have avoided.

His temperament, his background—in short, his character was the seed which ensured growth and proved the author's premise.

The important thing we wish the reader to remember is that Romeo was fashioned from that kind of stuff which made him what he was (impulsive, and so on) and forced him to do what he did later (murder and suicide). This characteristic was apparent in the first line uttered.

Another fine example of growth is found in *Mourning Becomes Electra,* by Eugene O'Neill. Lavinia, the daughter of a brigadier general, Ezra Mannon, and his wife Christine, says almost at the very beginning of the play, when a young man who loves her alludes to love:

LAVINIA: [*Stiffening, brusquely*] I don't know anything about love. I don't want to know anything. [*Intensely*] I hate love!

Lavinia is the pivotal character, and lives up to this statement throughout the play. Her mother's illicit love affair made her what she became later—relentless, vengeful to death.

We have no intention of stopping anyone from writing a pageant or imitating the indefatigable Saroyan, who writes limping cadences to the beauty of life. Any of these things can be moving, even beautiful to behold. We wouldn't eliminate Gertrude Stein, either, from the groaning arena of literature for the simple reason that we enormously enjoy her vagaries and her style (although, we confess, frequently we don't know what she is talking about). From decay springs a new, vibrant life. Somehow these formless things belong to life. Without disharmony there could never be harmony. But some playwrights obviously write about character and want to build it into a well-constructed edifice, and when it turns out to be a pageant or a pseudo-Saroyan, they insist that we treat their work as a play. We can't do that, no matter how hard we try, just as we can't compare the mental capacity of a child to an Einstein.

Robert E. Sherwood's *Idiot's Delight* is such a work. Although it won the Pulitzer Prize, it is far from being a well-constructed play.

Harry Van and Irene are supposed to be the leading characters in this play, but we can't discern any possible growth in them. Irene is a liar and Harry is a good-natured, happy-go-lucky fellow. Only at the end we see some growth, but then the play is over.

Lavinia, Hamlet, Nora, and Romeo, even without a magnificent production, are still characters; living, pulsating, dynamic personalities. They know what they want and fight for it. But poor Harry and Irene just amble around without a visible goal to pursue.

QUESTION: What do you mean, explicitly, when you say "growth"?

ANSWER: For example, King Lear is ready to distribute his kingdom among his daughters. This is a blunder, and the play must prove to the audience that it is folly. It does this through showing the effect of Lear's action on himself, his "growth," or logical development, as a consequence of his mistake. First, he *doubts* that the power he gave his children is being misused. Then he suspects that it is. Then he is sure, and becomes indignant. He is furious, next, and flies into a rage. He is stripped of all authority and is shamed. He wishes to kill himself. In shame and grief, he goes mad, and dies.

He planted a seed which grew and bore the kind of fruit that seed was bound to bear. He never dreamed the fruit would be so bitter—but that is the result of his character, which caused his original mistake. And he pays the price.

QUESTION: Would his growth have been the same if he had chosen the right person—his youngest daughter—as the most trustworthy?

ANSWER: Naturally not. Each mistake—and its reaction upon him—grew from the mistake before it. If Lear had made the right choice in the first place there would have been no motivation for the later action. His first blunder was in deciding to invest his authority in his children. He knew this authority was great, coupled with the highest honor, and he never doubted the ready assurance from his daughters that they loved and revered him. He was shocked by the relative coolness of Cordelia and so made his second mistake. He asked for words rather than deeds. Everything that happened thereafter grew from these roots.

QUESTION: Weren't his mistakes simply stupidity?

ANSWER: Yes, but don't forget that all blunders—yours and mine—are stupid *after* they are made. At the time they may grow out of pity, generosity, sympathy, understanding. What we term stupid at the last may have been a beautiful gesture at the first.

"Growth" is a character's reaction to a conflict in which he is involved. A character can grow through making the correct move, as well as the incorrect one—but he *must* grow, if he is a real character.

Take a couple. They are in love. Leave them for a while, and they may produce the elements of a drama. Perhaps they drift apart, and there is conflict between them; perhaps their love grows deeper, and conflict comes from *outside*. If you ask, "Does real love deepen through adversity?" or if you say, "Even a great love suffers in adversity," your characters will have a goal to achieve, and a chance to grow to prove the premise. The proving of a premise indicates growth on the part of the characters.

II

Every good play grows from pole to pole.

Let us examine a motion picture and see whether or not this is true.

"Professor Mamlock"

(*He will go from Isolation, Pole I, to Collective Action, Pole II*)

STEP 1. Isolation. He was unconcerned under the Nazi tyranny. He was an outstanding personality; he felt above politics. He never dreamed that anyone could harm him, although he saw terror all around.

STEP 2. Nazi power reaches into his own class and tortures his colleagues. He starts to worry. But he still doesn't believe that anything can happen to him. He sends away friends who beg him to escape.

STEP 3. At last, he senses that a tragic fate might smash him, as it did others. He calls his friends, and rationalizes that he had been justified in being an isolationist. He still is not ready to give up the ship.

STEP 4. Fear grips him. At last he realizes that his previous stand was sheer blindness.

STEP 5. He wishes to escape, but doesn't know how or where to turn.

STEP 6. He becomes *desperate*.

STEP 7. He *joins common struggle* against Nazism.

STEP 8. He becomes a member of the underground organization.

STEP 9. *Defies tyranny*.

STEP 10. Collective action and death.

Let us now take Nora and Helmer from *Doll's House*.

NORA: *From:* submissive, happy-go-lucky, naïve, trusting
      To: cynical, independent, adult, bitter, disillusioned

HELMER: *From:* bigoted, domineering, sure of himself, practical, precise, patronizing, conventional, ruthless
        To: bewildered, unsure, disillusioned, dependent, submissive, weak, tolerant, considerate, confused

III

HATRED TO LOVE

Before curtain	*Curtain*
1. Insecurity	5. Hatred
2. Humiliation	6. Causing injury
3. Resentment	7. Satisfaction
4. Fury	8. Remorse
	9. Humility
	10. False generosity
	11. Reevaluation
	12. Real generosity
	13. Sacrifice
	14. Love

LOVE TO HATRED

Before curtain	*Curtain*
1. Possessive love	5. Suspicion
2. Disappointment	6. Testing
3. Doubt	7. Hurt
4. Questioning	8. Realization
	9. Bitterness
	10. Reevaluation and failure to adjust
	11. Anger
	12. Fury (at self)
	13. Fury (at object)
	14. Hate

5. *Strength of Will in a Character*

A weak character cannot carry the burden of protracted conflict in a play. He cannot support a play. We are forced, then, to discard such a character as a protagonist. There is no sport if there is no competition; there is no play if there is no conflict. Without counterpoint there is no harmony. The dramatist needs not only characters who are willing to put up a fight for their convictions. He needs characters who have the strength, the stamina, to carry this fight to its logical conclusion.

We may start with a weak man who gathers strength as he goes along; we may start with a strong man who weakens through conflict, but even as he weakens he must have the stamina to bear his humiliation.

Here is an example, in O'Neill's *Mourning Becomes Electra*. Brant is talking to Lavinia. He is the illegitimate child of a servant girl and an almighty Mannon. He is an outcast, as far as the Mannons are concerned, and his mother brought him up in a distant place. But now he has returned,

under an assumed name, to avenge the humiliation his mother
and he have undergone. He is a captain, and he makes love
to Lavinia to hide his affair with her mother. But Lavinia's
servant puts her on her guard.

(Brant tries to take her hand, but at his touch she pulls
away and springs to her feet.)

LAVINIA: [*With cold fury*] Don't touch me! Don't you dare! You
liar! You—! [*Then, as he starts back in confusion, she seizes this
opportunity to follow Seth's (the servant's) advice—staring at
him with deliberately insulting scorn*] But I suppose it would be
foolish to expect anything but cheap romantic lies from the son
of a low Canuck nurse girl.

BRANT: [*Stunned*] What's that? [*Then, rage at the insult to his
mother overcoming all prudence, springs to his feet threaten-
ingly*] Belay, damn you!—or I'll forget you're a woman. No
Mannon can insult her while I—

LAVINIA: [*Appalled now she knows the truth*] So it is true—you are
her son! Oh!

BRANT: [*Fighting to control himself—with harsh defiance*] And
what if I am? I'm proud to be! My only shame is my dirty Mannon blood! So that's why you couldn't stand my touching you
just now, is it? You're too good for the son of a servant, eh? By
God, you were glad enough before—!

These characters are vital, full of fight, and they will easily
carry the play to a crescendo. Brant has been planning his
revenge for a long time, and now, when it is almost within
his grasp, he is thwarted. At this point the conflict ripens
into a crisis. We are really eager to know what he is going to
do when he is unmasked. Unfortunately, O'Neill bungles and
distorts his characters in this play—but more about this in our
analysis of plays.

Martha, one of the dead soldiers' wives, is speaking in
Irwin Shaw's *Bury the Dead:*

MARTHA: A house should have a baby. But it should be a clean house with a full icebox. Why shouldn't I have a baby? Other people have babies. They don't have to feel their skin crawl every time they tear a page off the calendar. They go off to beautiful hospitals in lovely ambulances and have babies between colored sheets. What's there about them that God likes that he makes it so easy for them to have babies?

WEBSTER: [*One of the soldiers*] They're not married to mechanics.

MARTHA: No! It's not eighteen-fifty for them. And now—now it's worse. Your twenty dollars a month. You hire yourself out to be killed and I get twenty dollars a month. I wait on line all day to get a loaf of bread. I've forgotten what butter tastes like. I wait on line with the rain soaking through my shoes for a pound of rotten meat once a week. At night I go home. Nobody to talk to, just sitting watching the bugs, with one little light because the government's got to save electricity. You had to go off and leave me to that! What's the war to me that I have to sit at night with nobody to talk to? What's the war to you that you had to go off and—

WEBSTER: That's why I'm standing up now, Martha.

MARTHA: What took you so long, then? Why now? Why not a month ago, a year ago, ten years ago? Why didn't you stand up then? Why wait until you're dead? You live on eighteen-fifty a week, with the roaches, not saying a word, and then when they kill you, you stand up! You fool!

WEBSTER: I didn't see it before.

MARTHA: Just like you! Wait until it's too late! There's plenty for live men to stand up for! All right, stand up! It's about time you talked back. It's about time all you poor, miserable, eighteen-fifty bastards stood up for themselves and their wives and the children they can't have! Tell 'em all to stand up! Tell 'em! Tell 'em! [*She shrieks. Blackout.*]

These characters, too, are pulsating with fighting strength; whatever they do, they'll force opposite wills to clash.

Go through all great dramas and you will find that the characters in them *force the issue* in question until they are beaten or reach their goal. Even Chekhov's characters are so strong in their passivity that the accumulated force of circumstance has a hard time crushing them.

Some weakness which seems inconsequential may easily provide the starting point of a powerful play.

Look at *Tobacco Road*. Jeeter Lester, the central figure, is a weak-kneed man, without the strength to live or die successfully. Poverty stares him in the face, his wife and children starve, and he twiddles his thumbs. No catastrophe is great enough to move him. This weak, useless man has phenomenal strength in waiting for a miracle; he can cling tenaciously to the past, he can ignore the fact that the present offers a new problem to be solved. He laments endlessly the great injustice done him in the past—it is his pet theme, yet he does nothing to correct it.

Is he a weak or a strong character? To our way of thinking he is one of the strongest characters we have seen in the theater in a long time. He typifies decay, disintegration, and still he is strong. This is a natural contradiction. Lester stubbornly maintains his *status quo*, or *seems* to maintain it, against the changes of time. Even to put up a noticeable fight against natural laws requires tremendous strength, and Jeeter Lester has that strength, although ever-changing conditions will liquidate him as they have liquidated all things which could not adapt themselves. Jeeter and the dinosaur are of one spirit.

Jeeter Lester represents a class: the dispossessed small farmers. Modern machinery, the accumulation of wealth in a few hands, competition, taxes, assessments have put him and his class out of business. He will not organize with the dispossessed because he is unaware of the value of organization. Because his ancestors never organized, he lives in miserable isolation, ignorant of the outside world. He is stubborn in his ignorance. His tradition is against change. But in his weakness he is exceptionally strong, and condemns himself and his class to slow death rather than change. Yes, Jeeter Lester is a strong man.

Can anyone imagine a sweeter and weaker character than the classic mother? Can one forget her eternal vigilance, tender care, anxious warnings? She subordinates herself to one goal, the success of her child, sacrificing even her life, if necessary. Isn't your mother like that? Enough mothers are, to have built up a maternal tradition. Haven't you been haunted in your dreams, at least once, by your mother's smile, her sullen silence, her persistent admonitions, her tears? Haven't you, at least once, felt like a murderer in going against your mother's wishes? All the sins in the world, put together, have never made mankind into greater liars than their sweet mothers.

Seemingly weak, always ready to retreat and give in, yet almost always the winner in the end, such is Mother. You don't always know how you have been roped and tied, but you find that you have made a promise your mind rebels at breaking.

Are mothers weak? Emphatically no! Think of *The Silver Cord*, by Sidney Howard. Here is a mother wrecking the lives of her own children—not with brutality, but with sweet, weak words, with bitter tears, with seemingly ineffectual silence. In the end she ruined the lives of all about her. Is she weak?

Who, then, are the weak characters as opposed to the strong ones? They are those who have no power to put up a fight.

Jeeter Lester, for instance, is inactive in the face of starvation. To go hungry without doing anything about it is queer, to say the least. The man has stamina, even if it is misdirected. Self-preservation is a natural law, and it leads both animals and men to hunt, steal, and murder, to get food. Jeeter Lester disobeys this law. He has his tradition, he has his ancestral home. The property belongs to him as it did to his ancestors, and he feels that to run away from it in adversity would be cowardly. He thinks it is fortitude to take all the punishment he gets for the sake of what belongs to him. It may be that basic laziness, even cowardice, has made him the tenacious man he is, but the resultant behavior is strong.

The truly weak character is the person who will not fight because the pressure is not strong enough. Take Hamlet. He is persistent and with bulldog tenacity proves the facts of his father's death. He has weaknesses, else he would not have had to hide behind assumed insanity. His sensitivity is a drawback in his fight, yet he kills Polonius who he thinks is spying on him. Hamlet is a complete character, hence he is ideal material for a play, as is Jeeter. Contradiction is the essence of conflict, and when a character can overcome his internal contradictions to win his goal, he is strong.

The stool pigeon in *Black Pit* offers a good example of a weak, badly drawn character. He could never make up his mind what to do. The author wanted us to see the danger of compromise, but the audience felt sympathy and pity for the man they were supposed to despise.

The man was never really a stool pigeon. He was not defiant, but ashamed. He knew he was doing something wrong, but couldn't help it. On the other hand, he wasn't a class-conscious worker, because he was unfaithful to his class—and he could not do anything about that, either.

Where there is no contradiction there is no conflict. In this case the contradiction was ill-defined, as was the conflict. The man let himself be entangled in a web and lacked the courage to get out. His shame was not deep enough to force him into a decision—the only compromise—nor was his love for his family great enough to overcome all opposition and make him a stool pigeon in earnest. He could not make up his mind one way or the other, and such a person is incapable of carrying a play. We can now define a weak character in another way: "A weak character is one who, for any reason, cannot make a decision to act."

Is Joe, the stool pigeon, so inherently weak that he would have remained undecided under any conditions? No. If the situation in which he finds himself is not pressing enough, it is the author's duty to find a more clearly defined premise. Under greater pressure Joe would have reacted more violently than he did. It was not enough to arouse Joe that his wife would have to give birth to her child without a midwife. That was an everyday occurrence in his world, and most of the women survived.

But there is no character who would not fight back *under the right circumstances.* If he is weak and unresisting, it is because the author has not found the psychological moment when he is not only ready, but eager to fight. The point of attack was miscalculated. Or it might be put this way: a decision must be permitted to mature. The author may catch a character in a period of *transition,* when he is not yet ready to act. Many a character fails because the author forces him into action he is not ready to take, action he will not be ready to take for an hour, or a year, or twenty years.

We find this little item in *The New York Times* of February 25, 1939, on the editorial page:

MURDER AND INSANITY

After studying some 500 murders, the Metropolitan Life Insurance Company expresses in its Bulletin mild astonishment at the reasons. An irate husband beats his wife to death because *dinner* is not ready; one friend kills another over a matter of *25 cents;* a lunchroom proprietor shoots a customer after an argument over *a sandwich;* a youth kills his mother because she upbraids him about his *drinking;* a barfly slashes another to death over a dispute as to who shall drop a nickel into a slot and *play* a mechanical piano first.

Were these people all mad? What could have motivated them to take human life over a pittance, for a grudge? Normal people do not commit such atrocities—perhaps they really were insane.

There is only one way to find out and that is to examine the physiological, sociological, and psychological make-up of a murderer in a case which, on the surface, is brutal and shocking.

Our man is fifty years old. He killed a man—stabbed him —because of a joke. Everyone thought him a vicious, unsocial creature, a beast. Let us see what he was.

The murderer's history shows that he was patient and harmless, a good provider, an excellent father, a respected citizen, an esteemed neighbor. He had worked as bookkeeper in one firm for thirty years. His employers found him honest, responsible, inoffensive. They were shocked when he was arrested for murder.

The groundwork for his crime began thirty-two years ago, when he was married. He was eighteen, and in love with his wife, although she was exactly his opposite in nature. She was vain, unreliable, flirtatious, untruthful. He had to close his eyes to her constant indiscretions, because he sincerely believed that she would someday change for the better. He never did anything decisive to stop her shameful behavior, although he threatened her now and again. But it remained only a threat.

A playwright, seeing him at this point, would have found him too weak and inoffensive to make a dramatic character. He felt the humiliation deeply, but he was powerless to do anything about it. There is no hint of what the man will become.

Years pass. His wife gives him three beautiful children, and he hopes that with advanced age she will finally change. She does. She becomes more careful, and seems really to settle down, to be a good wife and mother.

Then one day she disappears, never to return. At first, the poor man almost goes mad, but he recovers and takes over her duties around the house along with his work. He receives no thanks from his children for his sacrifice. They abuse him, and leave him at the first opportunity.

On the surface our man has been bearing all this stoically. Perhaps he is a coward, lacking the energy to resist or revolt. Perhaps he has superhuman energy and the courage to bear abuse and injustice.

Now he loses the house which was his pride. He is deeply moved and makes efforts to save it. But he cannot, and he is crushed, although not to the point where he would take drastic action. He is still the timid Milquetoast: changed, yes; bitter, yes; uneasy, yes. Looking for an answer, and not finding one, he is bewildered, alone. Instead of revolting, he becomes a recluse.

So far he's still not much good to a dramatist—he still has not made a decision.

Now only his job, which has lately become insecure, holds him to sanity. Then the last straw breaks his back. A younger man is put into the place where he slaved for thirty years. He is aroused to an unbelievable fury, for at last he has reached the breaking point. And when a man makes a harmless joke —about the depression, perhaps—he kills him. He murders for no apparent cause a man who never hurt him.

If you look hard enough, you will find that there is always a long chain of circumstances leading to a seemingly unmotivated crime. And these "circumstances" can be found in the criminal's physical, sociological, and mental make-up.

This is related to what has been said about miscalculation. An author must realize how vitally important it is to catch a character at the high point of mental development, a subject we'll discuss more fully when we speak of "Point of Attack." Suffice it to say here that every living creature is capable of doing anything, if the conditions around him are strong enough.

Hamlet is a different man at the end of the play from what
he was at the beginning. In fact, he changes on every page—
not illogically, but in a steady line of growth. We are all
changing with every passing minute, hour, day, week, month,
and year. The problem is to find the moment at which it is
most advantageous for the playwright to deal with a character.
What we call Hamlet's weakness is his delay in taking a step
(sometimes fatal) until he has full evidence. But his iron
determination, his devotion to his cause, are strong. He makes
a decision. Jeeter Lester, too, made a decision to *stay*, whether
or not this decision was conscious. As a matter of fact, Jeeter's
will was unconscious—subconscious, let us say—whereas
Hamlet's determination to prove that the king murdered his
father was conscious. Hamlet was acting in accordance with a
premise he was aware of, while Lester stayed because he did
not know what else to do.

The dramatist may use either type. This is the point at
which inventiveness comes to the fore. The trouble starts
when the author puts a Chekhovian character into a blood-
and-thunder play, or vice versa. You cannot force a character
to make a decision before he is good and ready. If you try
that, you will find that the action is superficial and trite—it
will not reflect the real character.

So as you see, there is really no such thing as weak character. The question is: did you catch your character at that
particular moment when he was ready for conflict?

6. *Plot or Character—Which?*

What is a weed? A plant whose virtues have not yet been discovered.   —EMERSON

Despite the frequent quotations from Aristotle, and the
work done by Freud on one of the three elements of a
human being, character has not been given the penetrat-

ing analysis which scientists give the atom or the cosmic ray.

William Archer, in his *Playmaking, a Manual of Crafts-manship,* says:

. . . To reproduce character can neither be acquired nor regulated by theoretical recommendations.

We readily agree that "theoretical recommendations" are of no use to anyone—but what of concrete recommendation? While it is true that the seemingly inanimate objects are easier to examine, the involved, ever-moving character of man must also be analyzed—and the task is organized, made simpler, by recommendations.

Specific directions for character-drawing would be like rules for becoming six feet high. Either you have it in you, or you have it not,

says Mr. Archer. This is a sweeping, and unscientific, statement. And it has a familiar ring. It is, in essence, the answer that was given to Leeuwenhoek, inventor of the microscope; to Galileo, who was almost burned as a heretic when he said the earth moved. Fulton's steamboat was received with derision. "It won't move!" the crowds shouted, and when it did move they cried, "It won't stop!"

Yet today cosmic rays are made to photograph and measure themselves.

"Either you have it in you, or you have it not," says Mr. Archer, thus admitting that one man has the ability to draw character, to peneterate the impenetrable, whereas another has not. But if one man can do it, and if we know how he did it, can we not learn from him? One man does it by observation. He is privileged to see things which others pass by. Is it that these less fortunate men cannot see the obvious? Perhaps. When we read a bad play carefully, we are struck by the author's ignorance of his characters; and when we read a good play carefully, we are struck by the wealth of information the writer displays. Then why may we not sug-

gest to the less-privileged playwright that he train his eye to
see, and his mind to understand? Why may we not recom-
mend observation?

If the "have-not" playwright has imagination, selectivity,
writing ability, he will be a better man for learning consciously what the "have" playwright knows only by instinct.
How is it that even the genius who has it within his power
to be six feet tall frequently misses the mark? Why is it that
the man who once knew how to draw character now makes
a fool of himself? Might it be because he relied solely upon
his instinctive powers? Why shouldn't these powers work all
the time? The privileged one either has the power in him or
he has not.

We trust you will admit that any number of geniuses have
written any number of bad plays—because they relied on an
instinctive power which is, at best, a hit-or-miss affair. One
is not supposed to conduct important business on a hunch,
a feeling, a whim—one is supposed to *act upon knowledge*.

Mr. Archer's definition of character follows:

. . . for the practical purposes of the dramatist it may be defined
as a *complex of intellectual, emotional,* and nervous habit.

This hardly seems enough, so we turn to *Webster's International Dictionary.* Perhaps Mr. Archer's words hold more
than appeared on the surface.

Complex: composed of two or more parts; composite; not simple.
Intellectual: apprehensible by intellect alone; hence of a spiritual nature; perceptible only to inspired vision or by spiritual insight.
Emotion: an agitation, disturbance, a tumultuous movement
whether physical or social.

Now we know. It is so simple and so complex at the same
time. Not much help, it's true, but refreshing, nevertheless.

It is not enough to know that a character consists of "complex intellectual, emotional, and nervous habit." We must know precisely what this "complex intellectual" means. We have found that every human being consists of three dimensions: physiological, sociological, and psychological. If we make a further breakdown of these dimensions, we shall perceive that the physical, social, and mental make-up contains the minute genes—the builder, the mover in all our actions which will motivate everything we do.

A shipbuilder knows the material he is working with, knows how well it can withstand the ravages of time, how much weight it can carry. He must know these things if he wishes to avoid disaster.

A dramatist should know the material he is working with: his characters. He should know how much weight they can carry, how well they can support his construction: the play.

There are so many conflicting ideas about character that it might be a good idea for us to review a few of them before we attempt to go further.

John Howard Lawson writes in his book, *The Theory and Technique of Playwriting:*

People find it curiously difficult to consider a story as something which is in the process of *becoming:* confusion on this point exists in all textbooks on playwriting, and is a stumbling block to all playwrights.

Yes, it is a stumbling block, because they start to build their house from the roof down, instead of starting with premise and showing a character in relation to his environment. Lawson says as much in his introduction:

A play is not a bundle of isolated elements: dialogue, characterization, etc., etc. It is a living thing, in which all of these elements have been fused.

This is true, but on the very next page he writes:

We can study the form, the *outwardness* of a play, but the *inwardness, the soul,* eludes our grasp.

It will elude us forever if we fail to understand a basic principle: the so-called "inwardness," the seemingly unpredictable soul, is nothing more nor less than character.

Lawson's fundamental mistake is using dialectics upside down. He accepts Aristotle's basic error, "character is subsidiary to action," and from this springs his confusion. It is vain for him to insist on a "social framework" when he puts the cart before the horse.

We contend that character is the most interesting phenomenon anywhere. Every character represents a world of his own, and the more you know of this person, the more interested you become. We have in mind just now George Kelly's *The Show-off*, and *Craig's Wife*. They are far from being well-constructed plays, but there is a conscious attempt to build character. Kelly shows us a world through the eyes of Craig's wife, a drab and monotonous world, but a real one.

George Bernard Shaw says that he is not governed by principle, but by inspiration. If any man, inspired or not, builds on character, he is going in the right direction and is employing the right principle, consciously or otherwise. The vital thing is not what the playwright says, but what he does. Every great literary work grew from character, even if the author planned the action first. As soon as his characters were created they took precedence, and the action had to be reshaped to suit them.

Let us suppose we were building a house. We started at the wrong end and it collapsed. We began again—at the top—and it collapsed. And so a third and a fourth time. But eventually we make it stand up, without the slightest idea of what change in our method was responsible for our success. Can we now, without compunction, give advice on the construction of houses? Can we honestly say: it must collapse four times before it can stand?

The great plays came down to us from men who had unlimited patience for work. Perhaps they started their plays at the wrong end, but they fought themselves back inch by inch, until they made character the foundation of their work, although they may not have been objectively conscious that character is the only element that could serve as the foundation.

Says Lawson:

Of course it is hard to think of situations, and this depends upon the power of the writer's "inspiration."

If we know that a character embodies in himself not only his environment, but his heredity, his likes and dislikes, even the climate of the town where he was born, we do not find it hard to think of situations. *The situations are inherent in the character.*

George P. Baker quotes Dumas the Younger:

Before every situation that a dramatist creates, he should ask himself three questions: What should *I* do? What would *other people* do? What *ought* to be done?

Isn't it strange to ask everyone what should be done in a situation, except the character who created the situation? Why not ask him? He is in a position to know the answer better than anyone else.

John Galsworthy seems to have grasped this simple truth, for he claims that character creates plot, not vice versa. Whatever Lessing had to say about the matter, he built on character. So did Ben Jonson—in fact, he sacrificed many theatrical devices to bring his characters into sharper relief. Chekhov has no story to tell, no situation to speak of, but his plays are popular and will be so in time to come, because he per-

mits his characters to reveal themselves and the time in which
they lived.

Engels says in *Anti-Dühring:*

Every organic being is at each moment both the same and not the
same; at each moment it is assimilating matter drawn from without
and excreting other matter; every moment the cells of its body are
dying and new ones are being formed; in fact, within a longer or
shorter period the matter of its body is completely removed and is
replaced by other atoms of matter, so that every organic thing is at
all times itself and yet something other than itself.

A character thus has the capacity to completely reverse himself
under internal and external stimulus. Like every other organic
being, he changes continuously.

If this is true, and we know it is true, how can one invent
a situation, or a story, which is a static thing, and force it
upon the character who is in a state of constant change?

Starting with the premise "Character is subsidiary to
action," it was inevitable that the textbook writers should
become confused. Baker quotes Sardou, who replied as follows to the question of how plays revealed themselves to him:

The problem is invariable. It appears as a kind of equation from
which the unknown quantity must be found. The problem gives
me no peace till I have found the answer.

Perhaps Sardou and Baker have found the answer, but
they have not given it to the young playwright.

Character and environment are so closely interrelated that
we have to consider them as one. They react upon each other.
If one is faulty, it affects the other, just as the disease of one
part of the body causes the whole to suffer.

The plot is the first consideration, and as it were, the soul of the
tragedy. Character holds the second place,

writes Aristotle in his *Poetics.*

Character comes in as subsidiary to the action. Hence the incidents and the plot are the end of a tragedy. . . . Without action there cannot be a tragedy; there may be without character. . . . The drama interests us, not predominantly by depicting of human nature, but primarily by the situations and only secondarily by the feelings of those therein involved.

After checking through volumes and volumes in search of the answer to which is more important, character or plot, we concluded that ninety-nine per cent of the writings on this issue are confused and barely understandable.

Consider these statements by Archer, in *Playmaking:* On page twenty-two:

A play can exist without anything that can be called character, but not without some sort of action.

But on page twenty-four:

Action ought to exist for the sake of character: when the relationship is reversed the play may be an ingenious toy, but scarcely a vital work of art.

To find the real answer is not an academic problem. It is an answer which will make a deep impression on the future of playwriting, since it is *not* the answer which was dictated by Aristotle.

We are going to take the oldest of all plots, a trite, worn-out triangle, a vaudeville skit, to prove our point.

A husband starts on a two-day trip, but forgets something and comes back to the house. He finds his wife in another man's arms. Let us suppose that the husband is a man of five feet three. The lover is a giant. The situation hinges on the husband—what will he do? If he is free of the author's interference, he will do what his character dictates, what his physical, social, and psychological make-up tell him to do.

If he is a coward, he may apologize, beg forgiveness for

his intrusion, and flee—grateful that the lover let him go unmolested.

But perhaps the husband's short stature has made him cocky, has forced him to be aggressive. He springs at the big man in a fury, unmindful that he may be the looser.

Perhaps he is a cynic, and sneers; perhaps he is imperturable, and laughs; perhaps any number of things—depending on the character.

A coward might create a farce, a brave man might create a tragedy.

Take Hamlet, the brooding Dane, and let him—not Romeo—fall in love with Juliet. What would have happened? He might have contemplated the matter too long, muttering to himself beautiful soliloquies about the immortality of the soul and the deathlessness of love, which, like the phoenix, rises anew every spring. He might have consulted his friends, his father, to make peace with the Capulets, and while these negotiations went on, Juliet, not suspecting that Hamlet loved her, would have been safely married to Paris. Then Hamlet could have brooded still more and cursed his fate.

While Romeo runs into trouble with reckless abandon, Hamlet looks into the mechanism of his problem. While Hamlet hesitates, Romeo acts.

Obviously their conflicts grew out of their character, and not vice versa.

If you try to force a character into a situation where he does not belong, you will be like Procrustes who cut the feet off the sleeper to make him fit the bed.

Which is more important, plot or character? Let us trade the sensitive, brooding Hamlet for a pleasure-loving prince, whose one reason for living is the privileges his princehood affords him. Would he avenge his father's death? Hardly. He would turn the tragedy to comedy.

Let us trade the naïve Nora, ignorant of money matters,

forging a note for her husband, for a mature woman, aware of finance, too honest to let her love for her husband lead her astray. This new Nora would not have forged the note, and Helmer would have died then and there.

The sun, along with its other activities, creates rain. If it is true that the characters are secondary in importance, there is no reason why we should not use the moon instead of the sun. Do we get the same plot results? Emphatically: *no!*

Something will happen, however. The moon will witness the slow death of the earth, in place of the turbulent life created by the sun. We substituted only one character. This, of course, changed our premise and made a considerable alteration in the outcome of the play. With the sun: life. With the moon: death.

The inference is unmistakable: character creates plot, not vice versa.

It is not difficult to understand why Aristotle thought of character as he did. When Sophocles wrote *Oedipus Rex,* when Aeschylus wrote *Agamemnon,* when Euripides wrote *Medea,* Fate was supposed to have played the chief role in the drama. The gods spoke, and men lived or died in accordance with what they said. "The structure of the incidents" was ordained by the gods—the characters were merely men who did what had been prearranged for them. But, while the audience believed this, and Aristotle based his theories upon it, *it does not hold true in the plays themselves.* In all important Greek plays, the characters create the action. The playwrights substituted the *Fates* for the *premise* as we know it today. The results, however, were identical.

If Oedipus had been any other type of man, tragedy would not have befallen him. Had he not been hot-tempered, he would not have killed a stranger on the road. Had he not been stubborn, he would not have forced the issue of who killed Laius. With rare perseverance he dug out the smallest details, continuing because he was honest, even when the accusing finger pointed at him. Had he not been honest, he would not have punished the murderer by blinding himself.

CHORUS: O doer of dread deeds, how couldst thou mar
Thy vision thus? What demon goaded thee?
OEDIPUS: Apollo, friends, Apollo, he it was
That brought these ills to pass;
But the right hand that dealt the blow
Was mine, none other.

Why should Oedipus blind himself if the gods had ordained that he should be punished anyway? They would certainly have taken care of their promise. But we know that he punished himself because of his rare character. He says:

How could I longer see when sight
Brought no delight?

A scoundrel would not have felt that way. He might have been exiled and the prophecy fulfilled—but that would have played havoc with the majesty of *Oedipus* as a drama.

Aristotle was mistaken in his time, and our scholars are mistaken today when they accept his rulings concerning character. Character was the great factor in Aristotle's time, and no fine play ever was or ever will be written without it.

Through Medea's conniving her brother was killed. She sacrificed him for the husband, Jason, who later brushed her aside to marry King Creon's daughter. Her grim deed brought its own poetic justice. What kind of man was it who would marry such a woman? Exactly the kind Jason proved to be —a ruthless betrayer. Both Jason and Medea were made of stuff that any playwright might envy. They stand on their own feet, without any help from Zeus. They are well drawn, tridimensional. They are constantly growing, which is one of the fundamental principles of great writing.

The Greek plays which have come down to us boast many extraordinary characters which disprove the Aristotelian contention. If character were subsidiary to action, Agamemnon would not inevitably have died by the hand of Clytemnestra.

Before the action starts, in *Oedipus Rex*, Laius, King of Thebes, knew *"of the prophecy that the child born to him by his queen, Jocasta, would slay his father and wed his mother."* So, when in time a son was born, the infant's feet were riveted together and he was left to die on Mount Cithaeron. But a shepherd found the child and tended him and delivered him to another shepherd who took him to his master, the King of Corinth. When Oedipus learned of the prophecy, he fled to thwart the fulfillment of the Delphic oracle. In his wanderings he killed his father, Laius, without knowing his identity, and entered the kingdom of Thebes.

But how did Oedipus learn of the prophecy? At a banquet, he was told by a drunkard, "Thou art no true son of thy sire." Disturbed, he sought to learn more.

So privily without their leave I went to Delphi, and Apollo sent me back, baulked of the knowledge that I came to seek.

Why did Apollo withhold the information Oedipus wanted?

But other grievous things he prophesied,
Woes, lamentations, mourning, portents dire,
To wit, I should defile my mother's bed,
And raise seed too loathsome to behold.

It would seem that Apollo deliberately withheld the real identity of Oedipus' father. Why? Because *"Fate," as premise, drives the character to the inevitable end,* and Sophocles needed that driving force. But let's take it for granted that Apollo wished to make Oedipus flee, and at the end fulfill the prophecy. We shan't ask the reasons for the dire fate of two innocent beings. Instead, let us go to the opening of the play and watch Oedipus' character grow.

He was traveling incognito, a grown warrior, just and noble, fleeing to escape his fate. He was in no easy mood when he drew near the triple-branching road where the murder occurred. He says:

> A herald met me and a man who sat
> In a car drawn by colts—as in the tale—
> The man in front and the old man himself
> Threatened to thrust me rudely from the path.

So they were rude to him and used force, and only then:

> I struck him, and the old man, seeing this,
> Watched till I passed and from his car brought down
> Full on my head the double-pointed goad.

Only then Oedipus struck.

> .... one stroke
> Of my good staff sufficed to fling him clean
> Out of the chariot seat and laid him prone.

The incident shows that the attack on Laius and his escorts was motivated. They were rude, Oedipus was in a bad mood, and hot-tempered besides, and he acted according to his character. Apollo is certainly secondary here. Again, you may say that Oedipus is still carrying out the desire of the *Fates*—when he is only proving the *premise*.

Once in Thebes, Oedipus answers the riddle of the Sphinx, at which thousands had failed. The Sphinx would ask those who entered or left the city: what was it which in the morning walks on four legs, at midday on two, in the evening on three? Oedipus answered: man, proving himself the wisest among them. The Sphinx departed in shame, and the Thebans, in joy at the end of their bondage, elected him their king.

So we know that Oedipus was brave, impulsive, wise—and by way of further proof, Sophocles tells us that the Thebans prospered under his rule. Anything that happened to Oedipus happened because of his character.

If you forget the "Argument" which states the ancient beliefs concerning the part played by the gods, and read the play as it stands, you will see the validity of our assertion. Character makes the plot.

The moment Molière established Orgon as Tartuffe's dupe, the plot automatically unfolded itself. Orgon represents a religious fanatic. It stands to reason that a converted bigot disapproves of everything he believed before.

Molière needed a man who was intolerant of everything worldly. Through conversion, Orgon became this man. This state of affairs suggests that such a man should have a family who indulged in all the innocent joys of life. Our man, Orgon, must necessarily regard all these earthly activities as sinful. Such a man will go the limit to change the ways of those under his influence or domination. He will try to reform them. They will resent it.

This determination forced the conflict, and, as the author had a clear-cut premise, the story grew out of this character.

When the author has a clear-cut premise, it is child's play to find the character who will carry the burden of that premise. When we accept the premise "Great love defies even death," we necessarily will think of a couple who defy tradition, parental objections, and death itself. What kind of person has the capacity to do all this? Certainly not Hamlet or a professor of mathematics. He must be young, proud, impetuous. He is Romeo. Romeo fits the part assigned to him as easily as Orgon does in *Tartuffe*. Their characters create the conflict. A plot without character is a makeshift contraption, dangling between heaven and earth like Mohammed's coffin.

What would the reader think of us if we were to announce that, after long and arduous study, we had come to the conclusion that honey is beneficial to mankind, but that the

bee's importance is secondary, and that the bee is therefore
subsidiary to its product? What would you think if we should
say that the fragrance is more important than the flower, the
song more important than the bird? We should like to alter the quotation from Emerson with
which we opened this chapter. For our purposes it should
read:

What is a character? A factor whose virtues have not yet been discovered.

7. *Characters Plotting Their Own Play*

"Shallow men believe in luck," said Emerson. There is
no luck involved in the success of Ibsen's plays. He studied,
he planned, he worked hard. Let us try to look into his
workroom and see him at work. Let us try to analyze Nora
and Helmer of *A Doll's House* as they start to plot their own
story, according to the premise and character principle.

There is no doubt that Ibsen was struck by the inequality
of women in his time. (The play was written in 1879.) Being a crusader of a sort, he wanted to prove that "Inequality
of the sexes in marriage breeds unhappiness."

To begin with, Ibsen knew he needed two characters to
prove his premise: a husband and a wife. But not any couple
would do. He had to have a husband who would epitomize
the selfishness of all the men of the time, and a wife who
would symbolize the subjugation of all the women. He was
looking for a self-centered man and a sacrificing woman.

He chose Helmer and Nora, but as yet they were only
names bearing the tags "selfish" and "unselfish." The next
natural step was to round them out. The author had to be
very careful in constructing his characters, because later, in
conflict, they would have to make their own decisions as to
what to do or what not to do. And since Ibsen had a clear-

cut premise which he was eager to prove, his characters had to be people who could stand alone without the author's help. Helmer became manager at a bank. He must have been a very industrious, conscientious man to earn the highest rank in an important institution. He oozes responsibility, suggesting a merciless superior who is a stickler for order. No doubt he demands punctuality and devotion from his subordinates. He has an overdose of civic pride; he knows the importance of his station and guards it with the utmost care. Respectability is his highest aim, and he is ready to sacrifice anything, even love, to gain it. In short, Helmer is a man who is hated by his subordinates and admired by his superiors. He is human only at home, and then with a vengeance. His love for his family is boundless, as is often the case with a man who is hated and feared by others, and he thus needs more love than the average man.

He is about thirty-eight years old, a man of average height with a determined nature. His speech, even at home, is unctuous, grave, constantly admonishing. He suggests a middle-class background, honest and not too well off. The constant thought he gives to his beloved bank seems to indicate that his ambition, as a youngster, was to hold just such a post in just such an organization. He is extremely satisfied with himself and has no doubts for the future.

He has no harmful habits, and does not smoke or drink except for a glass or two on special occasions. We see him, then, a self-centered man with high moral principles which he demands that others observe.

All these things can be seen in the play, and while they make only a sketchy character study, they indicate that Ibsen must have known a great deal about Helmer. He also must have known that the woman would have to oppose all the ideals the man represented.

So he sketched Nora. She is a child: spendthrift, irresponsible, lying, cheating as a child might. She is a skylark, dancing, singing, careless—but loving her husband and children sincerely. It is the crux of her character that she loves her husband enough to do things for him which she would not dream of doing for anyone else.

Nora has a fine, searching mind, but she knows little of the society in which she lives. Because of her love and admiration for Helmer she is willing to be a doll wife, and as a result her mental growth is retarded despite her intelligence. She was a pampered daughter, given over to her husband for further pampering.

She is twenty-eight or thirty years old, charming, attractive. Her background is not as spotless as Helmer's, for her father, too, was happy-go-lucky. He had peculiar ideas, and there was a hint of scandal in the family closet. Nora's one selfishness, perhaps, is her desire to see everyone as happy as she.

Here stand the two characters which will generate conflict. But how? There is not a single hint that a triangle situation can ever develop between them. What possible conflict can arise between a couple who love each other so? If we are in any doubt, we must go back to the character studies and to the premise. There we shall find a clue. We look, and find one. Since Nora represents unselfishness, love, she will do something for her family, preferably for her husband, which will be misunderstood by him. But what kind of act will it be? If we are stuck again, we can again read the character studies which must point the answer. Helmer represents *respectability*. Well and good. Nora's act should undermine or threaten the position he holds. But since she is unselfish, the deed must be done for *his* sake, and his reaction must show the hollowness of his love when it is matched against his respectability.

What type of act would throw this man off balance to such an extent that he forgets everything when his position is threatened? Only an act which he knows *from his own ex-*

perience to be most contemptible and most disgraceful: some-thing concerning money.

Theft? That might be it, but Nora is not a thief, nor does she have access to much money. But what she does must have something to do with securing money. She must need the money badly, and it must be an amount which is larger than she could put her hands on, but small enough for her to obtain without raising a great to-do.

Before we go further we must know her motive for obtaining money in some way annoying—to put it mildly!—to her husband. Perhaps he is in debt— No, no. Helmer would never contract debts which could not be taken care of. Perhaps she needs some household accessory? No, that would not be to Helmer's vital interest. Sickness? Excellent idea. Helmer himself is ill, and Nora needs money to take care of him.

Nora's reasoning is easy to follow. She knows little of money matters. She needs money for Helmer, but *Helmer would rather die than borrow.* She cannot go to friends, lest Helmer discover what she has done and be humiliated. She cannot steal, as we have seen. The only course open is to go to a professional money-lender. She is aware, however, that as a woman, her signature will not be enough. She cannot ask a friend to countersign without encountering the unpleasant questions she is trying to avoid. A stranger? She could hardly approach a man she does not know without leaving the way open for an immoral proposition. She loves her husband too much even to think of such a thing. Only one person would do it for her—her father. But he is a very sick man, on the verge of dying. Healthy, he would help her get money, but there would be no play then. The characters must prove the premise through conflict; therefore Nora's father is, of necessity, dead.

Nora bemoans this fact, and that gives her an idea. She

will forge her father's signature. She's elated, once she has found this only way out. The idea is so perfect that she bubbles with joy. She not only has a way of getting the money, but of concealing from Helmer the manner in which it will be obtained. She will tell him that her father left it to her, and he will not be able to refuse it. It will be his.

She goes through with it, receives the money, and is supremely happy.

There is one hitch in the scheme. The money-lender knows the family—he works in the same bank as Helmer. He has known all along that the signature was forged, but the forgery is worth more to him than the best guarantee or deposition. If Nora cannot pay it (live up to it) Helmer will do so a thousandfold. That's why he is Helmer. With his respectability at stake, his position to be considered, he would do anything. The money-lender is safe.

If you read over the character sketches of Nora and Helmer, you will see that their characters made the story possible.

QUESTION: Who forced Nora to do what she did? Why couldn't she have overcome the various considerations and borrowed money legally?

ANSWER: The premise forced her to choose only one direction—the one which will prove it. You will say—and we shall agree—that a person has the privilege of choosing a hundred different ways to achieve his purpose. But *not* when you have a clear premise which you wish to prove. After close scrutiny and elimination you must find the *one way* which will lead you to your goal—prove your premise. Ibsen chose that one way, by drawing characters who would naturally behave in a way to prove his premise.

QUESTION: I don't see why there should be only one way to build a conflict. I don't believe that there was nothing for Nora to do but forge her father's name.

ANSWER: What would you have her do instead?

QUESTION: I don't know, but there must be some other way.

ANSWER: If you refuse to think, the argument is over.

QUESTION: Well, why wouldn't stealing be as plausible as forging?

ANSWER: We have already pointed out that she had no access to money, but let us pretend that she did. From whom would she steal? Not Helmer, certainly, since he has no money. Relatives? All right—but would they expose her when they learned of the theft? They could not do so without disgracing the family name, and the chances are all in favor of their saying nothing. Would she steal from neighbors, strangers? That's foreign to her character. But suppose she does—it serves only to complicate matters.

QUESTION: Isn't that what you want—conflict?

ANSWER: Only when it proves the premise.

QUESTION: Doesn't stealing do that?

ANSWER: No. When she forged her father's name, she put only her husband and herself in jeopardy; by stealing she hurts innocent people, not otherwise involved in the story. Besides, by stealing she changes the premise. The fear of discovery and inevitable disgrace would overshadow the original premise. It would be a denunciation of theft, not a plea for woman's equality.

But, you ask, what if Nora stole and was not caught? That would prove her a good thief—but not a woman meriting equality. And if she were caught? A heroic struggle would ensue in which Helmer would fight to get her out of prison—and then discard her. This is what his respectability would force him to do, thereby proving the exact opposite of the premise with which you began. No, my friend. *You have a premise on the one side and a perfect character study on the other. You must stay on the straight road marked by these limits and not wander off on a byway.*

QUESTION: It seems you can't get away from that premise.
ANSWER: It seems so. *The premise is a tyrant who permits you to go only one way—the way of absolute proof.*
QUESTION: Why couldn't Nora prostitute herself?
ANSWER: Would that prove that she was carrying the burden and responsibility of the household? That she's equal with man? That there should be no doll's house? Would it?
QUESTION: How should I know?
ANSWER: If you don't know, the argument is over.

8. Pivotal Character

The pivotal character is the *protagonist*. According to Webster's dictionary, protagonist is—"one who takes the lead in any movement or cause."

Anyone who opposes the protagonist is an opponent or *antagonist*.

Without a pivotal character there is no play. The pivotal character is the one who creates conflict and makes the play move forward. The pivotal character knows what he wants. Without him the story flounders . . . in fact, there is no story.

In Othello, Iago (the pivotal character) is a man of action. Slighted by Othello, he revenges himself by sowing dissension and jealousy. He started the conflict.

In *A Doll's House*, Krogstad's insistence on rehabilitating his family almost drove Nora to suicide. He is the pivotal character.

In *Tartuffe*, Orgon's insistence to force Tartuffe on his family started the conflict.

A pivotal character must not merely desire something. He must want it so badly that he will destroy or be destroyed in the effort to attain his goal.

You might say: "Suppose Othello had given Iago the office he so passionately coveted?"

In that case there would not have been a play.

There must always be something a person wants more than anything else in life if he is to be a good pivotal character; revenge, honor, ambition, etc.

A good pivotal character *must have something very vital at stake.*

Not everyone can be a pivotal character.

A man whose fear is greater than his desire, or a man who has no great, all-consuming passion, or one who has patience and does not oppose, cannot be a pivotal character.

By the way, there are two types of patience; positive and negative.

Hamlet had no patience to *endure* (negative), but he did have patience to persevere (positive). Jeeter Lester, in *Tobacco Road,* had the kind of patience that made you marvel at human endurance. The patience of a martyr, despite torture, is a powerful force that we can use in a play or in any other type of writing.

There is a positive kind of patience which is relentless, death defying. Then there is a negative patience which has no resilience, no inner strength to endure hardship.

A pivotal character is necessarily aggressive, uncompromising, even ruthless.

Even though Jeeter Lester appears to be a "negative" character, he is nevertheless as provocative as the "aggressive" Iago. Both of them are pivotal characters.

We might as well clarify just what we mean when we say "negative" and "positive" (aggressive) pivotal characters.

Everybody understands what an aggressive character is, but we must explain the "negative" one. To withstand hunger, torture, physical and mental suffering for an ideal, whether real or fancied, is strength in Homeric proportions. This negative strength is really aggressive in the sense that it provokes counter-action. Hamlet's snooping, Jeeter Lester's maddening insistence to stay on his land and actually die from sheer hunger, are actions which certainly provoke counter-action. So a negative force, if it is enduring, becomes a positive force. Either one of these forces is good for any type of writing.

Once more, a pivotal character is necessarily aggressive, uncompromising, even ruthless, whether he is the "negative" or "positive" type.

A pivotal character is a driving force, not because he decided to be one. He becomes what he is for the simple reason that some inner or outer necessity forces him to act; there is something at stake for him, honor, health, money, protection, vengeance, or a mighty passion.

Oedipus, in *Oedipus Rex,* insists upon finding the King's murderer. He is the pivotal character and his aggressiveness is motivated by Apollo's threat to punish his Kingdom with pestilence if he doesn't find the murderer. It is the happiness of his people which forces him to become a pivotal character.

The six soldiers in *Bury the Dead,* refuse to be buried, not because of themselves, but because of the great injustice befallen on the majority of the working people. They refuse to be buried for the sake of mankind.

Krogstad in *A Doll's House,* is relentless for the sake of his children whom he wants to rehabilitate.

Hamlet ferrets out his father's murderers not to justify himself, but to bring the guilty to justice.

As we see, a pivotal character never becomes a pivotal character because *he wants to.* He is really forced by circumstances within him and outside of him to become what he is.

The growth of a pivotal character cannot be as extensive as that of the other characters. For instance, the *other* characters might go from *hate* to *love* or from *love* to *hate,* but not the pivotal character, because *when your play starts the pivotal character is already suspicious or planning to kill.* From suspicion to the discovery of unfaithfulness is a much shorter road than from absolute faith to the discovery of unfaithfulness. Therefore, if it would take the average character ten steps to go from love to hate, the pivotal character would only travel the last four, three, two or even just one step.

Hamlet starts with a certainty (his father's ghost tells him about the murder), and he ends with murder. Lavinia in *Mourning Becomes Electra*, starts with hatred, plots for revenge, and ends in desolation.

Macbeth starts with coveting the King's throne, and ends in murder and death.

The transition between blind obedience and open revolt is much greater than that between an oppressor's *anger* and his *vengeance* against a rebellious peon. Yet there is transition in both cases.

Romeo and Juliet experience hate, love, hope, despair, and death, while their parents, the pivotal characters, experience only hate and regret.

When we say that poverty encourages crime, we are not attacking an abstraction but the social forces which make poverty possible. These forces are ruthless, and their ruthlessness is represented by *a man*. In a play we attack the man and through him, the social forces which make him what he is. This representative *cannot* relent: the forces behind him back him up. And if he does weaken, you know he was a poor choice of character and another representative was needed who could faithfully serve the forces behind him.

The pivotal character can match the emotional intensity of his adversaries, but he has a smaller compass of development.

QUESTION: A few things still puzzle me about growth. I saw *Juarez* the other day. Every character in the picture went through a transition: Maximilian from vacillation to determination; Carlotta from love to madness; Diaz from faith in his cause to vacillation. Only Juarez did not grow; yet his stolidity, his unwavering faith, make him a monumental figure. What was wrong? Why didn't he grow?

ANSWER: He does grow, constantly, but not as obviously as the others. He is the pivotal character, whose strength, determination and leadership are responsible for the conflict. We shall come back to this and see why his central position makes his growth less apparent. But first let us show you that he does grow. He warns Maximilian—and then carries out his threat. Growth. When he finds that his forces cannot stand against the French, *he changes tactics,* disbands his army. Growth. We see him in transition. We know why he changes his mind when we hear the shepherd boy describe how his dogs unite to fight a wolf. We see how Juarez handles treachery and faces his enemies in their own camp. The scene in which he walks through a firing squad shows him in actual conflict and confirms our belief that he is a very brave man.

His depth of love for his people is proved by his relentlessness toward Maximilian. Through the constant exposition of his character we learn that his motivation is honest and unselfish.

An imperceptible transition is revealed on the surface when he murmurs, "Forgive me," over Maximilian's coffin. His love is revealed conclusively and we know that his cruelty was not directed against Maximilian, but against Imperialism.

QUESTION: Then his growth is from *resistance* to *stronger resistance,* instead of from *hate* to *forgiveness.* I see. Why wasn't it necessary for Juarez' change to be as great as Maximilian's?

ANSWER: Juarez is the pivotal character. Remember, the growth of the pivotal character is much less than that of the other characters for the simple reason that he has reached a decision *before the story starts.* He is the one who *forces the others to grow.* Juarez' strength is the strength of the masses who are willing to fight and die for their liberty. He is not alone. He is not fighting because he wants to fight. Necessity forces a liberty loving person to try to destroy his oppressor or die, rather than submit to slavery.

If a pivotal character has no inner or outer necessity to fight, except his own caprice as a motive, there is the danger that any minute he might stop being a driving force, thus betraying the premise, and with it, the play.

QUESTION: What about the people who want to write, act, sing, paint? Would you call this inner urge for self-expression a caprice?

ANSWER: With ninety-nine per cent of them it might be a caprice.

QUESTION: Why ninety-nine per cent?

ANSWER: Because ninety-nine per cent usually give up before they have a chance to achieve anything. They have no perseverence, no stamina, no physical or mental strength. Although there are people who have both physical and mental strength, the inner urge to create is not strong enough.

QUESTION: Is it possible for an element like cold, heat, fire, water, to be a pivotal character?

ANSWER: No. These elements were the absolute rulers on earth when man ambled along from the darkness of his primitive existence. It was the eternal status quo, a state of affairs which had existed unquestioned, unchallenged, for billions of years. The protozoa, pleuroccocus, bacteria, amoeba, did nothing to counteract the existing order. Man did. Man started the conflict. Man became the pivotal character in the drama for existence. He has not only harnassed the elements but is on the verge of conquering multiple sickness with the recently discovered Penicillin and Sulpha drugs.

Man's aggressiveness against the elements is not dependent upon a whim. It arises out of dire necessity and is implemented by intelligence. This necessity and intelligence forced him to split the atom and create the most frightfully destructive force in existence, the atom bomb; but if he is to survive, this very "frightfulness" will force him again to use it for the elevation of mankind instead of for destruction. He'll do this not from nobility, but because dire *"necessity"* will force his hand again.

Once more: a pivotal character is forced to be a pivotal character out of sheer necessity, and not because he wills it.

9. The Antagonist

Anyone who opposes a pivotal character necessarily becomes the opponent or *antagonist*. The antagonist is the one who holds back the ruthlessly onrushing protagonist. He is the one against whom the ruthless character exerts all his strength, all his cunning, all the resources of his inventive power.

If for any good reason the antagonist cannot put up a protracted fight, you might as well look for another character who will.

The antagonist in any play is necessarily as strong and, in time, as ruthless as the pivotal character. A fight is interesting only if the fighters are evenly matched. Helmer, in *Doll's House*, is the antagonist against Krogstad. The protagonist and the antagonist must be dangerous foes to each other. Both of them are ruthless. The mother in *The Silver Cord* finds a worthy opponent in the women her sons brought home. Iago, in *Othello*, is the ruthless, conniving protagonist. Othello is the antagonist. Othello's authority and power are so great that Iago cannot show his hand openly—but he courts great danger anyway, nay, his very life is in danger. Othello, then, is a worthy antagonist. The same is the case in *Hamlet*.

Let me now repeat it again: the antagonist must be as strong as the protagonist. The wills of conflicting personalities must clash.

If a big brute brutalizes a little man, we'll turn against him, but this will not mean that we shall wait with bated breath to see the outcome of this uneven encounter. We know it beforehand.

A novel, play, or any type of writing, really is a crisis from beginning to end growing to its necessary conclusion.

10. Orchestration

When you are ready to select characters for your play, be careful to orchestrate them right. If all the characters are the same type—for instance, if all of them are bullies—it will be like an orchestra of nothing but drums.

In *King Lear,* Cordelia is gentle, loving, faithful; Goneril and Regan, the older daughters, are cold, heartless, and deceitful plotters. The King himself is rash, headstrong, and given to unreasoning anger.

Good orchestration is one of the reasons for rising conflict in any play.

It is possible to choose two liars, two prostitutes, two thieves, for one play, but necessarily they will be different in temper, philosophy, and speech. One thief might be considerate, the other ruthless; one could be a coward, the other fearless; one might respect womanhood, the other might despise women. If both have the same temperament, the same outlook on life, there will be no conflict—and no play.

When Ibsen selected Nora and Helmer for *A Doll's House,* it was inevitable that he should choose a married couple, since the premise dealt with married life. This phase of selection is obvious to everyone.

The difficulty starts when the dramatist chooses people of the same type and tries to generate conflict between them.

We are thinking of Maltz' *Black Pit,* in which Joe and Iola are very much alike. They are both loving and considerate. They have the same ideals and desires and fears. No wonder, then, that Joe makes his fatal decision almost without conflict.

Nora and Helmer love each other, too. But Helmer is *domineering* where Nora is *obedient,* scrupulously *accurate and truthful* where Nora *lies and cheats* as a child would. Helmer is responsible for everything he does; Nora is careless. *Nora is everything Helmer is not; they are perfectly orchestrated.*

Suppose that Helmer had been married to Mrs. Linde. She is mentally mature, aware of Helmer's world and standards. She and Helmer might have quarreled, but they would never have created the great conflict which comes of the contrast between Nora and Helmer. A woman like Mrs. Linde would scarcely have committed the forgery, but if she had done so, she would have been aware of the seriousness of her deed.

Just as Mrs. Linde is different from Nora, Krogstad is different from Helmer. And Dr. Rank is different from all of them. Together, these contrasting characters are instruments which work together to give a well-orchestrated composition.

Orchestration demands well-defined and uncompromising characters in opposition, moving from one pole toward another through conflict. When we say "uncompromising," we think of Hamlet, who goes after his objective—to ferret out his father's murderer—as a bloodhound follows his quarry. We think of Helmer, whose rigid principle of civic pride causes the drama. We think of Orgon, in *Tartuffe,* who in his religious fanaticism deeds his fortune to a villain and willingly exposes his young wife to his advances.

Whenever you see a play, try to find out how the forces are lined up. The forces may be groups, as well as individuals; Fascism vs. democracy, freedom vs. slavery, religion vs. atheism. Not all religious persons who fight atheism are the same. The divergencies between their characters can be as wide as between heaven and purgatory.

In *Dinner at Eight,* Kitty and Packard are well orchestrated. Although Kitty resembles Packard in many ways, a world separates them. They both wish to be accepted in high society, but Packard wishes to reach the top in politics. Kitty abhors politics and Washington. She has nothing to do; he has no moment for relaxation. She lies in bed awaiting her lover; he rushes from place to place to do business. Between such characters there are endless possibilities for conflict.

In every big movement there are smaller movements. Let us suppose that the big movement in a play is from *love* to *hate.* What are the smaller movements within it? *Tolerance* to *intolerance* is one, and it can be broken down into *indifference* to *annoyance.* Now, whichever movement you choose for your play will affect the orchestration of your characters. Characters orchestrated for the *love*-to-*hate* movement would be far too violent for the smaller movement from *indifference* to *annoyance.* Chekhov's characters fit the movements he chose for his plays.

Kitty and Packard, for instance, would never do for *The Cherry Orchard,* and *The Cherry Orchard* characters would never get to first base in *King Lear.* Your characters should be as contrasted as the movement you are using will permit. Fine plays can be written on the smaller movements, but even on this smaller scale the conflict must be sharp, as the plays of Chekhov indicate.

When someone says, "It is a rainy day," we really don't know what kind of rain he refers to. It can be:

> mizzle (mistlike rain)
> drizzle (fine drops)
> rain (steady fall)
> downpour (heavy rain)
> storm (rain plus disturbed atmosphere).

Similarly, someone might remark, "So-and-so is a bad person." We haven't the slightest idea what that "bad" means. Is he:

                           unreliable
                           untrustworthy
                           a liar
                           a thief
                           a racketeer
                           a rapist
                           a killer?
We have to know exactly in what category every character
belongs. As the author, you have to know every character's
exact status, because you will orchestrate him with his opposites. Different orchestration is necessary for different movements. But there must be orchestration—*well-defined, strong,
uncompromising characters in conflict commensurate to the
movement of the play.*
    If, for instance, the movement was
                           from
                           indifference
                                 to
                           boredom
                                 to
                           impatience
                                 to
                           irritation
                                 to
                           annoyance
                                 to
                           anger
your characters could not be black and white. They would
be light gray against dark gray, perhaps—*but they would be
orchestrated.*
    If your characters are correctly orchestrated, as are those
in *A Doll's House* or *Tartuffe* or *Hamlet,* their speech will
necessarily be contrasted also. For instance, if one of your
characters is virginal and the other a rake, their dialogue will

reflect their respective natures. The first has no experience, and her ideas will be naïve. Casanova, in contrast, has had a wealth of experience, which will be reflected in everything he says. Any meeting between the two is sure to reveal the knowledge of one, the ignorance of the other. If you are faithful to your tridimensional character outlines, your characters will be faithful to themselves in speech and manner, and you need have no fear about contrast. If you bring a professor of English face to face with a man who never utters a sentence without mangling it, you'll have all the contrast you need without going out of your way to find it. If these two characters happen to be in conflict, trying to prove the premise of a play, the conflict will be more colorful and exciting because of the contrast in speech. *Contrast must be inherent in character.*

Conflict is sustained through growth. The naïve virgin may become wiser. She may teach a lesson, in marriage, to Casanova, who becomes unsure of himself. The professor may become careless with his speech, while the other man turns into an eloquent speaker. Remember what growth did to Eliza in Shaw's *Pygmalion.* A thief may become honest—and an honest man may turn thief. The philanderer learns to be faithful, the faithful wife turns to philandering. The unorganized worker becomes strong through organization. These are bold outlines, of course. There are infinite variations of growth possible for any character—but growth there must be. Without growth you'll lose whatever contrast you had at the beginning of the play. The absence of growth signals the lack of conflict; and the lack of conflict indicates that your characters were not well orchestrated.

11. *Unity of Opposites*

Even assuming a play is well orchestrated, what assurance have we that the antagonists won't make a truce in the middle and call it quits? The answer to this question is to be found in the "unity of opposites." It is a phrase that many people apply wrongly or misunderstand in the first place. Unity of opposites does not refer to any opposing forces or wills in a clash. Misapplication of this unity leads to a condition in which the characters cannot carry a conflict through to the finish. Our first insurance against this catastrophe is to define our terms—what is the unity of opposites?

If a man in a crowd is pushed by a stranger, and, after some insulting remarks on both sides, hits him, will the resulting fight be the result of a unity of opposites?

Only superficially, not fundamentally. The men have a desire to fight. Their egos have been slighted, they want physical revenge, *but the difference between them is not so deep-rooted that only an injury or death would straighten it out.* These are antagonists who might quit in the middle of a play. They might rationalize, explain, apologize, and shake hands. *The real unity of opposites is one in which compromise is impossible.*

We must go to nature again for an example before we apply the rule to human beings. Can anyone imagine a compromise between a deadly disease germ and the white corpuscles in a human body? It will be a fight to the finish, because the opposites are so constituted that they must destroy each other to live. There is no choice. A germ cannot say: "Oh, well, this white corpuscle is too tough for me. I'll find another place to live." Nor can the corpuscle let the germ alone, without sacrificing itself. They are opposites, united to destroy each other.

Now let's apply this same principle to the theater. Nora and Helmer were united by many things: love, home, children, law, society, desire. Yet they were opposites. It was necessary for their individual characters that this unity should be broken, or that one of them should succumb completely to the other—thus killing his individuality.

Like the germ and the corpuscle, the unity could be broken and the play ended *only by the "death" of some dominant quality in one of the characters*—Nora's docility, in the play. Naturally, death in the theater need not apply to the death of a human being. The severing of the unity between Nora and Helmer was a very painful thing, not at all easy. The closer the unity, the more difficult the breaking. And this unity, despite the qualitative change that has taken place in it, still affects the characters it has bound. In *Idiot's Delight,* the characters had nothing to bind them to each other. If one person was disagreeable he could leave.

In *Journey's End,* on the other hand, the ironclad unity of the soldiers was established beyond doubt. We were convinced that they had to stay in the trenches, perhaps die there, although they wished to be thousands of miles away. Some drank to keep up the courage that would enable them to do what was expected of them. Let us analyze their situation. These men lived in a society in which certain contradictions culminated in war. The men did not wish to fight, having no interests to safeguard, but they were sent to kill because they were subject to the desires of those who decided to solve their economic problem with war. Moreover, these young men had been taught since childhood that to die for one's country is heroic. They are torn between conflicting emotions: to escape and live will mean being stamped as a coward and despised; to stay will mean distinction—and death. Between these desires lies drama. The play is a good example of the unity of opposites.

In nature nothing is ever "destroyed" or "dead." It is transformed into another shape, substance, or element. Nora's love for Helmer was transformed into liberation and thirst for more knowledge. His smugness was transformed into a search for the truth about himself and his relation to society. A lost equilibrium tries to find a new equilibrium for itself.

Take the case of Jack the Ripper. This man, who killed so

indiscriminately, was never caught by the police, because his motivation was obscure. He seemed to have no relationship, no unity with his victims. No rancor, no anger, no jealousy, no revenge was connected with his acts. He and his victim represented opposites without unity. The motivation was missing. This same lack of motivation explains why so many bad crime plays are written. Theft, or murder, for money so that one can show off before a woman is never a real motivation. It is superficial. We do not see the irresistible force behind the crime. Criminals are people whose backgrounds have thwarted them, making crime necessary in the absence of more normal action. *If we are given the opportunity of seeing how a murderer is forced by necessity, environment, and inner and outer contradictions to commit a crime, we are witnessing the unity of opposites in action.* Proper motivation establishes unity between the opposites.

A pimp asks more money from a prostitute. Shall she give it to him? She has to. She has a sick husband whom she adores. If she refuses the pimp, he might give her secret away.

You insult your friend. He is angry and leaves, never to return. But if he lent you ten thousand dollars, can he leave so easily, never to return?

Your daughter falls in love with a man whom you abhor. Can she leave your home? Of course she can. But will she, if she expected you to put her future husband into business with your backing?

You are in partnership with your father-in-law. You don't like the old man's way of doing business. Can you dissolve this union? We don't see any reason why not. The only trouble is that the old man holds a check you have forged, and he can turn you into prison at his pleasure.

You are living with your stepfather. You hate him and still insist on staying in his house. Why? You have a horrible suspicion that he killed your father, and you stay to prove it.

You divided your fortune between your children, and in
return you ask only one room in their spacious house. Later
they become disagreeable, even insulting. Can you pack up
and leave them, when you have no means left to support
yourself?

(The last two examples may seem familiar. They should be,
since they are *Hamlet* and *King Lear* again.)

Fascism and democracy in a death grip are a perfect unity
of opposites. One has to be destroyed so that the other may
live. Here are still others:

> science—superstition
> religion—atheism
> capitalism—communism

We could go on endlessly, citing unities of opposites in
which the characters are so bound to each other that compromise is impossible. Of course, the characters have to be
made of such stuff that they will go the limit. The unity between opposites must be so strong that the deadlock can be
broken only if one of the adversaries or both are exhausted,
beaten, or annihilated completely at the end.

If King Lear's daughters had understood the King's plight,
there would have been no drama. If Helmer could have seen
the motivation of Nora's forgery, that it was done for him,
A Doll's House would never have been written. If a warring
country's government could only fathom the abysmal fear of
the soldiers, they might let them go home and stop the war,
but can they let them do such a thing? Of course not. King
Lear's daughters are unrelenting because it is in their nature
and because they have set their hearts on a goal. Governments
are at war because inner contradictions force them on the road
to destruction.

Here is a synopsis for a skit which establishes the unity of
opposites as the story goes along:

It is a brisk winter evening, and you are going home from
work. A little dog attaches himself to you. You say, "Nice

doggie," and since there is no unity between you two, you go on, forgetting about the dog. At the door you see that he is still there. He adopted you, so to speak. But you want no part of him, and say, "Go away, doggie, go away."

You go up, eat supper with your wife, read, listen to the radio, and go to bed. Next morning, with a shock, you see that the dog is still there, waiting hopefully for you, wagging his tail.

"What persistence!" you say, and pity him. You go to the subway, the dog trailing behind. You lose him at the entrance, and a few minutes later you forget him. But in the evening, coming home, just when you are about to go into your house, you stumble over him again. Apparently he was waiting, and greets you as a long-lost friend. He is freezing and emaciated by now, but happy and hopeful that you will take him in. You will, if your heart is in the right place. You don't want a dog, but this maddening persistence from a dumb animal wears you down. He wants you, he loves you, and it seems he is willing to die at your doorstep rather than give you up.

You take him upstairs. With his stubbornness, he has established a unity of opposites between you two.

But your wife is outraged. She wants no part of the dog. You defend your act, but to no avail. She is adamant. She says, "The dog or me—choose," so you give in. After feeding your little friend, you tell your wife "You take him out—I haven't the heart." She puts him out with alacrity, but afterwards feels a little sad as she remembers the sniveling animal out in the cold.

She starts to have misgivings. She is angry that she is forced to be heartless, but after all, she never wanted a dog, and she doesn't want one now.

The evening is ruined. You look at your wife with a strange, hostile eye, as if you saw her for the first time in her true colors.

In the morning you meet the dog again, but now you are really angry. He caused the first real breach between you and your wife. You try to chase the darned animal away, but the dog refuses to be chased. He escorts you to the subway again, but now you are sure that you will stumble into him when you come back in the evening.

All day long you think of the dog and your wife. He is frozen to death by now, you think. You decide you have to do something about it, and can hardly wait to go home.

When you arrive home, there is no dog, and instead of going home, you start to look for him. But there is no sign of the animal. You are terribly disappointed. You wanted to bring him up again into your house and defy your wife. If she wants to leave you on account of the dog, let her—she never loved you, anyway.

You go up, bitterness in your heart, and you are confronted with the strangest spectacle you ever saw. You see the little stray dog sitting on your best armchair, washed, combed; and before him kneels your wife, talking baby talk to him.

The dog is the pivotal character in this case. His determination changed two human beings. One equilibrium was lost, but another was found. Even if your wife would not have taken the dog in, the old relationship would have been broken just the same.

The real unity of opposites can be broken only if a trait or dominant quality in one or more characters is fundamentally changed. In a real unity of opposites, compromise is impossible.

After you have found your premise, you had better find out immediately—testing if necessary—whether the characters have the unity of opposites between them. If they do not have this strong, unbreakable bond between them, your conflict will never rise to a climax.

III

CONFLICT

◇◇

1. Origin of Action

THE blowing of the *wind* is action, even if it is only a breeze.

And *rain* is action, even to its name. The verb and the noun are one.

Our ancestor, the cave man, killed that he might eat—that was certainly action.

The walking of a man is action, the flight of a bird, the burning of a house, the reading of a book. Every manifestation of life is "action."

Can we, then, treat action as an independent phenomenon?

Let's look at *wind*. What we call wind is the mass contraction and expansion of the invisible ocean of air which surrounds us. Cold and heat create this movement called "wind." It is the result of varied contributing factors which make action possible. Wind, inactive, alone, is impossible.

Rain is the product of the sun and other factors. Without them there would be no rain.

The cave man killed. Killing is an action, but behind it there is a man who lives under conditions which force him to kill: for food, self-defense, or glory. Killing, although an "action," is only the result of important factors.

There is no action under the sun which is the origin and the result in one. Everything results from something else; *action cannot come of itself.*

Let us look further for the origin of action.

Motion, we know, is equivalent to action. Where does motion come from? We are told that motion is matter, and matter energy, but since energy is generally recognized as motion, we're back where we started.

Let us take a concrete example: the protozoon. This one-celled creature is active. It eats and digests by absorption; it moves. It performs the necessary life activities, and they are, obviously, the outgrowth of something specific: the protozoon.

Is the action of the protozoon inherent or acquired? We find that the chemical composition of the animal includes oxygen, hydrogen, phosphorus, iron, calcium. These are all complex elements—*each highly active in its composition*. It seems, then, that the protozoon inherited "action," with its other characteristics, from its multiple parents.

We had best halt our search right here, before it entangles us in the solar system. We cannot find action in a pure, isolated form, although it is always present as the result of other conditions. It is safe to say, we conclude, that action is not more important than the contributing factors which give rise to it.

2. *Cause and Effect*

In this chapter we shall divide conflict into four major divisions: the first will be "static," the second "jumping," the third "slowly rising," and the fourth "foreshadowing." We shall examine these different conflicts to see why one is static, and remains static regardless of what you do, why the second jumps, defying reality and common sense, why the third, the slowly rising, grows naturally without obvious effort from the playwright, and why without foreshadowing conflict no play can exist.

But first let us trace a conflict and see how it comes into being.

Assume that you are a gentle, inoffensive young man. You have never hurt anyone, nor have you any intention of breaking laws in the future. You are single, and you meet a girl who pleases you at a party to which you had not meant to go. You like her smile, the tone of her voice, her dress. Her tastes and yours coincide. In short, this seems to be the beginning of a deep-rooted love.

With great trepidation you invite her to see a show with you. She accepts. There is nothing wrong in this, nothing unusual, and yet it may be a turning point in your life.

At home you look over your wardrobe, which consists of the single suit you wear on all gala occasions. Under your critical eyes it sheds all the requirements you think necessary for such a suit. For one thing, you decide it is out of style; for another, it looks cheap and shabby. She is not blind; she is sure to notice.

You decide that you must have a new suit. But how? There is no money. What you earn you hand over to your mother, who keeps house for you and your two small sisters. Your father is dead, and your salary must take care of all the family expenses, the shoes for the children, the doctor bills for your mother. The rent is due. . . . No, you cannot buy a suit.

For the first time, you feel old. You remember that you are over twenty-five, that it will be years before either of your sisters is old enough to work. What's the use of planning—of living—of taking your girl to the theater. Nothing can come of it, anyway. So, you drop her.

This step makes you cross at home, listless at business. You may brood over your condition; you will be despondent. You cannot stop thinking of the girl, of what she must think of you, of whether you dare call her up, of the impossibility of your ever seeing her again. You are negligent at the office, and before you realize it, you are out of a job. This does not improve your temper. You go on a frantic job hunt and find nothing. You apply for relief—and get it, after a harrowing, long-drawn-out, shameful experience. You feel as useless as a squeezed lemon. After you get on relief you discover that you receive too little to sustain life well, but just enough to keep you from dying of hunger.

As you see, this conflict, and almost all conflict, can be traced to the environment, the social conditions of the individual.

Now the question is of what material you are made. How determined are you? How much stamina have you? What amount of suffering can you endure? What was your hope for the future? How farseeing are you? Have you imagination? Have you the ability to plan a long-range program for yourself? Are you physically able to carry out any program you may plan?

If you are sufficiently aroused, you will make a decision. And this decision will set in motion forces to thwart itself, foreshadowing a counteraction which will oppose you. You may never be aware of the process, but the playwright must be. You never knew, when you invited this girl to the theater, that you had started a long chain of events which would culminate in your desperate decision to take action now. If you are strong enough, conflict is born, the result of a long, evolutionary process which might have begun with an everyday occurrence—an invitation, perhaps.

If the young man makes a decision, but lacks the strength to carry it through, or if he is a coward, the play will be static, moving very slowly, and then on an even plane. The author would do best to leave such a character alone. He is not yet ripe enough to carry on a protracted conflict. If the dramatist has vision, he may be able to visualize this character at the psychological moment—the point of attack—when the weakling or coward is not only able to face a battle, but can meet his adversary more than halfway. This will be discussed further under "Point of Attack."

A jumping conflict would occur if the young man decided, upon seeing the shabbiness of his suit, to rob a bank, or hold up a passer-by. It is illogical that an inoffensive boy would arrive at such a conclusion so rapidly. There would have to be more crushing events, each more urgent and painful than the one before, to force him to take this fatal step. It is possible that at a moment of frustration and despair a man will do the unexpected in real life—but never in the theater. There we wish to see the natural sequence, the step-by-step development of a character. We want to see how the cloak of decency, high moral standards, is torn away from a character shred by shred by the forces emanating from him and from his surroundings.

Every rising conflict should be foreshadowed first by the determined forces lined up against each other. We shall make this clearer as we go along, but there is one thing we wish to emphasize here: all the conflicts within the big, major conflict will be crystallized in the premise of the play. The small conflicts, which we call "transition," lead the character from one state of mind to another, until he is compelled to make a decision. (*See* "Transition.") Through these transitions, or small conflicts, the character will grow in a slow, even tempo.

In another chapter we have discussed the complexity of the word "happiness." Take away a small fraction of any part, and you see how the whole structure of "happiness" loses its unity and undergoes a radical change, which, in the process of reshifting, may turn "happiness" into "unhappiness." This law governs infinitesimal cells, humans, and the solar system.

Dr. Milislaw Demerec read a paper on *Heredity* before the annual meeting of the American Association for the Advancement of Science, in Richmond, Virginia, on December 30, 1938. He wrote:

The balance within a gene system is so sensitive that the absence of even one gene out of a total of several thousand may upset it to such an extent that this system is not able to function and the organism does not survive. Moreover, numerous cases of interaction between genes are on record where *a change in one gene affects the functioning of another seemingly unrelated gene.* Considering all the evidence, it seems apparent that the activity of a gene is determined by three internal factors: (1) the chemical constitution of the gene itself, (2) the genetic constitution of the gene system in which it acts, and (3) by the position of the gene in the gene system. These three internal factors, together with the external factors forming the environment, determine the phenotype (totality of inheritable characteristics) of the organism.

A gene, therefore, should be considered as a unit part of a well-organized system and a chromosome a higher step in that organization. In that sense genes as individual units with fixed properties do not exist, but their existence as component units of a larger system, with properties partially determined by that system, cannot be denied.

Just as a gene is a unit, but part of a well-organized society of genes, a human being is a unit, part of a well-organized society of human beings. Whatever change comes over the society will affect him; whatever happens to him will affect the society.

You can find conflict all around you. Watch the members of your family, your friends, your relatives, your acquaintances, your business associates, and see if you can discover one of the following traits: affection, abusiveness, arrogance, avarice, accuracy, awkwardness, brazenness, bragging, craftiness, confusion, cunning, conceit, contemptuousness, cleverness, clumsiness, curiosity, cowardice, cruelty, dignity, dishonesty, dissipation, envy, eagerness, egotism, extravagance, fickleness, fidelity, frugality, gaiety, garrulity, gallantry, generosity, honesty, hesitance, hysteria, heedlessness, ill-temper, idealism, impulsiveness, indolence, impotence, impudence, kindness, loyalty, lucidity, morbidity, maliciousness, mysticism, modesty, obstinacy, prudishness, placidity, patience, pretentiousness, passion, restlessness, submission, sarcasm, simplicity, skepticism, savagery, solemnity, suspicion, stoicism, secretiveness, sensitivity, snobbery, treachery, tenderness, untidyness, versatility, vindictiveness, vulgarity, zealousness.

Any of these, and thousands of other traits, can be the soil from which a conflict springs. Let a skeptic oppose a militant believer and you have a conflict.

Cold and heat create conflict: thunder and lightning. Bring opposites face to face and conflict is inevitable. Let each of these adjectives represent a man, and imagine the possible conflicts when they meet:

> frugal—spendthrift
> moral—immoral
> dirty—immaculate
> optimistic—pessimistic
> gentle—ruthless
> faithful—fickle
> clever—stupid
> calm—violent
> cheerful—morbid
> healthy—hypochondriac
> humorous—humorless
> sensitive—insensitive
> dainty—vulgar
> naïve—worldly
> brave—cowardly.

When our cave-man ancestor went after food, he fought with a tangible enemy: a huge beast which meant food—a conflict. He threw his life into the balance, and the fight was to the death. This was rising conflict: conflict, crisis, conclusion.

A football game represents conflict. The teams are evenly

matched—two strong groups face each other. (*See* "Orchestration.") But since victory is the goal, the fight will be bitter and hard won.

Boxing is conflict. All competitive sports are conflict. A saloon brawl is conflict. A fight for supremacy among men or nations is conflict. Every manifestation of life, from birth to death, is conflict.

There are more complex forms of conflict, but they all rise on this simple basis: attack and counterattack. *We see real, rising conflict when the antagonists are evenly matched.* There is no thrill in watching a strong, skillful man fighting a sickly, awkward one. When two people are evenly matched, whether in the prize ring or on the stage, each is forced to utilize all that is in him. Each will reveal how much he knows about generalship; how his mind works in an emergency; what kind of defense he is capable of; how strong he really is; whether he has any reserve to marshal as a defense when he's in danger. Attack, counterattack; conflict.

If we try to isolate and examine conflict as an independent phenomenon, we are in danger of being led up a blind alley. There is nothing in existence which is out of touch with its surroundings or the social order in which it exists. Nothing lives for its own sake; everything is supplementary to every other thing.

The germ of conflict can be traced in anything, anywhere. Not everyone knows the answer when he is asked to name his ambition in life. Yet he has one, no matter how humble, perhaps for that very day, week, or month. And out of that small, seemingly inconsequential ambition, a rising conflict may grow. The conflict may become increasingly serious, reach a crisis, then come to a climax, and the individual is forced to make a decision which will alter his life considerably.

Nature has an elaborate system of distributing the seeds of

various plants. If every single seed were given a chance to develop in its year, mankind would be choked out of existence—and the plants as well.

Every human being has an ambition of some sort, depending on the character of the individual. If a hundred people have similar ambitions, the odds are that only one of them will have the perfect combination of circumstances, in himself and in the world about him, which will permit him to achieve his goal. We are thus brought back to character, to the reason why one will persist and another will not.

There is no doubt that conflict grows out of character. *The intensity of the conflict will be determined by the strength of will of the three-dimensional individual who is the protagonist.*

A seed may fall at any given point—but it will not necessarily germinate. And ambition may be found anywhere, but whether or not it germinates will depend upon the physical, sociological, and psychological condition of the person in whom it exists.

If ambition were to flourish with the same intensity in every man, that too would spell mankind's doom.

On the surface, a healthy conflict consists of two forces in opposition. At bottom, each of these forces is the product of many complicated circumstances in a chronological sequence, creating tension so terrific that it must culminate in an explosion.

Let us witness another example of how conflict comes into being.

Brass Ankle, a play by Du Bose Heyward, offers intimate insight into how conflict is born.

LARRY [*the husband, startled*]: Ruth and I aren't goin' to keep that kid, Doctor. You surely don't think we're goin' to keep a nigger in the family.

DR. WAINWRIGHT: That, of course, is your affair, yours and Ruth's.
After all, he is your son.
LARRY: My son—a nigger!

Larry is the leading citizen of a small town, and he is
fighting to segregate the Negro from the white. He believes
that even a drop of Negro blood makes a man unfit to associate with whites, and now his wife, white, has given birth
to a Negro. It is a personal tragedy. If the town gets wind of
it, he will become a laughingstock for life. This is an aggra-
vated conflict. Larry will be forced to make a decision: admit
the child is his own, or deny his fatherhood. But at this moment we are not interested in what will happen; we wish to
trace the origin of the conflict. We want to know how conflicts come into being.

The author says:

Larry is about thirty years of age, tall, straight and good-looking,
with fair hair and high color. His quick nervous gestures indicate
a high-strung and emotional nature.

Before his marriage he was lazy, we dare say. He was pampered by women, and perhaps had many affairs. But there
was one girl, Ruth, John Chaldon's granddaughter, a dark,
compelling beauty, a lady, different from the other women
in the village. She never paid any attention to Larry, but he
wooed her persistently, mended his ways, and at last she gave
in and married him.

Is there any clue thus far which would indicate a conflict
to come? There are many, but they would mean nothing if
the locale happened to be New York. Don't forget the vital
importance of the location—we shall see why, later.

Once more, Larry's physical make-up: good-looking. He
is spoiled, he has a way with women. Otherwise he would
never have married Ruth, and the tragedy would not have occurred.

Now the environment, the particular time of the event. It is two generations after the Civil War. Liberated Negroes live in the town, as do mulattoes, and part Negroes who pass as whites. There are more than a few nice, respectable families, apparently white, who are known to the village doctor to be Negro. Having brought most of them into the world, he alone knows who is who. He knows that Ruth has Negro blood in her, although she has passed for white. As a matter of fact, she has thought herself white. She has an eight-year-old daughter who is apparently white. The second child is one of those rare throwbacks.

That Ruth is good-looking and a lady is also an important factor in the coming conflict.

LARRY: I always swore I'd marry a lady. I ain't got no kick comin'.

And in another place:

LARRY: . . . and I owe it all to you. I never had any ambition until I married you.

Larry is now the proprietor of a successful store, thanks to Ruth's influence.

Their physical qualities attracted them to each other. The environment made Larry what he was: lazy, arrogant, spoiled; it also made Ruth dignified, soft-spoken. To him, she was an ideal; to her, he was a child. Her dignity appealed to him, since he lacked dignity; his devil-may-care manner appealed to her, since she lacked ease. His great love assured her that she could make a man of him.

The environment again: a small town, few young people. If there had been more girls, Larry might not have married Ruth. But there weren't many girls—and he is supremely happy with his wife. He is more and more ambitious, and the townsfolk want him to be the first mayor of the growing community.

AGNES [*a neighbor*]: Lee [*her husband*] says you've got the case on the Jackson children all ready for the Superintendent of Education. I've had a lot to do with that, you know. If I hadn't kept after him he never would have stirred himself. I say, if he expects me to give him children, he's got to see that they can go to school without havin' to sit by people we all know's got nigger blood.

LARRY [*in a tired voice*]: Yes, Agnes, we know you had a lot to do with it.

This dialogue indicates the town's anti-Negro sentiment which forces Larry to take an anti-Negro stand, too. It also shows that he is the leader, and we know he wishes to remain the leader *for the love of Ruth.* So he runs and barks with the pack, aggravating, building, strengthening the coming conflict which will crush him.

So it seems that conflict does spring from character after all, and that if we wish to know the structure of conflict, we must first know character. But since character is influenced by environment, we must know that, too. It might seem that conflict springs spontaneously from one single cause, but this is not true. A complexity of many reasons makes one solitary conflict.

3. Static

Characters who cannot make a decision in a play are responsible for static conflict—or, rather, let us blame the dramatist who chooses the characters. *You cannot expect a rising conflict from a man who wants nothing or does not know what he wants.*

Static means not moving, not exerting force of any kind. Since we intend to go into a detailed analysis of what makes dramatic action static, we must point out right here that even the most static conflict has movement of some kind. Nothing in nature is absolutely static. An inanimate object is full of movement which the naked eye cannot see; a dead scene in a play also contains movement, but so slow that it seems to be standing still.

No dialogue, even the cleverest, can move a play if it does not further the conflict. Only conflict can generate more conflict, and the first conflict comes from a conscious will striving to achieve a goal which was determined by the premise of the play.

A play can have only one major premise, but each character has his own premise which clashes with the others. Currents and undercurrents will cross and recross—but all of them must further the life line, the main premise of the play.

If, for instance, a woman perceives that her life is sterile, and cries her heart out, pacing her room, but does nothing about it, she is a static character. The dramatist may put the most haunting lines in her mouth, but she remains impotent and static. Grief is not enough to create conflict; we need a *will* which can consciously do something about the problem.

Here is a good example of static conflict:

HE: Do you love me?
SHE: Oh, I don't know.
HE: Can't you make up your mind?
SHE: I will.
HE: When?
SHE: Oh . . . soon.
HE: How soon?
SHE: Oh, I don't know.
HE: May I help?
SHE: That wouldn't be fair, would it?
HE: Everything is fair in love, especially if I can convince you that I am the one man you want.
SHE: How would you do that?
HE: First of all I would kiss you—
SHE: Oh, but I won't let you until we are engaged.
HE: If you don't let me kiss you, how on earth are you going to find out whether you love me or not?

SHE: If I like your company . . .
HE: Do you like my company?
SHE: Oh, I don't know—yet.
HE: That settles the argument.
SHE: How?
HE: You said—
SHE: Later on I might learn to like your company, though.
HE: How long will that take?
SHE: How am I to know?

We can go on and on, and still there will be no substantial
change in these characters. There is conflict, all right, but it
is static. They remain on the same level. We can attribute this
staticness to bad orchestration. Both are the same type—there
is no deep conviction in either of them. Even the man who
pursues the woman lacks the drive, the determination of a
deep-rooted conviction that this is the only woman he wants
for his mate. They can go on like this for months. They might
drift apart, or the man might force a decision at the end—the
Lord knows when. As they stand right now, they are no happy
choice for a dramatic composition.

Without attack, counterattack, there can be no rising conflict.

She started from the pole of "uncertainty," and at the end,
she is still uncertain. He started from the pole of hope, and
at the end, he is still in the same state of mind.

If a character starts from "virtuousness" and goes to "vil-
lainy," let us see what intervening steps she has to take:

1. Virtuous (chaste, pure)
2. Thwarted (frustrated in her virtue)
3. Incorrect (faulty, unbecoming behavior)
4. Improper (she becomes indecorous, almost indecent)
5. Disorderly (unmanageable)
6. Immoral (licentious)
7. Villainous (depraved, wretched)

If a character stops at the first or second step and lingers there too long before taking the next step, the play will become static. Such staticness usually occurs when the play lacks the driving force which is the premise.

Here is an interesting static play, *Idiot's Delight*, by Robert E. Sherwood. Although the play's moral is highly commendable and the author is deservedly a well-known playwright, it is a classic example of how not to write a play. (See synopsis on page 285.)

The premise of this play is: Do armament manufacturers stir up trouble and war? The author's answer is yes.

The premise is unfortunate—it is superficial. The play has direction, but the moment the author chooses a segregated minority group as the archenemy of peace, he negates the truth. Can we say that only the sun is responsible for rain? Of course not. There can be no rain without the oceans and other factors. No armament maker can stir up trouble if there is economic stability and contentment in the world. Armament manufacturing is the outgrowth of militarism, insufficient domestic and foreign markets, unemployment, and the like. Although Mr. Sherwood speaks about the people in the postscript of the printed version of his play, he sadly neglected them in *Idiot's Delight*.

There are no people in his play, no people who really matter. We see Mr. Weber, the sinister armament manufacturer, who says he wouldn't sell armaments if there were no buyers. This is true. The crux of the point is, why do they buy armaments? Mr. Sherwood has nothing to say about it. Since the conception of his premise is superficial, his characters necessarily become colored photographs.

His two main characters are Harry and Irene. Harry moves from *callousness* to *sincerity* and *fearlessness of death*. Irene starts from *loose morals,* and ends up on the same lofty heights as Harry.

If there are eight steps between these two poles, then they started at the first, stayed on it for two and one-half acts, leaped over the intervening second, third, fourth, fifth, and sixth steps as if they had never existed, and started to move again from the seventh to the eighth step during the last part of the play.

Characters wander in and out with no particular motivation. They enter, introduce themselves, and leave because the author wishes to introduce someone else. They re-enter for some artificial reason, tell what they think and how they feel, and wander out again so that the next batch may come on.

One thing on which we hope our critics will agree with us is that a play should have conflict. *Idiot's Delight* has it only in rare spots. Characters, instead of engaging in conflict, tell us about themselves, which is contrary to all standards of drama. What a pity that Harry, jovial and good-natured, and Irene, with a colorful background, were not used more advantageously. Here are a few, typical excerpts:

We are in the cocktail lounge of the Hotel Monte Gabriele. A war is expected at any moment. The borders have been closed, and the guests cannot leave. We turn to page six and read:

DON: It's lovely there, too.
CHERRY: But I hear it has become too crowded there now. I—my wife and I hoped it would be quieter here.
DON: Well, at the moment—it is rather quiet here. [*No conflict.*]

Now we turn to page thirty-two. People are still wandering in and out, aimlessly. Quillery enters, sits down. Five officers come in and talk in Italian. Harry comes in and talks to the Doctor about nothing in particular. The Doctor leaves, and Harry talks to Quillery. After a moment or so the latter, without apparent cause, addresses Harry as "Comrade." The author says, when Quillery comes in, "an extreme radical-socialist, but still, French." What the audience sees is that he is mad, except at a very few rational moments. Why should he be mad? Because, apparently, he is a radical-socialist, and extreme radical-socialists are all mad. Later he is killed for taunting the Fascists, but now he and Harry talk of pigs, cigarettes, and war. It is all empty talk, and then he says—this socialist—"This is not 1914, remember. Since then, some new voices have been heard—loud voices. I need mention only one of them—Lenin—Nikolai Lenin." Since this extreme radical-socialist is a madman, and is treated as such by his fellow characters, the audience may believe they are hearing of another extreme radical-socialist (synonym: madman). Then Quillery talks of revolution, futile idealism to Harry, who doesn't know what it's all about. But that just shows you how crazy these extreme radical-socialists are.

Now we are on page forty-four. The cast is still coming in and going out. The Doctor bewails the bad fortune that keeps him here. They drink, they talk. A war may break out, but there is still no sign of even static conflict. There is no sign of a character, with the exception of a certain madman to whom we have referred.

We turn to page sixty-six, sure that we shall have some action this far along in the play.

WEBER: Will you have a drink, Irene?
IRENE: No, thank you.
WEBER: Will you, Captain Locicero?
CAPT.: Thank you. Brandy and soda, Dumptsy.
DUMPTSY: Si, Signor.
BEBE: [yells] Edna! We're going to have a drink!
  [Edna comes in.]
WEBER: For me, Cinzano.
DUMPTSY: Oui, Monsieur. [He goes into the bar.]
DOCTOR: It is all incredible.
HARRY: Nevertheless, Doctor, I remain an optimist. [He looks at Irene.] Let doubt prevail—throughout this night—with dawn

will come again the light of truth! [*He turns to Shirley.*] Come
on, honey—let's dance. [*They dance.*]

Curtain

We rub our eyes, but this remains the end of the first act.
Should any young playwright dare to submit a play such as
this to any manager, he would risk being thrown out on his
ear. The audience must share Harry's optimism if it is to
overcome such a dose of hopelessness.

Sherwood must have seen or read *Journey's End*, in which
soldiers in the front-line trenches go to pieces in the nerve-
racking wait before they go over the top. The people in
Idiot's Delight are also waiting for war, but there is a difference. In *Journey's End* we have characters, flesh-and-blood
people, whom we know. They are striving to keep up their
courage. We feel, we know, the "Big Push" may come any
minute, and they have no choice but to face it and die. In
Idiot's Delight the characters are not in immediate danger.

There is no doubt that Sherwood had the best of intentions
when he wrote the play, but good intentions are not enough.

The greatest dramatic moment of *Idiot's Delight* is in the
second act. It is worth while to glance at it. Quillery heard
from a mechanic, who may have been wrong, that the Italians
have bombarded Paris. He goes berserk. He shouts.

QUILLERY: I say God damn you, assassins!
MAJOR AND SOLDIERS [*jump up*]: Assassins!
HARRY: Now listen, pal . . .
SHIRLEY: Harry! Don't get yourself mixed up in this mess!
QUILLERY: You see, we stand together! France, England, America!
    Allies!
HARRY: Shut up, France! It's O.K., Captain. We can handle this.
QUILLERY: They don't dare fight against the power of England and
    France! The free democracies against the Fascist tyranny!
HARRY: Now, for God's sake, stop fluctuating!

QUILLERY: England and France are fighting for the hopes of mankind!

HARRY: A minute ago, England was a butcher in a dress suit. Now we're allies!

QUILLERY: We stand together. We stand together, forever! [*Turns to officers.*]

The author makes this pitiful figure turn toward the Italian officers. He is afraid they will not take offense, in which case the great dramatic scene will collapse. So the poor fool turns toward the officers.

QUILLERY: I say God damn you. God damn the villains that sent you on this errand of death.

CAPTAIN: If you don't close your mouth, Frenchman, we shall be forced to arrest you.

The first step toward conflict. Of course, it isn't quite fair to fight a demented man, but it's better than nothing.

HARRY: It's all right, Captain. Mr. Quillery is for peace. He's going back to France to stop the war.

QUILLERY [*to Harry*]: You're not authorized to speak for me. I'm competent to say what I feel, and what I say is "Down with Fascism! *Abaso Fascismo!*"

After this, of course, they shoot him. The others go on dancing and pretend they are not very much impressed. But they can't fool us.

At one point Irene delivers a *splendid speech* to Achille, but before that point—and after it—nothing.

Another, less obvious example of static conflict can be found in Noel Coward's *Design for Living.*

Gilda has alternated between two lovers until her marriage to a friend of her lovers. All three men are friends. The two lovers come back to claim Gilda. Her husband is naturally outraged. The four are together now, at the end of the third act.

GILDA [*blandly*]: Now then!
LEO: Now then *indeed!*
GILDA: What's going to happen?
OTTO: Social poise again. Oh dear! Oh dear, oh dear!
GILDA: You know you both look figures of fun in pajamas!
ERNEST [*the husband*]: I don't believe I've ever been so acutely
   irritated in my whole life.
LEO: It is annoying for you, Ernest. I do see that. I am so sorry.
OTTO: Yes, we're both sorry.
ERNEST: I think your arrogance is insufferable. I don't know what
   to say. I don't know what to do. I am very, very angry. Gilda, for
   heaven's sake, tell them to go!
GILDA: They wouldn't. Not if I told them until I was black in the
   face!
LEO: Quite right.
OTTO: Not without you, we wouldn't.
GILDA [*smiling*]: That's very sweet of you both.

There is no visible development in character, hence the
conflict is static. If a character, for any reason, loses its reality,
it becomes incapable of creating rising conflict.

If we wish to portray a bore, it is not necessary to bore the
audience. Nor is it necessary to be superficial to show a superficial personality. We must know what motivates a character,
even if he does not know himself. The author must not write
in a vacuum to show characters who live in one. No sophistry
will explain away this fact.

GILDA [*blandly*]: Now then!

"Now then" means "what is going to happen now?" and
no more than that. There is nothing in it of provocation, of
attack leading to counterattack. Even for the shallow Gilda
it is too ineffectual, and it gets the right answer: "Now then
indeed."

If Gilda's remark had imperceptible movement, Leo's re-
sponse had none at all. It not only fails to take up the tiny

challenge she offered; it leaves it as it was. No movement to be seen.

The next line is sarcastic, but the three "oh dears" are not only *not* a challenge, but an admission of the speaker's impotence to remedy the situation. If you doubt this, look at the next line: "You both look figures of fun in those pajamas." Apparently Otto's sarcasm passed unnoticed. Gilda has not been touched, and the play refuses to move.

The very least the author could have done at this point was show another facet of Gilda's character. We might have seen the motivation behind Gilda's love life, her flippancy. But we see nothing but a superfluous comment—to be expected from "characters" who are simply manikins through whom the author speaks.

ERNEST: I don't believe I've ever been so acutely irritated in my whole life.

Anyone who says such a line is harmless. He can whine, but he cannot add or detract from the sum of the play. His exclamation does not aggravate the situation. There is no threat, no action. What is a weak character? One who, for any reason, cannot make a decision.

LEO: It is annoying for you, Ernest. I do see that. I am sorry.

There is something in this line—a trace of heartlessness. Leo doesn't give a damn about Ernest. But the conflict stays where it was. Then Otto steps in and assures Ernest that he too is sorry. If this is funny at all, it is because such an attitude, in life, would be brutal and unfeeling. The character who can employ such humor and still be heroic does not exist—and cannot create conflict.

Ernest's next speech is revealing. The antagonist admits that he cannot put up any sort of a fight, that he must appeal to the goal (Gilda) to fight his battle for him. Gilda, Otto, and Leo want what they want and there is no one even to try to stop them. This may be funny in a two-line gag, but it isn't the conflict necessary for a play.

If you reread the whole quotation, you will see that at the last line the play is almost in the same position as when it started. The movement is negligible, particularly when you remember that the act goes on like this for several pages.

In *Brass Ankle,* by Du Bose Heyward, almost the whole first act is taken up with exposition. But the second and third acts make up for the bad first one. In *Design for Living* there is cause for conflict in the initial situation, but it never materializes because of the superficiality of the characters. The result is a static conflict.

4. Jumping

One of the chief dangers in any jumping conflict is that the author believes the conflict is rising smoothly. He resents any critic who insists that the conflict jumps. What are the danger signals which an author can look for? How can he tell when he is going in the wrong direction? Here are a few pointers:

No honest man will become a thief overnight; no thief will become honest in the same period of time. No sane woman will leave her husband on the spur of the moment, without previous motivation. No burglar contemplates a robbery and carries it out at the same time. No violent physical act was ever carried out without *mental preparation.* No shipwreck has ever occurred without a sound reason. Some essential part of the ship may be missing; the captain may be overworked or inexperienced or ill. Even when a ship collides with an iceberg, human negligence is involved. Read *Good Hope* by Heijermans, and see how a ship thus goes under and human tragedy reaches a new height.

If you want to avoid jumping or static conflicts, you might

as well know beforehand what road your characters have to travel.

Here are a few examples. They might go from:

> drunkenness to sobriety
> sobriety to drunkenness
> timidity to brazenness
> brazenness to timidity
> simplicity to pretentiousness
> pretentiousness to simplicity
> fidelity to infidelity, and so on.

If you know your character has to travel from one pole to another, you are in an advantageous position to see that he or she grows at a steady rate. You are not fumbling around; instead, your characters have a destination and they fight every inch of the way to reach it.

If your character starts from "fidelity," and with a Gargantuan leap arrives at "infidelity," omitting the intervening steps, it will be a jumping conflict, and your play will suffer.

Here is a jumping conflict:

HE: Do you love me?
SHE: Oh, I don't know.
HE: Don't be a dumbbell. Make up your mind, will you?
SHE: Smart guy, huh?
HE: Not so smart if I can fall for a dame like you.
SHE: I'll smack your face in a minute. [*She walks away.*]

He in this instance started from "fondness," and arrived at "sneering," without any transition at all. *She* started from "uncertainty" and leaped to "anger."

The man's character was false at the start—false because if he loved her, he could not ask for her love and say in the same breath that she is a dumbbell. If he thought her dumb in the first place, he wouldn't want her love.

Both are of the same type again—impetuous, excitable.

Transition in such characters moves with lightning speed. Before you knew it, the scene was over. Yes, you can prolong it, but since they are moving with leaps and bounds, they'll be in each other's hair in no time. Liliom, in Ferenc Molnar's play, is the same type as "He" in this scene. But Liliom's counterpart is exactly the opposite. Julie is subservient, patient, and loving.

Badly orchestrated characters usually create static or jumping conflict, although even well-orchestrated characters can jump—and frequently do—*if the proper transition is missing.*

If you wish to create jumping conflict, you have only to force the characters into action which is alien to them. Make them act without thinking, and you will be successful in your own way, but unsuccessful with your play.

If, for instance, you have as your premise: "A dishonored man can redeem himself through self-sacrifice," the starting point will be a dishonored man. The goal, the same man honored, cleansed, perhaps glorified. Between these two poles lies a space, "empty" as yet. How he is going to fill this space is up to the character. If the author chooses characters who believe in, and are willing to fight for, the premise, he is on the right road. The next step will be to study them as thoroughly as possible. This study will show—a double check—if they are really capable of doing what the premise expects of them.

It is not enough if the "dishonored man" saves an old woman from fire, *à la* Hollywood, and is redeemed instantaneously. There must be a logical chain of events leading up to the sacrifice.

Between winter and summer come autumn and spring. Between honor and dishonor there are steps which lead from one to the other. Every step must be taken.

When Nora, in *A Doll's House,* wants to leave Helmer and her children, she lets us know why. More than that, we are convinced that this is the only step she could have taken.

In life, she might have been tight-lipped; might never have said a word—just banged the door after her. If she were to do that on the stage it would be a jumping conflict. We should not understand her, although her motives might be of the best.

We must be completely in the know, and in jumping conflict our knowledge is only superficial. *Real characters must be given a chance to reveal themselves, and we must be given a chance to observe the significant changes which take place in them.*

We propose to strip the last part of the third act in A Doll's House, *leaving the essentials, but still rendering it ineffectual.* This is the grand finale of the play. Helmer has just told Nora that he would not permit her to bring up the children. But the bell rings and a letter arrives, containing a note and the forged bond. Helmer cries out that he is saved.

NORA: And I?

HELMER: You too, of course. We're both saved, both you and I. I have forgiven you, Nora.

NORA: Thank you for your forgiveness. [*She goes out.*]

HELMER: No, don't go— [*looks in*] What are you doing in there?

NORA [*from within*]: Taking off my fancy dress.

HELMER: Yes, do. Try and calm yourself and make your mind easy again, my frightened little singing bird.

NORA [*enters, in everyday dress*]: I have changed my things now.

HELMER: But what for? So late as this.

NORA: It is for the reason that I cannot remain with you any longer.

HELMER: Nora! Nora! You are out of your mind! I won't allow it! I forbid you!

NORA: It is no use to forbid me anything any longer.

HELMER: You do not love me any more.

NORA: No.

HELMER: Nora! And you can say that!

NORA: It gives me great pain, but I cannot help it.

HELMER: I see, I see. An abyss has opened between us—there is no denying it. But, Nora, would it not be possible to fill it up?

NORA: As I am now, I am no wife for you. [*She takes cloak and hat and a small bag.*]

HELMER: Nora, not now! Wait till tomorrow.

NORA [*putting on her cloak*]: I cannot spend the night in a strange man's room.

HELMER: All over! All over! Nora, shall you never think of me again?

NORA: I know I shall often think of you and the children and this house. Good-by. [*She goes out through the hall.*]

HELMER [*sinks down on a chair at the door and buries his face in his hands*]: Nora! Nora! [*looks round and rises*] Empty. She's gone. [*The sound of a door shutting is heard from below.*]

The End

What we have here is a hybrid conflict of the worst kind. It is not static, nor is it always jumping. It is a combination of jumping and rising conflict, which might easily confuse the young author. Therefore we shall examine it more closely.

There is rising conflict when Nora announces that she will leave. Helmer forbids her, but she goes just the same. This is all right. But there is jumping conflict elsewhere. The first jump is Nora's reaction to Helmer's forgiveness. She thanks him and leaves the room—leaping over an abyss to do so. Does she really mean that she is grateful, or is she being subtly sarcastic? Nora is not much good at sarcasm. She is acutely aware of the injustice done to her and therefore would not be likely to joke about it, bitterly or otherwise. Yet it does not seem like a moment for gratitude on her part. We are left wondering when she leaves the room.

When she returns and announces that she cannot remain with Helmer any longer, it is far too sudden. There has been no preparation for such a step.

But the greatest jump is Helmer's reaction to the fact that Nora no longer loves him:

I see, I see. An abyss has opened between us.

It is almost unbelievable that a man of Helmer's character would arrive at such understanding without presenting a powerful rebuttal beforehand. If you will read the original version at the end of this chapter, you will see what we mean.

Nora leaves, at the end of the scene (in our version), but it is no decision of her problem. It is a jump—an impulse. We feel no absolute necessity for her action. Perhaps it is a caprice which she will regret—and retract—tomorrow. Leaving Helmer as she does (in our version again), Nora fails to convince us, regardless of her justification. This is the inevitable result of a jumping conflict.

Whenever a conflict lags, rises jerkily, stops, or jumps, look to your premise. Is it clear cut? Is it active? Remedy any fault here, and then turn to your characters. Perhaps your protagonist is too weak to carry the burden of the play (bad orchestration). *Perhaps some of your characters are not growing constantly.* Don't forget that staticness is the direct result of a static character who cannot make up his mind. And don't forget that he may be static because he is not tridimensional. The genuine rising conflict is the product of characters who are well rounded in terms of the premise. Every action of such a character will be understandable and dramatic to the audience.

If your premise is "Jealousy not only destroys itself, but destroys the object of its love," you know, or should know, that every line of your play, every move your characters make, must further the premise. Granted that there are many solutions for any given situation, *your characters are permitted to choose only those which will help prove the premise.* The moment you decide upon a premise, you and your characters become its slave. Each character must feel, intensely, that the action dictated by the premise is the *only action possible.* Moreover, the dramatist must be convinced of the absolute truth of his premise, or his characters will be the pale repetition of his undigested, superficial conviction. Remember, a play is not an imitation of life, but the essence of life. You must condense all that is important, all that is necessary. You will see, in the last part of *A Doll's House,* how every possibility is exhausted before Nora leaves her husband. Even if you disagree with her final decision, you understand it. For Nora, it is absolutely necessary that she leave.

When characters go round and round, *without making any decision,* the play will undoubtedly be a bore. But if they are in a process of growth, there is nothing to fear.

The pivotal character is responsible for the growth through conflict. Be sure that your pivotal character is relentless, cannot and will not compromise. Hamlet, Krogstad, Lavinia, Hedda Gabler, Macbeth, Iago, Manders in *Ghosts,* the doctors in *Yellow Jack*—these are such pivotal forces that compromise is out of the question. If your play jumps or becomes static, see to it that the unity of opposites is solidly established. The point is that the bond between the characters cannot be broken, except through the transformation of a trait or a characteristic in a person, or by death itself.

But let us go back to Nora once more. Step by step, Nora approached a minor climax. She builds on top of it, arriving at another climax, this time on a higher plane. She goes still higher, constantly fighting, clearing the way until she reaches the ultimate goal, which was contained in the premise.

And now, perhaps, you should read the original for yourself. *The sentences italicized* (disregarding stage directions, of course) *are those we used in our example of jumping conflict.*

A DOLL'S HOUSE

Act III

MAID: [*half-dressed, comes to the door*] A letter for the mistress.
HELMER: Give it to me. [*Takes the letter and shuts the door.*] Yes, it is from him. You shall not have it; I will read it myself.

NORA: Yes, read it.

HELMER: [*standing by the lamp*] I scarcely have the courage to do it. It may mean ruin for both of us. No, I must know. [*Tears open the letter, runs his eye over a few lines, looks at a paper enclosed, and gives a shout of joy.*] Nora! [*She looks at him questioningly.*] Nora!— No, I must read it once again— Yes, it is true! *I am saved! Nora, I am saved!*

NORA: *And I?*

HELMER: *You too, of course; we are both saved, both you and I.* Look, he sends you your bond back. He says he regrets and repents—that a happy change in his life—never mind what he says! We are saved, Nora! No one can do anything to you. Oh, Nora, Nora!—no, first I must destroy these hateful things— [*Takes a look at the bond.*] No, no, I won't look at it. The whole thing shall be nothing but a bad dream to me. [*Tears up the bond and both letters, throws them all into the stove, and watches them burn.*] There—now it doesn't exist any longer. He says that since Christmas Eve you— These must have been three dreadful days for you, Nora.

NORA: I have fought a hard fight these three days.

HELMER: And suffered agonies, and seen no way out but— No, we won't call any of those horrors to mind. We will only shout with joy, and keep saying, "It's all over! It's all over!" Listen to me, Nora. You don't seem to realize that it is all over. What is this?—such a cold, set face! My poor little Nora, I quite understand; you don't feel as if you could believe that I have forgiven you. But it is true, Nora, I swear it; I have forgiven you everything. I know that what you did, you did out of love for me.

NORA: That is true.

HELMER: You have loved me as a wife ought to love her husband. Only you had not sufficient knowledge to judge by the means you used. But do you suppose you are any the less dear to me, because you don't understand how to act on your own responsibility? No, no; only lean on me; I will advise you and direct you. I should not be a man if this womanly helplessness did not just give you a double attractiveness in my eyes. You must not think any more about the hard things I said in my first moment of consternation, when I thought everything was going to overwhelm me. *I have forgiven you, Nora;* I swear to you that I have forgiven you.

NORA: *Thank you for your forgiveness.* [*She goes out through the door to the right.*]

HELMER: No, don't go— [*Looks in.*] *What are you doing in there?*

NORA: [*from within*] *Taking off my fancy dress.*

HELMER: [*standing at the open door*] *Yes, do. Try and calm yourself, and make your mind easy again, my frightened little singing bird.* Be at rest, and feel secure; I have broad wings to shelter you under. [*Walks up and down by the door.*] How warm and cozy our home is, Nora. Here is the shelter for you; here I will protect you like a hunted dove that I have saved from a hawk's claws; I will bring peace to your poor beating heart. It will come, little by little, Nora, believe me. Tomorrow morning you will look upon it all quite differently; soon everything will be just as it was before. Very soon you won't need me to assure you that I have forgiven you; you will yourself feel the certainty that I have done so. Can you suppose I should ever think of such a thing as repudiating you, or even reproaching you? You have no idea what a true man's heart is like, Nora. There is something so indescribably sweet and satisfying, to a man, in the knowledge that he has forgiven his wife—forgiven her freely, and with all his heart. It seems as if that had made her, as it were, doubly his own; he has given her a new life, so to speak; and she has, in a way, become both wife and child to him. So you shall be for me after this, my little scared, helpless darling. Have no anxiety about anything, Nora; only be frank and open with me, and I will serve as will and conscience both to you— What is this? Not gone to bed? Have you changed your things?

NORA: [*in everyday dress*] Yes, Torvald, *I have changed my things now.*

HELMER: *But what for?—so late as this.*

NORA: I shall not sleep tonight.

HELMER: But, my dear Nora—

NORA: [*looking at her watch*] It is not so very late. Sit down here, Torvald. You and I have much to say to one another. [*She sits down at one side of the table.*]

HELMER: Nora—what is this—this cold, set face?

NORA: Sit down. It will take some time; I have a lot to talk over with you.

HELMER: [*sits down at the opposite side of the table.*] You alarm me, Nora!—and I don't understand you.

NORA: No, that is just it. You don't understand me, and I have never understood you either—before tonight. No, you mustn't interrupt me. You must simply listen to what I say. Torvald, this is a settling of accounts.

HELMER: What do you mean by that?

NORA: [*after a short silence*] Isn't there one thing that strikes you as strange in our sitting here like this?

HELMER: What is that?

NORA: We have been married now eight years. Does it not occur to you that this is the first time we two, you and I, husband and wife, have had a serious conversation?

HELMER: What do you mean by serious?

NORA: In all these eight years—longer than that—from the very beginning of our acquaintance, we have never exchanged a word on any serious subject.

HELMER: Was it likely that I would be continually and forever telling you about worries that you could not help me to bear?

NORA: I am not speaking about business matters. I say that we have never sat down in earnest together to try and get at the bottom of anything.

HELMER: But, dearest Nora, would it have been any good to you?

NORA: That is just it; you have never understood me. I have been greatly wronged, Torvald—first by Papa and then by you.

HELMER: What! by us two—by us two, who have loved you better than anyone else in the world?

NORA: [*shaking her head*] You have never loved me. You have only thought it pleasant to be in love with me.

HELMER: Nora, what do I hear you saying?

NORA: It is perfectly true, Torvald. When I was at home with Papa, he told me his opinion about everything, and so I had the same opinions; and if I differed from him I concealed the fact, because he would not have liked it. He called me his doll-child, and he played with me just as I used to play with my dolls. And when I came to live with you—

HELMER: What sort of an expression is that to use about our marriage?

NORA: [*undisturbed*] I mean that I was simply transferred from Papa's hands into yours. You arranged everything according to your own taste, and so I got the same tastes as you—or else I pretended to, I am really not quite sure which—I think, sometimes the one and sometimes the other. When I look back on it, it seems to me as if I had been living here like a poor woman—just from hand to mouth. I have existed merely to perform tricks for you, Torvald. But you would have it so. You and Papa have committed a great sin against me. It is your fault that I have made nothing of my life.

HELMER: How unreasonable and how ungrateful you are. Nora! Have you not been happy here?

NORA: No, I have never been happy. I thought I was, but it has never really been so.

HELMER: Not—not happy!

NORA: No, only merry. And you have always been so kind to me. But our home has been nothing but a playroom. I have been your doll-wife, just as at home I was Papa's doll-child, and here the children have been my dolls. I thought it great fun when you played with me, just as they thought it great fun when I played with them. That is what our marriage has been, Torvald.

HELMER: There is some truth in what you say—exaggerated and strained as your view of it is. But for the future it will be different. Playtime shall be over, and lesson time shall begin.

NORA: Whose lessons? Mine, or the children's?

HELMER: Both yours and the children's, my darling Nora.

NORA: Alas, Torvald, you are not the man to educate me into being a proper wife for you.

HELMER: And you can say that!

NORA: And I—how am I fitted to bring up the children?

HELMER: Nora!

NORA: Didn't you say so yourself a little while ago—that you dare not trust me to bring them up?

HELMER: In a moment of anger! Why do you pay any heed to that?

NORA: Indeed, you were perfectly right. I am not fit for the task. There is another task I must undertake first. I must try and educate myself—you are not the man to help me in that. I must do that for myself. And that is why I am going to leave you now.

HELMER: [*springing up*] What do you say?

NORA: I must stand quite alone, if I am to understand myself and everything about me. *It is for that reason that I cannot remain with you any longer.*

HELMER: Nora, Nora!

NORA: I am going away from here now, at once. I am sure Christine will take me in for the night—

HELMER: *You are out of your mind! I won't allow it! I forbid you!*

NORA: *It is no use forbidding me anything any longer.* I will take with me what belongs to myself. I will take nothing from you, either now or later.

HELMER: What sort of madness is this!

NORA: Tomorrow I shall go home— I mean to my old home. It will be easiest for me to find something to do there.

HELMER: You blind, foolish woman!

NORA: I must try and get some sense, Torvald.

HELMER: To desert your home, your husband and your children! And you don't consider what people will say!

NORA: I cannot consider that at all. I only know that it is necessary for me.

HELMER: It's shocking. This is how you would neglect your most sacred duties.

NORA: What do you consider my most sacred duties?

HELMER: Do I need to tell you that? Are they not your duties to your husband and your children?

NORA: I have other duties just as sacred.

HELMER: That you have not. What duties could those be?

NORA: Duties to myself.

HELMER: Before all else, you are a wife and a mother.

NORA: I don't believe that any longer. I believe that before all else I am a reasonable human being, just as you are—or, at all events, that I must try and become one. I know quite well, Torvald, that most people would think you right, and that views of that kind are to be found in books; but I can no longer content myself with what most people say, or what is found in books. I must think over things for myself and get to understand them.

HELMER: Can you not understand your place in your own home? Have you not a reliable guide in such matters as that—have you no religion?

NORA: I am afraid, Torvald, I do not exactly know what religion is.

HELMER: What are you saying?

NORA: I know nothing but what the clergyman said, when I went to be confirmed. He told me that religion was this, and that, and the other. When I am away from all this, and am alone, I will look into that matter too. I will see if what the clergyman said is true, or, at all events, if it is true for me.

HELMER: This is unheard of in a girl of your age! But if religion cannot lead you aright, let me try and waken your conscience. I suppose you have some moral sense? Or—answer me—am I to think you have none?

NORA: I assure you, Torvald, that is not an easy question to answer. I really don't know. The thing perplexes me altogether. I only know that you and I look at it in quite a different light. I am learning, too, that the law is quite another thing from what I supposed; but I find it impossible to convince myself that the law is right. According to it a woman has no right to spare her old dying father, or to save her husband's life. I can't believe that.

HELMER: You talk like a child. You don't understand the conditions of the world in which you live.

NORA: No, I don't. But now I am going to try. I am going to see if I can make out who is right, the world or I.

HELMER: You are ill, Nora; you are delirious; I almost think you are out of your mind.

NORA: I have never felt my mind so clear and certain as tonight.

HELMER: And is it with a clear and certain mind that you forsake your husband and your children?

NORA: Yes, it is.

HELMER: Then there is only one possible explanation.

NORA: What is that?

HELMER: *You do not love me any more.*

NORA: *No, that is just it.*

HELMER: *Nora!—and you can say that?*

NORA: *It gives me great pain, Torvald,* for you have always been so kind to me, *but I cannot help it.* I do not love you any more.

HELMER: [*regaining his composure*] Is that a clear and certain conviction too?

NORA: Yes, absolutely clear and certain. That is the reason why I will not stay here any longer.

HELMER: And can you tell me what I have done to forfeit your love?

NORA: Yes, indeed I can. It was tonight, when the wonderful thing did not happen; then I saw you were not the man I had thought you.

HELMER: Explain yourself better—I don't understand you.

NORA: I have waited so patiently for eight years; for goodness knows, I knew very well that wonderful things don't happen every day. Then this horrible misfortune came upon me; and then I felt quite certain that the wonderful thing was going to happen at last. When Krogstad's letter was lying out there, never for a moment did I imagine that you would consent to accept this man's conditions. I was so absolutely certain that you would say to him: publish the thing to the whole world. And when that was done—

HELMER: Yes, what then—when I had exposed my wife to shame and disgrace?

NORA: When that was done, I was so absolutely certain, you would come forward and take everything upon yourself, and say: I am the guilty one.

HELMER: Nora—!

NORA: You mean that I would never have accepted such a sacrifice on your part? No, of course not. But what would my assurances have been worth against yours? That is the wonderful thing which I hoped for and feared; and it was to prevent that that I wanted to kill myself.

HELMER: I would gladly work night and day for you, Nora—bear sorrow and want for your sake. But no one would sacrifice his honor for the one he loves.

NORA: It is a thing hundreds of thousands of women have done.

HELMER: Oh, you think and talk like a heedless child.

NORA: Maybe. But you neither think nor talk like the man I could bind myself to. As soon as your fear was over—and it was not fear for what threatened me, but for what might happen to you—when the whole thing was past, as far as you were concerned it was exactly as if nothing at all had happened. Exactly as before, I was your little skylark, your doll, which you would in future treat with doubly gentle care, because it was so brittle and fragile. [*Getting up*] Torvald, it was then it dawned upon me that for eight years I had been living here with a strange man, and had borne him three children— Oh, I can't bear to think of it! I could tear myself into little bits!

HELMER: [*sadly*] *I see, I see. An abyss has opened between us— there is no denying it. But, Nora, would it not be possible to fill it up?*

NORA: *As I am now, I am no wife for you.*

HELMER: I have it in me to become a different man.

NORA: Perhaps—if your doll is taken away from you.

HELMER: But to part!—to part from you! No, no, Nora, I can't understand that idea.

NORA: [*going out to the right*] That makes it all the more certain that it must be done. [*She comes back with her cloak and hat and a small bag which she puts on a chair by the table.*]

HELMER: *Nora, Nora, not now! Wait till tomorrow.*

NORA: [*putting on her cloak*] *I cannot spend the night in a strange man's room.*

HELMER: But can't we live here like brother and sister—?

NORA: [*putting on her hat*] You know very well that would not last long. [*Puts the shawl around her.*] Good-by, Torvald. I won't see the little ones. I know they are in better hands than mine. As I am now, I can be of no use to them.

HELMER: But some day, Nora—some day?

NORA: How can I tell? I have no idea what is going to become of me.

HELMER: But you are my wife, whatever becomes of you.

NORA: Listen, Torvald. I have heard that when a wife deserts her husband's house, as I am doing now, he is legally freed from all obligations toward her. In any case, I set you free from all your obligations. You are not to feel yourself bound in the slightest way, any more than I shall. There must be perfect freedom on both sides. See, here is your ring back. Give me mine.

HELMER: That too?

NORA: That too.

HELMER: Here it is.

NORA: That's right. Now it is all over. I have put the keys here. The maids know all about everything in the house—better than I do. Tomorrow, after I have left her, Christine will come here and pack up my own things that I brought with me from home. I will have them sent after me.

HELMER: *All over! All over!—Nora, shall you never think of me again?*

NORA: *I know I shall often think of you and the children and the house.*

HELMER: May I write to you, Nora?

NORA: No—never. You must not do that.

HELMER: But at least let me send you—

NORA: Nothing—nothing—

HELMER: Let me help you if you are in want.

NORA: No. I can receive nothing from a stranger.

HELMER: Nora, can I never be anything more than stranger to you?

NORA: [*taking her bag*] Ah, Torvald, the most wonderful thing of all would have to happen.

HELMER: Tell me what that would be!

NORA: Both you and I would have to be so changed that— Oh, Torvald, I don't believe any longer in wonderful things happening.

HELMER: But I will believe in it. Tell me. So changed that?

NORA: That our life together would be a real wedlock. Good-by. [*She goes out through the hall.*]

HELMER: [*sinks down on a chair at the door and buries his face in his hands*] Nora! Nora! [*looks round, and rises*] Empty. She is gone. [*A hope flashes across his mind.*] The most wonderful thing of all—? [*The sound of a door shutting is heard from below.*]

Curtain

Now reread the jumping conflict once more. It is worth while to see how the elimination of transition can turn a rising conflict into a jumping one.

5. Rising

Rising conflict is the result of a clear-cut premise and
well-orchestrated, three-dimensional characters, among whom
unity is strongly established.

"Inflated egotism destroys itself" is the premise of Ibsen's
Hedda Gabler. In the end, Hedda kills herself because un-
wittingly she was caught in the web of her own making.

As the play opens, Tesman and Hedda, his wife, have returned from their honeymoon the preceding night. Miss
Tesman, the aunt with whom he had lived, arrives early in
the morning to see if everything is all right. She and her
bedridden sister have mortgaged their small annuity to secure a house for the newlyweds. She thinks of Tesman as her
son, and he feels that she is both father and mother to him.

TESMAN: Why, what a gorgeous bonnet you've been investing in!
   [*The bonnet is in his hand; he looks at it from all sides.*]
MISS T.: I bought it on Hedda's account.
TESMAN: On Hedda's account? Eh?
MISS T.: Yes, so that Hedda needn't be ashamed of me if we hap-
   pened to go out together. [*Tesman puts down the bonnet, and
   Hedda at last enters. She's irritable. Miss Tesman gives a pack-
   age to Tesman.*]
TESMAN: Well, I declare! Have you really saved them for me, Aunt
   Julia? Hedda! Isn't this touching?
HEDDA: Well, what is it?
TESMAN: My old morning shoes! My slippers!
HEDDA: Indeed. I remember you often spoke of them while we were
   abroad.
TESMAN: Yes, I missed them terribly. [*Goes up to her.*] Now you
   shall see them, Hedda!
HEDDA: [*going toward the stove*] Thanks, I really don't care about
   it.
TESMAN: [*following her*] Only think—ill as she was, Aunt Rina

embroidered these for me. Oh, you can't think of how many associations cling to them.

HEDDA: [*at the table*] Scarcely for me.

MISS T.: Of course not for Hedda, George.

TESMAN: Well, but now that she belongs to the family, I thought—

HEDDA: [*interrupting*] We shall never get on with this servant, Tesman. [*The servant has practically mothered Tesman.*]

MISS T.: Not get on with Bertha?

TESMAN: Why, dear, what puts that in your head, eh?

HEDDA: [*pointing*] Look there! She has left her bonnet lying about on a chair.

TESMAN: [*In consternation, drops the slippers on the floor.*] Why, Hedda—

HEDDA: Just fancy, if anyone should come in and see it.

TESMAN: But Hedda—that's Aunt Julia's bonnet!

HEDDA: Is it!

MISS T.: [*taking up the bonnet*] Yes, indeed it's mine. And, what's more, it's not old, Madame Hedda.

HEDDA: I really did not look closely at it, Miss Tesman.

MISS T.: [*tying on the bonnet*] Let me tell you, it's the first time I have worn it—the very first time.

TESMAN: And a very nice bonnet it is too—quite a beauty.

MISS T.: Oh, it's no such great thing, George. [*Looks around her.*] My parasol—? Oh, here. [*Takes it.*] For this is mine, too—[*mutters*]—not Bertha's.

TESMAN: A new bonnet and new parasol! Only think, Hedda!

HEDDA: Very handsome indeed.

TESMAN: Yes, isn't it, eh? But, Aunty, take a good look at Hedda before you go. See how handsome she is!

MISS T.: Oh, my dear boy, there's nothing new in that. Hedda was always lovely. [*She moves away.*]

TESMAN: [*following*] Yes, but have you noticed what splendid condition she is in? How she has filled out on the journey?

HEDDA: [*crossing room*] Oh, do be quiet!

Only a few pages at the very beginning of the play, and three full, rounded characters stand before us. We know them; they breathe and live, whereas in *Idiot's Delight* the author needs two and one-half acts to bring his two main characters together to defy a hostile world in the closing scene of the play.

Why does the conflict rise in *Hedda Gabler?* First of all, there is unity of opposites; then the characters are well-rounded persons with *strong convictions.* Hedda despises Tesman and everything he stands for. She is unrelenting. She married him for convenience and uses him to attain a higher place in society. Can she corrupt him—the soul of purity and scrupulous honesty?

No playwright can line up such people—all of them so utterly different—without a well-defined premise.

Tension can be achieved through uncompromising characters in a death struggle. The premise should show the goal, and the characters should be driven to this goal, as Fate did in the Greek drama.

In *Tartuffe,* the rising conflict is attributable to Orgon, the pivotal character, who forces the conflict. He is uncompromising. To start with, he declares:

He [Tartuffe] detached my soul from these and taught me to set my heart on nothing that is here below. And now, were I to see my mother, wife, or children die, I should do so without so much as a pang.

Any man who can make such statements will create conflict—and he does.

As Helmer's belief in scrupulous honesty and civic pride precipitated his drama, Orgon's rabid intolerance brought on himself all the mishaps that befell him. We want to emphasize the "rabid intolerance." Iago in *Othello* is *relentless.* Hamlet's *bulldog tenacity* drives him on to the bitter end. Oedipus' *deep-rooted desire* to find the murderer of the king brought tragedy upon himself. Such iron-willed characters, driven by a well-understood and clearly defined premise, cannot help but lift the play to the highest pitch.

*Two determined, uncompromising forces in combat will
create a virile rising conflict.* Don't let anyone tell you that only certain types of conflict possess dramatic or theatrical value. Any type will do,
if you have tridimensional characters with a clear-cut premise. Through conflict, these characters will reveal themselves,
assume dramatic value, suspense, and all the other attributes
which theatrical jargon terms "dramatic."

In *Ghosts,* Manders' opposition to Mrs. Alving is gentle,
at first. but it slowly develops into a rising conflict.

MANDERS: Ah! There we have the outcome of your reading. Fine
fruit it has borne—this abominable, subversive, free-thinking literature!

(Poor Manders. How righteous he is in his condemnation.
He feels that he has uttered the last word, and Mrs. Alving
will be crushed. His attack was condemnation. Now we have
the counterattack, constituting conflict. The condemnation
alone could not grow into conflict if the person condemned
accepted it. But Mrs. Alving rejects it, hurls it back in his
face.)

MRS. ALVING: You are wrong there, my friend. You are the one who
made me begin to think, and I owe you my best thanks for it.

(No wonder Manders cries out in consternation, "I!" The
counterattack must be stronger than the attack in order that
the conflict may not be static. Mrs. Alving, therefore, ac-
knowledges the deed, but puts the blame on her accuser.)

MRS. ALVING: Yes! By forcing me to submit to what you call my
duty, and my obligations, by praising as right and just what my
whole soul revolted against as it would against something abominable. That was what led me to examine your teachings criti-
cally. I only wanted to unravel one point in them, but as soon
as I had got them unraveled the whole fabric came to pieces and
then I realized that it was only machine-made.

(She forces him into a defensive position. He is staggered for a moment. Attack, counterattack.)

MANDERS: [*softly and with emotion*] Is that all that I accomplished by the hardest struggle of my life?

(Mrs. Alving offered herself to him at a critical moment. He is reminding her of his sacrifice in refusing her. This soft question is a challenge, and Mrs. Alving meets it.)

MRS. ALVING: Call it rather the most ignominious defeat of your life.

Every word carries the conflict further.

If I call someone a thief, it is an invitation to conflict, but nothing more. Just as the male is needed, with the female, for conception, so something is needed, with the challenge, for a conflict. The accused might answer, "Look who's talking," and refuse to take offense, thus creating an abortion, so far as conflict is concerned. But if he calls *you* a thief, in retaliation, there is the promise of a conflict.

The drama is not the image of life, but the essence. We must condense. In life, people quarrel year in, year out, without once deciding to remove the factor which causes the trouble. In drama this must be condensed to the essentials, giving the illusion of years of bickering without the superfluous dialogue.

It is interesting to note that rising conflict was achieved in *Tartuffe* by a method different from that in *A Doll's House*. Whereas in Ibsen's plays, conflict means actual combat between characters, in *Tartuffe* Molière starts with group lined up against group. Orgon's insistence to be ruined by himself cannot be considered conflict. Nevertheless, it achieves rising tension. Let us watch him.

ORGON: It is a deed of gift, drawn up with all formality by which I make over my whole estate to you.

(This statement is certainly not an attack.)

TARTUFFE: [*recoiling*] To *me?* Oh, brother, brother, how came you to think of this?

(And this is not a counterattack, either.)

ORGON: Why, to tell you the truth, it was your story that put it into my head.

TARTUFFE: My story?

ORGON: Yes—about your friend at Lyons—I mean Limoges. Surely you have not forgotten that?

TARTUFFE: It comes back to me now. But had I thought it would prompt you to this, brother, I would have cut out my tongue ere I had told you.

ORGON: But you don't—you can't mean that you refuse?

TARTUFFE: Nay, how can I accept so heavy a responsibility.

ORGON: Why not? The other man did.

TARTUFFE: Ah, brother, but he was a saint, whereas I am but an unworthy vessel.

ORGON: I know none saintlier, none I would trust more entirely than you.

TARTUFFE: Were I to accept this trust, men—men of Belial—would say that I had taken a base advantage of your simplicity.

ORGON: Men know me better than that, my friend. I am not one who can be easily duped.

TARTUFFE: Not what they may say of *me*, brother, but of you.

ORGON: Then dismiss your fear, my friend, for it is my delight to set them gabbling. And think—think of the power for good that deed would give you. By it you could reform my unruly household, rid it altogether of the laxity and profusion that have so long vexed your tender soul.

TARTUFFE: It would indeed give me great opportunities.

ORGON: Ha! You admit that. Then is it not your duty to accept—for their sakes and mine?

TARTUFFE: I had not looked on it in that light before. It may be even as you say.

ORGON: It *is* so. Brother, their salvation is in your hands. Can you leave them to perish utterly?

TARTUFFE: Your arguments have overcome me, dear friend. I did
  wrong to hesitate.
ORGON: Then you accept the trust?
TARTUFFE: The will of heaven be done in this as in all other things.
  I accept. [*He puts the deed in his breast.*]

There is no conflict so far, but we know that not only
Orgon, the dupe, will be ruined by this deed, but his lovable
and decent family also. We'll watch with bated breath how
Tartuffe will use this newly acquired power. This scene really
is a preparation for conflict: foreshadowing conflict.

We are confronted here with a different rising conflict
than we have heretofore expounded. Which approach is better? The answer is: either is good if it helps the conflict to
rise. Molière achieved his rising conflict by welding the family
together to defeat Tartuffe (group against group). Tartuffe's
reluctance to accept Orgon's offer is hypocritical and weak.
It is really no conflict at all. *But the very offer of Orgon to
transfer his fortune to Tartuffe constitutes the tension and
foreshadows a death struggle between him and the family.*

Come back to *Ghosts* for a moment. Manders says:

Ah! There we have the outcome of your reading. Fine fruit it has
borne—this abominable, subversive, free-thinking literature!

If Mrs. Alving answered, "Really?" or "What affair is it of
yours?" or "What do you know about books?" or anything of
the kind which would rebuke Manders without attacking
him, the conflict would at once be static. But she answers:

You are wrong there, my friend.

She gives a general denial, first, adding irony with "my
friend." The next sentence is a bombshell, carrying the attack to enemy territory. It is a body blow, almost paralyzing.

You are the one who made me begin to think, and I owe you my
best thanks for it.

Manders' "I!" is equivalent to "Ouch!" in the ring, or even "Foul!"

Mrs. Alving follows up her advantage, showering blows on the unfortunate Manders, winding up with an upper-cut which just misses its mark. If Mrs. Alving had succeeded in annihilating her antagonist, the play would have been over. But Manders is not a mean fighter, either. When he is staggered he spars to get his wind back, and then counter-attacks fiercely. This is rising conflict.

MRS. ALVING: Call it rather the most ignominious defeat of your life.

(The blow that glanced off Manders' chin.)

MANDERS: [sparring] It was the greatest victory of my life, Helen. Victory over myself.
MRS. ALVING: [tired but game] It was a wrong done to both of us.
MANDERS: [seeing an opening, rushes in] A wrong? Wrong for me to entreat you as a wife to go back to your lawful husband when you came to me, half distracted, and cried, "Here I am. Take me." Was that wrong?

The conflict is still going higher and higher, revealing the characters' inmost feelings; the forces that made them act as they did; the position in which they now stand; the direction in which they are going. Each character has a well-defined premise in life. They know what they want—and fight for it.

Eugene O'Neill's *Mourning Becomes Electra* is a splendid example of rising conflict. The only trouble is that the characters, although involved in a death struggle, are not deeply motivated.

If you read the synopsis at the end of this book, you will find a dynamic, irresistible force driving the characters toward their inevitable end—Lavinia to revenge her father, and Christine to free herself from her husband's bondage.

Conflict comes in waves, rising higher and higher to an awesome crescendo, overwhelming in its power—until we start to scrutinize the characters. Then, to our sorrow, we realize that all this blood and thunder was just sham. We can't believe them. They weren't living people. They were the creation of an author who has extraordinary vitality and power to make them behave as conscious living beings should. But the moment he leaves them alone they collapse from the sheer weight of their existence.

The characters go relentlessly where the author tells them to go. They have no will of their own. Lavinia hates her mother with a cold hate because that will create conflict. She finds out things about her father which would mitigate her fierce protective love for him, but she dismisses it as something nonexistent. She had to, if she was to go through with the part the author assigned to her.

Captain Brent hates the Mannons because they let his mother starve to death. But that he left her himself for years, abandoning her to her fate, is not important either. The conflict has to go on.

Christine hates her husband because her love turned to hate, and she kills him. But what made this love turn to hate? The author never explains.

O'Neill has a good reason not to divulge his secret: he doesn't know himself. He has no premise.

He imitated the Greek pattern. He thought if he substituted Fate instead of premise, he would secure a driving force which would match the classics of the Hellenic drama. He failed, because the Greek dramas have premise under the disguise of Fate, whereas O'Neill has blind Fate only, without a premise.

As we see, rising conflict can be achieved with superficial, badly motivated characters also, but this is not the play we are after. Such plays may impress us, even terrorize us, while we are in the theater. But such plays soon become only a memory because they bear no resemblance to life as we know it. The characters are not three-dimensional.

Once more, then: rising conflict means a clear-cut premise and unity of opposites, with three-dimensional characters.

6. Movement

It is simple enough to recognize a storm as a conflict, yet what we experience and call "storm," or "tornado," is actually a climax, the result of hundreds and thousands of small conflicts, each bigger and more dangerous than the last, until they arrive at the crisis—the lull before the storm. In that last moment the decision is made, and the storm either moves on or breaks in all its fury.

When we think of any manifestation of nature, we are likely to think of it as having only one possible cause. We say that a storm starts in such and such a way, forgetting that each storm has a different background, although the results are essentially the same, just as each death arises from different conditions, although, in essence, death is death.

Every conflict consists of attack and counterattack, yet every conflict differs from every other conflict. There are small, almost inperceptible movements in every conflict—transitions—which determine the type of rising conflict you will employ. These transitions, in their turn, are determined by the individual characters. If a character is a slow thinker, or sluggish, his transition will affect the conflict by its resultant sluggishness; and since no two individuals ever think exactly alike, no two transitions, and no two conflicts, will ever be identical.

Let us watch Nora and Helmer for a while. Let us see the motivation that they themselves do not know. Why does Nora assent when that clinches Helmer's argument *against* her? What goes into a simple sentence?

Helmer has just found out about the forgery. He is in a rage.

HELMER: Miserable creature—what have you done?

(This is not an attack. He knows quite well what she has done, but is too horrified to believe it. He is struggling with himself and needs a breathing spell. But the line *foreshadows* a vicious attack to come.)

NORA: Let me go. You shall not suffer for my sake. You shall not take it upon yourself.

(And this is not a counterattack, yet the conflict continues to rise. She is not yet aware that Helmer has no intention of taking the blame upon himself, nor does she fully realize that he is angry with her. He has flared up, she knows, but he does not mean it. She retains that last shred of naïveté which makes her so appealing in the face of the onrushing danger. This is not a fighting sentence, then, but a transition which helps the conflict rise.)

If we did not know Helmer, his character, his moral scruples, his fanatical honesty, Nora's struggle with Krogstad would not be conflict at all. There would be nothing to look forward to. The one question would be who will outsmart whom. *The small movement, then, becomes important only in its relation to the big movement.*

Hay Fever is a play which offers material for illustration. The scene we have taken from it contains no big movements. There is nothing at stake, nothing to make the little movements important. If one character loses out there is no harm done—tomorrow is another day. The fact that this is a comedy is no excuse for so serious a flaw—as proved by the further fact that this is not a good comedy.

The parenthetical comments after each speech—attack, rise, counterattack—indicate that speech's potentialities for development into each conflict.

From *Hay Fever*, by Noel Coward:
(A family, consisting of a charming mother who is a retired actress, a charming father who is a novelist, and two charming children who are just charming, has invited guests for the week end. Mother Judith has invited her latest. Father David has invited his latest, Daughter Sorel has invited her latest, and Son Simon has invited guess who. They quarrel about sleeping arrangements until the guests arrive—four ordinary people who serve as stooges for the family.)

SOREL: I should have thought you'd be above encouraging silly, shallow young men who are infatuated by your name. [*Attack.*]

JUDITH: That may be true, but I shall allow no one but myself to say it. I hoped you'd grow up a good daughter to me, not a critical aunt. [*Counterattack. Rise.*]

SOREL: It's so terribly cheap. [*Attack. Rise.*]

JUDITH: Cheap? Nonsense. What about your diplomatist? [*Counterattack.*]

SOREL: Surely that's a little different, dear? [*Static.*]

JUDITH: If you mean that because you happen to be a vigorous ingenue of nineteen you have the complete monopoly of any amorous adventure there may be about, I feel it my firm duty to disillusion you. [*Attack.*]

SOREL: But, Mother— [*Rise.*]

JUDITH: Anyone would think I was eighty the way you go on. It was a great mistake not sending you to boarding schools, and you coming back and my being your elder sister. [*Static.*]

SIMON: It wouldn't have been any use; everyone knows we're your son and daughter. [*Static.*]

JUDITH: Only because I was stupid enough to dandle you about in front of cameras when you were little. I knew I should regret it. [*Static.*]

SIMON: I don't see any point in trying to be younger than you are. [*Attack. Rise.*]

JUDITH: At your age, dear, it would be indecent if you did. [*Counterattack.*]

SOREL: But, Mother dear, don't you see, it's awfully undignified for you to go flaunting about with young men. [*Attack.*]

JUDITH: I don't flaunt about, I never have. I've been morally an extremely nice woman, all my life, more or less, and if dabbling gives me pleasure I don't see why I shouldn't dabble. [*Static.*]

SOREL: But it oughtn't give you pleasure any more. [*Attack.*]

JUDITH: You know, Sorel, you grow more damnably feminine every day. I wish I'd brought you up differently. [*Counterattack.*]

SOREL: I'm proud of being feminine. [*Attack.*]

JUDITH: You're a darling and I adore you [*kissing her*], and you're very pretty and I'm madly jealous of you. [*Static.*]

SOREL: Are you really, how lovely. [*Static.*]

JUDITH: You will be nice to Sandy, won't you? [*Static.*]

SOREL: Can't he sleep in "little hell"? [*Static.*]

JUDITH: My dear, he's frightfully athletic and all those water pipes will sap his vitality. [*Static.*]

SOREL: They'll sap Richard's vitality too. [*Static.*]

JUDITH: He won't notice them, he's probably used to scorching tropical embassies with punkahs waving and everything. [*Static.*]

SIMON: He's sure to be deadly anyhow. [*Static.*]

SOREL: You're getting too blasé and exclusive, Simon. [*Jump.*]

SIMON: Nothing of the sort, only I loathe being hearty with your men friends. [*Attack.*]

SOREL: You've never been civil to any of my friends, men or women. [*Counterattack.*]

SIMON: Anyhow, the Japanese room's a woman's room, and a woman ought to have it. [*Static even for the transition it is intended to be.*]

JUDITH: I promised it to Sandy—he loves everything Japanese. [*Static.*]

SIMON: So does Myra. [*Jump.*]

JUDITH: Myra! [*Rise.*]

SIMON: Myra Arundel, I've asked her down. [*Rise.*]

JUDITH: You've what? [*Rise.*]

Surprise! Surprise! Nobody but the audience suspected that Simon might have invited someone too. This is the point which was reached by the scene—a clear waste of several pages because there is no big movement to give meaning to the small movements. There is not much transition, either, due to the transparency and two-dimensionality of the characters. You wish to start an automobile—this is your premise. First you ignite the gas. A drop of gasoline will explode. If for any reason there is no further explosion (conflict), the car will remain static (as will your play). But if the gasoline flows freely, one explosion will set off another explosion (conflict creates conflict) and the engine will vibrate with a steady hum. The car (and your play) is moving.

The many small explosions will move the car ahead. Not one, or two, but many explosions are necessary to start the big movement of the wheels.

In a play, each conflict causes the one after it. Each is more intense than the one before. The play moves, propelled by the conflict created by the characters in their desire to reach their goal: *the proof of the premise.*

But let's go back to our old friends, Nora and Helmer. Let us see how their conflict moves and changes.

HELMER: No tragedy airs, please. [*Locks the hall door*] Here you shall stay and give me an explanation. Do you understand what you have done? Answer me. Do you understand what you have done?

(The lines suggest the increasing tempo. The locking of the door adds weight to his words. The whole speech is an attack.)

NORA: [*Looks steadily at him and says with a growing look of coldness in her face*] Yes, now I am beginning to understand thoroughly.

(Nora's answer is not a counterattack. True, attack and counterattack is the most direct, the shortest method of building a conflict. But it cannot be employed exclusively throughout a play without becoming tiresome and without ending the play far too rapidly.

(Nora's answer is negative, but we must understand why.

She is *refusing to obey* her lord's impatient demand for an
explanation. She explains nothing, but there is the first ray
of awakening in her answer, the first sign that Helmer will
receive more than he bargained for. Is Nora's line a fighting
one, then? Definitely. The coldness, the tone, give warning
of danger ahead. But Helmer, in his fury, does not see it.
Step by step he drives himself into an uncontrollable rage.)

HELMER: [*walking about the room*] What a horrible awakening!
   All these eight years—she who was my joy and pride—a hypocrite, a liar—worse, worse—a criminal! The unutterable ugliness of it all! For shame! For shame! [*Nora is silent and looks
   steadily at him. He stops in front of her.*]

(Helmer's attack is now so vicious that any interruption on
Nora's part would kill the effect Ibsen has achieved. Her
silence is sufficiently eloquent and speaks for her better than
any line even a Shakespeare might conceive.

   We see then that the conflict becomes a variation on the
straight attack, counterattack. Nora's silence is a subtle
counterattack, in that it is resistance in preparation for action.)

HELMER: I ought to have suspected that something of the sort would
   happen. I ought to have foreseen it. All your father's want of
   principle—be silent!—all your father's want of principle has
   come out in you. No religion, no morality, no sense of duty.
   Now I am punished for having winked at what he did! I did it
   for your sake, and this is how you repay me.

(Helmer's attack is direct, overwhelming. Nora's answer is
interesting.)

NORA: Yes, that's just it.

(Her agreement proves his point—but there is a reason. She
wishes to leave. She sees for the first time that the past eight
years have been a bad dream. Her answer is negative again

—not an orthodox counterattack, but the first sign of an awakening resistance. Moreover, it serves to infuriate Helmer. The man who wishes to fight and finds no opponent becomes increasingly dangerous. We do not wish to imply that Nora's intention is to anger her husband. On the contrary. She sees, now, the hopelessness of life with him. She agrees because she is strengthened in her determination to leave, and because what he says is true, but only now does she see the implications of the truth. Ibsen uses her state to further the conflict.)

As we read on we see how Helmer, with overpowering arguments, tramples Nora down. The battle seems one-sided —seems like a prize fight in which one fighter showers blows on an apparently defenseless opponent. But Nora, instead of weakening, is waiting her turn patiently. Every blow strengthens her position, and her resistance is a counterattack in itself.

This type of conflict differs from that which we discussed earlier. It is different, but no less effective.

QUESTION: It is effective, all right, but I see no "difference."
ANSWER: Do you remember the scene we quoted from *Ghosts?* The scene between Manders and Mrs. Alving contained all the elements of direct conflict. The entire play was written on that line—attack, counterattack—with few exceptions. Yet we cannot make a flat statement to the effect that all superior plays should be built on that principle, because it was successful in *Ghosts.*
QUESTION: Why not?
ANSWER: Because the situation and the characters are not the same. Every conflict must be treated with regard to the characters and the situation involved. *Ghosts* starts at a high pitch. Mrs. Alving is a bitter person, worldly-wise, disillusioned. She is exactly the opposite of the gullible, spoiled, childlike Nora. These characters will certainly generate

different kinds of conflict. Mrs. Alving's conflict comes at the *beginning* of the play, and arises from her patience, her efforts to keep up appearances. Nora's big conflict comes at the *end* of the play, and arises from her ignorance of money matters. Certainly they require different treatment. But, although the type of conflict varies with the characters, there must be conflict throughout.

7. *Foreshadowing Conflict*

If you feel that you must read your script to a relative or friend, do so. But don't ask him to comment on it. He may know infinitely less than you do and is likely to do more harm than good. He does not have the qualifications needed to give expert advice, and you will be forcing him into an unfortunate and painful position.

If you must read your work to someone, ask that person to tell you the moment he begins to feel tired or bored. It denotes lack of conflict; lack of conflict is a dead give-away that your characters are badly orchestrated. They are not militant; they do not have unity of opposites, and there is no uncompromising pivotal character in your composition. If all these are missing, then you have no unified work,—just an accumulation of words.

You may argue that your audience is not on the high intellectual level that your writing demands for intelligent appreciation. What then? Will the above statement still stand? Yes, it still stands because the more intelligent the person the quicker he will be bored, if he can't detect a *foreshadowing conflict* from the very beginning.

Conflict is the heartbeat of all writing. No conflict ever existed without first foreshadowing itself. Conflict is that titanic atomic energy whereby one explosion creates a chain of explosions.

There never was a night without a twilight; a morning without a dawn; a winter without an autumn; a summer without a spring first; they all foreshadow a coming event. The foreshadowing is not necessarily the same. In fact, there never were two springs or two twilights alike.

A play without conflict creates the atmosphere of desolation, the imminence of decomposition.

Without conflict life could not be possible on earth, or, for that matter, anywhere in the universe. The technique of writing is only a replica of the universal law which governs an atom or a constellation above us.

Oppose any two fanatics or groups against each other and you will foreshadow conflict of breathtaking intensity.

The motion picture, *Thirty Seconds over Tokyo*, perfectly illustrates what we have in mind. The first two-thirds of the picture was devoid of any conflict whatsoever and still the audience sat through it as if hypnotized. What happened? What magic did the authors weave over the audience to arrest their eternal restlessness? It is really very simple. They foreshadowed conflict.

An officer tells the assembled fliers: "Boys, you're all volunteers to perform an exceedingly dangerous mission. It is so dangerous that it would be best for the safety of all of you not to discuss your possible destination even among yourselves."

This warning is the springboard for the story. Then the characters busy themselves with a long-drawn-out training program for their promised dangerous journey ahead.

Foreshadowing is really promising; in our case, conflict.

Whether in this particular story the prolonged waiting was justified or not is beside the point. The important thing to remember is that the audience remained breathless and waited for two hours for that foreshadowed thirty seconds over Tokyo.

When a well-matched pair of fighters face each other in

the ring, the expectation runs high. The same thing goes for the stage.

This is true, you admit, but how can you line up strong uncompromising characters on the stage, foreshadowing conflict at the very beginning of a play or story?

We think this is the easiest job a writer has to face. Take Helmer in *A Doll's House,* for instance. His uncompromising attitude toward the slightest delinquency, foreshadows trouble with the certainty of death. What will he do when he discovers that Nora forged a signature on his behalf? Will he relent? We don't know. One thing is certain; there will be trouble. *Any uncompromising character could create the same expectancy.*

The six dead soldiers in *Bury the Dead* protest against injustice. Their very act foreshadows conflict. (They are uncompromising.)

Foreshadowing conflict is really *tension* in theatrical parlance.

The public generally calls psychology "common sense," or "horse sense." Any author who underestimates the "horse sense" of his audience, will face a rude awakening.

A man who never heard of Freud will pass judgment on your play while sitting alongside of a trained critic. If your play lacks conflict no subterfuge or slick dialogue will influence this primitive member of your audience. He knows the play is bad. How? He was bored. His horse sense, his inborn quality to differentiate between good and bad, told him so. He fell asleep, didn't he? This is a sure sign the play is bad as far as he is concerned. To us his reaction means the play lacked conflict, or even the foreshadowing of conflict.

People distrust strangers. Only in conflict can you "prove" yourself. In conflict your true self is revealed. On the stage, as well as in life, every one is a stranger who does not first "prove" himself. A person who stands by you in adversity is a proven person. No, you cannot fool the audience. Even an illiterate knows that politeness and smart talk are not signs of sincerity or friendship. But sacrifice is. Again, foreshadowing *any quality* of a character is as necessary as breathing to a man.

Now, if you foreshadow conflict you're promising the very substance of existence. Since most of us play possum and hide our true selves from the world, we are interested in witnessing the things happening to those who are forced to reveal their true characters under the stress of conflict. Foreshadowing conflict is not conflict yet, but we are eagerly waiting for the fulfillment of the promise of it. In conflict we are *forced* to reveal ourselves. It seems that self-revelation of others or ourselves holds a fatal fascination for everyone.

We don't think it is necessary to sell the idea to writers that foreshadowing is an absolute must. The important and most difficult thing is how to use it. In *Waiting for Lefty*, by Clifford Odets, for instance, the very first line promised a mounting tension.

Fatt: You're so wrong I ain't laughing.

Fatt and the gangsters on the platform are *against* a strike. The audience members,—characters in the play,—are *for* the strike.

Poverty forces the would-be strikers to do something for themselves. They're bitter, determined. They're starving. They have nothing to lose. They *have* to strike if they want to live.

On the other hand, there is Fatt and the gangster boys. If the union goes on strike, the gunmen will lose their usefulness. You see, they're not ordinary gangsters. They are worse. They represent crooked union leadership. The fat union dues will be lost to them if a strike is called. This strike is not just a plain, everyday strike—it is a revolution.

Both sides are on the verge of losing or winning *everything*. The very determined set-up between these people creates tension, which, in our lingo foreshadows conflict.

Unrelenting people facing each other in a show-down fight foreshadows merciless conflict to the bitter end.

Determined foes, under no circumstances, can or will compromise. One must destroy the other in order to live. Add this all up; it certainly foreshadows conflict.

8. Point of Attack

When should the curtain rise? What is point of attack? When the curtain goes up, the audience wishes to know as soon as possible who these people on the stage are, what they want, why they are there. What is the relationship between them? But the characters in some plays prattle a long time before we are given a chance to know who they are and what they want.

In *George and Margaret,* by Gerald Savory, the author consumes 40 pages introducing us to the family. Then we have a hint on page 46 that one of the sons was seen going into the maid's room. The subject is then dropped. The family life moves in a well-oiled groove. Everyone is a little touched in the head. No one gives a hoot about anybody else, and on page 82, at last, we find out definitely that one of the sons was in the maid's room. Nothing serious, you know— just a casual affair.

Although the characters are well drawn—like good charcoal drawings—we wondered why they were on the stage. What did they hope to accomplish? The play is a slightly exaggerated but meticulously drawn portrait of the family in repose. The author knows how to draw, but lacks even an elementary knowledge of composition.

It is pointless to write about a person who doesn't know what he wants, or wants something only halfheartedly. Even if a person knows what he wants, but has no internal and external necessity to achieve this desire *immediately*, that character will be a liability to your play.

What makes a character start a chain of events which might destroy him or help him to succeed? There is only one answer: *necessity*. There must be something at stake—something pressingly important.

If you have one or more characters of this kind, your point of attack cannot but be good.

A play might start exactly at the point where a conflict will lead up to a crisis.

A play might start at a point where at least one character has reached a turning point in his life.

A play might start with a decision which will precipitate conflict.

A good point of attack is where something vital is at stake at the very beginning of a play.

The beginning of *Oedipus Rex* is Oedipus' *decision* to find the murderer. In *Hedda Gabler*, Hedda's contempt for her husband and all he stands for is a good start. She is so positive in her contempt that it amounts to a decision *not* to be satisfied with anything the poor man does. Knowing Tesman's character, we wonder how long he will stand for the abuse. We wonder if his love will cause him to submit, or if he will rebel.

In *Antony and Cleopatra* we hear Antony's soldiers worrying over Cleopatra's domination of their general. We see immediately the conflict between his love and his leadership. Their meeting came when his career was at its height; it proves the turning point of that career. As a member of the triumvirs, he had summoned her to answer for her conduct in aiding Cassius and Brutus in the war in which they were defeated. Antony is the accuser, Cleopatra the defendant, but he falls in love with her, against his and Rome's interests.

In each of these plays—in every work which one can unblushingly call a play—the curtain rises when at least one character has reached a *turning point in his life.*

In *Macbeth* a general hears a prophecy that he will become king. It preys on his mind until he kills the rightful king. The play starts when Macbeth begins to covet the kingship (turning point).

Once in a Lifetime starts when the leading characters decide to break with their former activities and go to Hollywood. (This is a turning point because their savings are at stake.)

Bury the Dead starts when six dead soldiers decide not to let themselves be buried. (Turning point—the happiness of mankind is at stake.)

Room Service begins when the hotel manager decides that his brother-in-law must pay the bill which has been run up by his theatrical company. (Turning point—his job is in danger.)

They Shall Not Die starts when the sheriff convinces two girls that they should accuse the Scottsboro boys of rape. They decide to tell the hideous lie in order to escape going to jail for various offenses. (Turning point—their freedom is at stake.)

Liliom starts when the hero turns against his employees and, against his better judgment, goes to live with a little servant girl. (Turning point—his job is in danger.)

The Tragedy of Man, by Madach, begins when Adam breaks his promise to the Lord and eats of the forbidden fruit. (Turning point—his happiness is in danger.)

Faust, by Goethe, starts when Faust sells his soul to Lucifer. (Turning point—his soul is in danger.)

Doctor Faustus, by Marlowe, starts the same way.

The Guardsman starts when the actor-husband, driven by jealousy, decides to impersonate a guardsman and test his wife's fidelity. The point of attack is that point at which a character must make a momentous decision.

QUESTION: What is a momentous decision?

ANSWER: One that constitutes a turning point in the character's life.

QUESTION: Yet there are plays which do not begin that way —Schnitzler's plays, for instance.

ANSWER: True. We were talking about plays in which the movement covers all the steps between two opposing poles, as, let us say, love and hate. Between these two poles there are many steps. You might decide to utilize one, two, or three steps only in that big movement, but even then you have to have a decision to start with. Necessarily the type of decision or just preparation for a decision cannot be as sweeping as in the big movement. Look in the chapter on transition, and you'll see that before one can arrive at a decision there are minutiae: doubts, hopes, vacillations. If you wish to write a drama around a transition, utilizing this preparatory state of mind, you must amplify these minutiae, enlarge them so that they are visible to the audience. A supreme knowledge of human behavior is necessary for one to write such a play.

QUESTION: Would you advise me to write such a play?

ANSWER: You should know your own strength, your own ability to cope with the problem.

QUESTION: In other words, you're not encouraging me.

ANSWER: Nor discouraging you. It is our function to tell you how to go about writing or criticizing a play—not whether you should choose a particular topic.

QUESTION: Fair enough. Can a play be written which is a combination of the preparatory and the immediate-decision types?

ANSWER: Great plays have been written in every combination.

QUESTION: Now, let me see if I've got all this straight. We must start a play at a point of decision, because that is the point at which the conflict starts and the characters are given a chance to expose themselves and the premise.

ANSWER: Right.

QUESTION: The point of attack must be a point of decision
or preparation for a decision.

ANSWER: Yes.

QUESTION: Good orchestration and unity of opposites ensure
conflict; the point of attack starts conflict. Right?

ANSWER: Yes, go on.

QUESTION: Do you think conflict is the most vital part of a
play?

ANSWER: We think that no character can reveal himself without conflict—and no conflict matters without character.
There is conflict simply in the choice of characters in
Othello. A Moor wishes to wed the daughter of a patrician
senator. Yet it would be pointless for Shakespeare to begin
with an account of identities, as Sherwood does in *Idiot's
Delight,* for instance. We shall learn who Othello and
Desdemona are from their courtship. Their dialogue will
tell us their backgrounds and their characters. So Shakespeare begins with Iago, from whose character conflict
stems. In one brief scene we learn that he hates Othello,
we learn what Othello's position is and that Othello and
Desdemona have eloped. We begin, in other words, with
the knowledge of the great love between Othello and
Desdemona, with an inkling of the obstacles that love has
faced, and with a realization of Iago's intention to tear
down Othello's happiness and position. If a man contemplates murder, he is not particularly interesting. But if he
plots with others or alone, and decides to commit the murder, the play is started. If a man tells a woman he loves her,
they can continue in that vein for hours and days. But if
he says "Let's elope," it may be the beginning of a play.
The one sentence suggests many things. Why should they
elope? If she answers, "But what about your wife?" we
have the key to the situation. If the man has the strength

of will to go through with his decision, conflict will follow every move he makes.

QUESTION: Why didn't Ibsen start his play when Nora was frightened by Helmer's illness and frantically looked for help? There was plenty of conflict while she was deciding to forge her father's signature.

ANSWER: True. But the conflict was *inside her mind,* invisible. *There was no antagonist.*

QUESTION: There was. Helmer and Krogstad.

ANSWER: Krogstad was very willing to lend the money just because he knew the signature was forged. He wanted Helmer in his power and placed no obstacle in Nora's way. And Helmer is the reason for the forgery, not an obstacle to it. The only thing he does at the time is suffer, which encourages Nora to get the money.

Ibsen's choice of a point of attack was unfortunate in *A Doll's House.* He should have started the play when Krogstad becomes impatient and demands his money. This pressure upon Nora reveals her character and speeds the conflict.

A play should start with the first line uttered. The characters involved will expose their natures in the course of conflict. It is bad playwriting first to marshal your evidences, drawing in the background, creating an atmosphere, before you begin the conflict. Whatever your premise, whatever the make-up of your characters, the first line spoken should start the conflict and the inevitable drive toward the proving of the premise.

QUESTION: As you know, I am writing a play—a one-act play. I have my premise, my characters are lined up and orchestrated. I have the synopsis, but still something is wrong. There is no tension in my play.

ANSWER: Let's here your premise.

QUESTION: Desperation leads to success.

ANSWER: Tell me the synopsis.

QUESTION: A young college boy, extremely shy, is madly in love with a lawyer's daughter. She loves him but respects and adores her father, too. She makes the boy understand that if her father disapproves of him, she won't marry him. The boy meets her father, who is a great wit and makes a laughingstock out of the poor boy.

ANSWER: And then what?

QUESTION: She's sorry for him, and declares that she will marry him just the same.

ANSWER: Tell me your point of attack.

QUESTION: The girl tries to persuade the boy to come to her home to meet her father. The boy resents this interference by the father and—

ANSWER: What's at stake?

QUESTION: The girl, of course.

ANSWER: Not true. If her marriage depends on her father's approval, she can't be very much in love.

QUESTION: But it is the turning point in their lives.

ANSWER: How?

QUESTION: If the father disapproves they might be separated and their happiness will be at stake.

ANSWER: I don't believe it. She's undecided, and therefore she cannot be the cause of a rising conflict.

QUESTION: But there is a rising conflict. The boy resents going there—

ANSWER: Just a moment. If I remember correctly, you established your premise as "Desperation leads to success." As you know by now, a premise is a thumbnail synopsis of your play. You have no tension because you have forgotten your premise. Your premise says one thing, your synopsis another. The premise indicates that *someone's life is at stake*, but not the synopsis. Why not start your play in the girl's home, with the boy waiting for the father? The boy is desperate, and reminds the girl what he swore to before the curtain went up.

QUESTION: What did he swear to?

ANSWER: That he would kill himself if her father disapproved of him, and his death would be on her conscience.

QUESTION: And then what?

ANSWER: You can follow your synopsis. The father is a famous wit and very shrewd. He puts the boy through the third degree. We know now the boy is so desperate that he is ready to throw away his life if he fails. His very life is at stake, and certainly this will be a turning point in his life. Everything the father or the boy say becomes important. After all, the boy will fight for his life and might do the unexpected. His shyness might vanish in the face of danger, and he might attack and confound the father. The girl is impressed and defies her father.

QUESTION: But can't he do this without threatening to kill himself?

ANSWER: Yes, but if I remember correctly, you were complaining before that your play had no tension.

QUESTION: True.

ANSWER: It had no tension because there was nothing *important at stake*. The point of attack was wrong. There are thousands of youngsters in the same predicament. Some of them forget their infatuation after a while and others seemingly consent to the wishes of their elders while seeing each other on the sly. In either case no serious thing is at stake. They are not ready to have a play written about them. Your lovers, on the other hand, are deadly serious. The boy, at least, has reached a turning point in his life. He puts everything on one card. He is worth while writing about.

Even if your premise is good, the characters well orchestrated, without the right point of attack, the play will drag. It will drag because there was nothing vital at stake at the beginning of the play.

No doubt you have heard the old adage: "Every story must have a beginning, a middle and an end."

Any writer who has the naïveté to take this advice seriously is bound to run into trouble.

If it is true that every story has to have a beginning, then every story might have started at the conception of the characters and ended with their death.

You may protest that this is a too literal interpretation of Aristotle. Perhaps it is, but many plays met their Waterloo for the very reason that their authors, consciously or otherwise, obeyed this Aristotelian dictum.

Hamlet did not start when the curtain went up. Far from it. A murder had been committed before, and the murdered man's ghost had just come back to demand justice.

This play opens, then, not in the beginning, but in the *middle,* after a dastardly act had been committed first.

You may argue that Aristotle meant that even the "middle" must have a beginning and an end. Perhaps, but if that is what he wanted to say, he certainly could have expressed himself more clearly than he did.

Doll's House did not start when Helmer was taken ill, nor when Nora frantically tried to get money to save his life. The play did not start even when Nora forged her father's signature to secure money, nor when Helmer returned home jobless, after recuperating. No, the play did not start during the years Nora pinched to repay the loan. The play actually started when Krogstad found out that Helmer was being given the job as manager of the bank. Then Krogstad started his blackmail, and with this, the play.

Romeo and Juliet did not start when the Montagues and Capulets started their feud. The play did not start when Romeo fell in love with Rosalind, but when Romeo, defying death, went to the home of the Capulets and saw Juliet, the play really began.

Ghosts did not start when Mrs. Alving left her husband and went to Manders, offering herself to him and imploring help; nor when Regina's mother became pregnant through Captain Alving. The play did not start when Captain Alving died. It really started when Oswald came home, broken in body and spirit, and the ghost of his father started to haunt them again.

An author must find a character who wants *something* so desperately that he can't wait any longer. His needs are immediate.

Why? You have your story or play the moment you can answer authoritatively why this man must do something so urgently and immediately. Whatever it is, the motivation must have grown out of what happened *before* the story started. In fact, your story is *possible only because it grew out of the very thing that happened before.*

It is imperative that your story starts in the middle, and not under any circumstances, at the beginning.

9. *Transition*

I

Two or three billion years ago, the earth was a ball of fire, revolving around its own axis. It took millions of years to cool under the constant downpour of rain. The process was slow, imperceptible, but the gradual change—transition—came to pass, the crust of the earth hardened; great cataclysms pushed up hills, created valleys and ravines through which rivers could flow. Then came the unicellular forms of life, and the globe began to swarm with living things.

Near the botton of the scale of life are the plants called thallogens, which lack proper stems and leaves. After these come the acrogens, or flowerless plants, such as the ferns which possess stems and leaves. Farther up are the flowering plants, then the polycotyledonous trees, and then what are known as our "forest trees" and fruit-bearing trees.

Nature never jumps. She works in a leisurely manner, experimenting continuously. The same natural transition can be seen in mammals.

The gap between terrestrial and aquatic mammals is bridged by the muskrat, beavers, otters and seals, which are more or less equally at home on land and in water,

says Woodruff in *Animal Biology.*

There are connecting links between the fish and the mammal; between the bird and the mammal; between the cave man and man today. The gradual change, transition, works everywhere, silently building storms and destroying solar systems. It helps the human embryo to become an infant, an adolescent, a young man, a middle-aged man, an old man.

Leonardo da Vinci writes in his *Notebooks:*

. . . And this old man, a few hours before his death, told me that he had lived a hundred years, and that he did not feel any bodily ailment other than weakness, and thus, while sitting up on a bed in the hospital of Santa Maria Nuova at Florence, without any movement or sign of anything amiss, he passed away from this life. And I made an autopsy in order to ascertain the cause of so peaceful a death, and found that it proceeded from weakness through failure of blood and of the artery that feeds the heart and the other lower members, which I found to be very parched and shrunk and withered; and the result of this autopsy I wrote down very carefully and with great ease, for the body was devoid of either fat or moisture, and these form the chief hindrance to the knowledge of its parts. . . . The old who enjoy good health die through *lack of sustenance.* And this is brought about by the passage to the mesaraic veins becoming continually restricted by the thickening of the skin of these veins [hardening of the arteries— L.E.]: *and the process continues until it affects the capillary veins* which are the first to close up altogether; and from this it comes to pass that the old dread the cold more than the young, and that those who are very old have their skin the color of wood or of dried chestnut, because this is almost completely deprived of sustenance.

Here, too, transition works stealthily. The arteries are gradually blocked, through the years, the skin withers and loses its natural color.

There are two main poles in every life: birth and death. In between there is transition:

> birth—childhood
> childhood—adolescence
> adolescence—youth
> youth—manhood
> manhood—middle age
> middle age—old age
> old age—death.

Now let us see the transition between *friendship* and *murder:*

friendship—disappointment
disappointment—annoyance
annoyance—irritation
irritation—anger
anger—assault
assault—threat (to greater harm)
threat—premeditation
premeditation—murder.

Between "friendship" and "disappointment," for instance, as between the others, there are still other smaller poles with their own transitions.

If your play will go from love to hate, you have to find all the steps leading up to hate.

If you try to leap from "friendship" to "anger," you necessarily leave out "disappointment" and "annoyance." This is a jump, because you left out two steps which belong to the dramatic construction as your lungs or liver belong to your body.

Here is a scene from *Ghosts* where transition is handled in a masterly fashion. Manders, the priest, is greatly incensed against Engstrand, the lovable but incurable liar. Manders feels that he must even his score, once and for all, with this man who has misused his credulity.

The probable transitions will be:

anger—repudiation
or
anger—forgiveness.

Knowing Manders' character, one knows that he will forgive. Watch the natural, smooth transition in this *small conflict:*

ENGSTRAND: [*Appears in the doorway*] I humbly beg pardon, but—
MANDERS: Aha! Hm!—
MRS. ALVING: Oh, it's you, Engstrand!
ENGSTRAND: There were none of the maids about, so I took the great liberty of knocking.

MRS. ALVING: That's all right. Come in. Do you want to speak to me?

ENGSTRAND: [*Coming in*] No, thank you very much, ma'am. It was Mr. Manders I wanted to speak to for a moment.

MANDERS: [*Stopping in front of him*] Well, may I ask what it is you want?

ENGSTRAND: It's this way, Mr. Manders. We are being paid off now. And many thanks to you, Mrs. Alving. And now the work is quite finished, I thought it would be so nice and suitable if all of us, who have worked so honestly together all this time, were to finish up with a few prayers this evening.

(The consummate liar! He wants something from Manders, and knowing he can be approached only through piety, offers to pray.)

MANDERS: Prayers? Up at the orphanage?

ENGSTRAND: Yes, sir, but if it isn't agreeable to you, then—

(He is willing to withdraw. It is enough that Manders knows he has the good intention.)

MANDERS: Oh, certainly, but—hm!—

(Poor Manders! He was so angry—but what can one do when the object of his wrath approached him for prayer?)

ENGSTRAND: I have made a practice of saying a few prayers there myself each evening—

MRS. ALVING: Have you?

(Mrs. Alving knows too well his true color. She knows he is lying.)

ENGSTRAND: Yes, ma'am, now and then—just as a little edification, so to speak. But I am only a poor common man, and haven't rightly the gift, alas—and so I thought that as Mr. Manders happened to be here, perhaps—

MANDERS: Look here, Engstrand. First of all I must ask you a question. Are you in a proper frame of mind for such a thing? Is your conscience free and untroubled?

(Manders wasn't entirely taken in by Engstrand's hypocritical clamor for prayer.)

ENGSTRAND: Heaven have mercy on me a sinner! My conscience isn't worth our speaking about, Mr. Manders.

MANDERS: But it is just what we must think about. What do you say to my question?

ENGSTRAND: My conscience? Well—it's uneasy sometimes, of course.

MANDERS: Ah, you admit that at all events. Now will you tell me, without any concealment—what is your relationship to Regina?

(Engstrand always maintained that Regina was his daughter, when in reality she is the illegitimate child of the departed Captain Alving. Engstrand received seventy pounds to overlook this deficiency in his wife when he married her.)

MRS. ALVING: [Hastily] Mr. Manders!

MANDERS: [Calming her] Leave it to me!

ENGSTRAND: With Regina? Good Lord, how you frightened me! [Looks at Mrs. Alving] There is nothing wrong with Regina, is there?

MANDERS: Let us hope not. What I want to know is, what is your relationship to her? You pass as her father, don't you?

ENGSTRAND: [Unsteadily] Well—hm!—you know, sir, what happened between me and my poor Joanna.

MANDERS: No more distortion of the truth! Your late wife made a full confession to Mrs. Alving, before she left her service.

ENGSTRAND: What!—do you mean to say—? Did she do that after all?

MANDERS: You see it has all come out, Engstrand.

ENGSTRAND: Do you mean to say that she, who gave me her solemn oath—

MANDERS: Did she take an oath?

ENGSTRAND: Well, no—she only gave me her word, but as seriously as a woman could.

MANDERS: And all these years you have been hiding the truth from me—from me, who have had such complete and absolute faith in you.

ENGSTRAND: I am sorry to say I have, sir.

MANDERS: Did I deserve that from you, Engstrand? Haven't I been always ready to help you in word and deed as far as it lay in my power? Answer me! Is it not so?

ENGSTRAND: Indeed there's many a time I should have been very badly off without you, sir.

MANDERS: And this is the way you repay me—by causing me to make false entries in the church registers, and afterwards keeping back from me for years the information which you owed it both to me and to your sense of the truth to divulge. Your conduct has been absolutely inexcusable, Engstrand, and from today everything is at an end between us.

ENGSTRAND: [*With a sigh*] Yes, I can see that's what it means.

MANDERS: Yes, because how can you possibly justify what you did?

ENGSTRAND: Was the poor girl to go and increase her load of shame by talking about it? Just suppose, sir, for a moment, that your reverence was in the same predicament as my poor Joanna—

MANDERS: I!

(And he will be in a similarly shameful position later. The scene has a direct bearing on his future conduct.)

ENGSTRAND: Good Lord, sir, I don't mean the same predicament, I mean, suppose there were something your reverence were ashamed of in the eyes of the world, so to speak. We men oughtn't to judge a poor woman too harshly, Mr. Manders.

MANDERS: But I am not doing so at all. It is you I am blaming.

ENGSTRAND: Will your reverence grant me leave to ask you a small question?

MANDERS: Ask away.

ENGSTRAND: Shouldn't you say it was right for a man to raise up the fallen?

MANDERS: Of course it is.

ENGSTRAND: And isn't a man bound to keep his word of honor?

MANDERS: Certainly he is, but—

ENGSTRAND: At the time when Joanna had her misfortune with this Englishman—or maybe he was an American or a Russian, as they call 'em— [*He was not aware that the man was Captain Alving.*] Well, sir, then she came to town. Poor thing, she had refused me once or twice before; she only had eyes for good-looking men in those days, and I had this crooked leg then. Your reverence will remember how I had ventured up into a dancing saloon where seafaring men were reveling in drunkenness and intoxication, as they say. And when I tried to exhort them to turn from their evil ways—

MRS. ALVING: Ahem!

(This lying is sufficiently obvious to make even Mrs. Alving utter a sound.)

MANDERS: I know, Engstrand, I know—the rough brutes threw you downstairs. You have told me about that incident before. The affliction to your leg is a credit to you.

(Manders is willing to swallow anything with a religious intent.)

ENGSTRAND: I don't want to claim credit for it, your reverence. But what I wanted to tell you was that she came there and confided in me with tears and gnashing of teeth. I can tell you, sir, it went to my heart to hear her.

MANDERS: Did it indeed, Engstrand? Well, what then?

(Manders is beginning to forget that he is angry, and transition starts.)

ENGSTRAND: Well, then I said to her, "The American is roaming about on the high seas, he is. And you, Joanna," I said, "you have committed a sin and are a fallen woman. But here stands Jacob Engstrand," I said, "on two strong legs,"—of course that was only speaking in a kind of metaphor, as it were, your reverence.

MANDERS: I quite understand. Go on.

ENGSTRAND: Well, sir, that was how I rescued her and made her

my lawful wife, so that no one should know how recklessly she
had carried on with the stranger.

MANDERS: That was all very kindly done. The only thing I cannot
justify was your bringing yourself to accept the money—

ENGSTRAND: Money? I? Not a farthing.

MANDERS: But—

ENGSTRAND: Ah, yes! Wait a bit; I remember now. Joanna did have
a trifle of money, you are quite right. But I didn't want to know
anything about that. "Fie," I said, "on the mammon of un-
righteousness, it's the price of your sin; as for this tainted gold"
—or notes, or whatever it was—"we will throw it back in the
American's face," I said. But he had gone away and disappeared
on the stormy seas, your reverence.

MANDERS: Was that how it was, my good fellow?

(Manders is softening perceptibly.)

ENGSTRAND: It was, sir. So then Joanna and I decided that the
money should go toward the child's bringing up, and that's what
became of it; and I can give a faithful account of every single
penny of it.

MANDERS: This alters the complexion of the affair very considerably.

ENGSTRAND: That's how it was, your reverence. And I make bold
to say that I have been a good father to Regina—as far as was
in my power—for I am a poor erring mortal, alas!

MANDERS: There, there, my dear Engstrand—

ENGSTRAND: Yes, I do make bold to say that I brought up the child,
and made my poor Joanna a loving and careful husband, as the
Bible says we ought. But it never occurred to me to go to your
reverence and claim credit for it or boast about it because I had
done one good deed in this world. No; when Jacob Engstrand
does a thing like that, he holds his tongue about it. Unfortunately, it doesn't often happen, I know it only too well. And
whenever I do come to see your reverence, I never seem to have
anything but trouble and wickedness to talk about. Because, as
I said just now—and I say it again—conscience can be hard on
us sometimes.

MANDERS: Give me your hand, Jacob Engstrand.

The movement is complete. The poles were "anger" and "forgiveness." In between: transition.

Both characters are absolutely clear. Engstrand, besides being a liar, is as good a psychologist as Manders is naïve. Later, when Engstrand leaves, Mrs. Alving tells Manders, "You always will remain a big baby."

Nora, however, is a baby who grows up—and we have seen a great part of that growth in her scene with Helmer. A less skillful writer would have turned the last scene of *A Doll's House* into a grand display of fireworks—thus creating a jumping conflict on Nora's part. We have seen Helmer's slow development, but we have not seen Nora's in that case, and if she were to present her intention of leaving without a suitable period of transition, she would surprise us—and leave us unconvinced. It is possible, in life, that such a transition would take place in a split second of thought. But Ibsen has translated that thought into action, so that the audience can see and understand it.

It is possible that a person flares up instantaneously at the very moment the insult occurred. Even then subconsciously the person went through a mental transition. The mind received the insult, weighed the relationship between the insulter and himself; found that the insulter was an ingrate, misused their friendship and on top of it insulted him. This lightning review of their relationship made him resent his attitude. Anger and explosion followed. This mental process might have happened in a split second. The instantaneous flare up as we see it, then, wasn't a jump, but the result of a mental process, however quick.

Since there is no jump in nature there cannot be one on the stage either. A good playwright will record the minute movements of the mind as a seismograph jots down the slightest oscillation of the earth thousands of miles away.

Nora decided to leave Helmer after his terrific outburst on finding the letter from Krogstad. She might have looked at him, in real life, horror-stricken, without saying a word. She might have turned and walked out on the raving Helmer. It is possible, but it would have been a jumping conflict and bad playwriting. The author has to take all the steps which lead to the conclusion, whether that conflict happened in just that way or in the person's mind.

You can write a play around a single transition. *The Sea Gull* and *The Cherry Orchard* are made of just such material, although we have designated the poles as a single step in a drama. Of course, such transitional plays are slow-moving, but they contain conflict, crisis, climax, on a smaller scale.

Now, between "ambition thwarted" and "resentment," there is a transition. Many authors leap from one to the other of these without a pause, feeling that the reaction is immediate. But even when the resentment is spontaneous, there is a series of minute movements, a transition, which causes the reaction.

It is these tiny, split-second movements with which we are concerned. Analyze a transition and you will find that you know the characters better.

There is a fine transition in *Tartuffe*, when this sublime villain at last has the opportunity to be alone with Orgon's wife. He has been masquerading as a saint, but at the same time he has designs on the lovely Elmire. Let us watch him —how will he bridge saintliness to proposal of illicit love and at the same time remain in character?

After desiring Elmire so long, he naturally loses control of his emotions after finding himself alone with her. He fingers her dress absent-mindedly. But Elmire is on the alert.

ELMIRE: Monsieur Tartuffe!
TARTUFFE: Satin, unless I am mistaken? And of so deliciously soft a texture! In such fine raiment doubtless was arrayed the Bride of Solomon's Song when—
ELMIRE: However she was arrayed, Monsieur, can be no concern of either of us!

(This rebuff cools his ardor a bit, and Tartuffe becomes more cautious.)

ELMIRE: We have other matters than lace to discuss. I want to hear from you whether it is true that you are proposing to marry my stepdaughter?

TARTUFFE: I would ask in return if such a marriage would incur your disapproval.

(He moves warily now. After the first disappointment he has to be more careful.)

ELMIRE: Why, can you possibly suppose I could approve of it?

TARTUFFE: To say the truth, Madame, I have been led to doubt it. And you must permit me to reassure you on that head. It is true that Monsieur Orgon did broach this alliance to me. But, Madame, you do not need to be told that my hopes are fixed on a far other, far higher happiness!

ELMIRE: [Relieved] Ah yes, of course. You mean that your heart is set on joys that are not of this world.

TARTUFFE: Do not misunderstand me, or perhaps I should say, do not affect to misunderstand me, Madame. That was *not* my meaning.

(He presupposes that she has an inkling of his intention. No jump. He goes smoothly toward his goal: to declare his love.)

ELMIRE: Then perhaps you will tell me what you *did* mean.

TARTUFFE: I meant, Madame, that my heart is not of marble.

ELMIRE: And is that so remarkable?

TARTUFFE: So far is it from marble, Madame, that, however it may aspire heavenward, it is not proof against the desire for earthly felicity.

(He is on the way.)

ELMIRE: If it is not, it should surely be your endeavor to make it so, Monsieur Tartuffe.

TARTUFFE: How strive against the irresistible, Madame? When we behold some perfect work of the Creator can we refrain from worshiping Him in His own image? No—and with good reason, for to refrain would be undevout.

(The ground is prepared. Now he can move to attack.)

ELMIRE: I see, you are a lover of nature.

TARTUFFE: An ardent one, Madame, when it takes so divine a shape, so enchanting a beauty as in the dazzling form I am privileged to behold. For a season I wrestled against your charms, regarding them as snares set by the Evil One for my undoing. And then it was revealed to me that, since my passion was pure, I could indulge it without either sin or shame, and offer you a heart so little worthy of your acceptance. But, such as it is, Madame, I lay it at your dainty feet, and await the decision which will either raise me to bliss unspeakable or doom me to utter despair.

(He mitigates his audacity by envisaging his possible doom if rejected. Surely, this man Tartuffe knows his psychology.)

ELMIRE: Surely, Monsieur Tartuffe, this is a somewhat surprising outburst from one of your rigid principles!

TARTUFFE: Ah, Madame, what principles would withstand such beauty! Alas! I am no Joseph!

(He skillfully puts the blame on her. No woman can be outraged if she is thought so irresistible.)

ELMIRE: Too evidently. But neither am I a Madame Potiphar, as you seem to be suggesting.

TARTUFFE: But you *are*, Madame, you are! Unconsciously, I am willing to believe, but a temptress none the less, and one against whom all my fastings, all my supplications on my bended knees have availed me naught! Now at last my pent-up passion hath burst its bounds, and I implore you for some sign that it is not altogether disdained. Reflect that I offer you not only a devotion without parallel, but a discretion that you may be sure will never

tarnish your fair name by so much as a breath. You need have
no fear that I am one of those who boast of their good fortune.

(This very assurance of secrecy gives Tartuffe away as a
designing scoundrel. But he is in character.)

ELMIRE: And have *you* no fear, Monsieur Tartuffe, that I may alter
my husband's opinion of you by repeating this conversation to
him?

TARTUFFE: Madame, I think too highly of your discretion—I mean
that you have too kind a heart to injure one whose only offense
is that he is unable to help adoring you.

ELMIRE: Well, how another woman might act in my place I cannot
say, but I shall say nothing to my husband of this—incident,
Monsieur Tartuffe.

TARTUFFE: I should be the last to advise your doing so, Madame—
in the circumstances.

ELMIRE: But I shall name a price for my silence. You in return
must renounce all claim to my stepdaughter's hand—however
my husband may urge.

TARTUFFE: Ah, Madame, must I again assure you that you and you
alone—?

ELMIRE: Wait, Monsieur Tartuffe. You are to do more than that—
you are to use all your influence to bring about her marriage
with Valère.

TARTUFFE: And if I do, Madame, if I do, what may I hope for as
my reward?

ELMIRE: Why, my silence, to be sure.

(After this transition the scene naturally arrived where conflict had to burst forth. Damis, Orgon's son, suddenly steps
between them. Damis had overheard their conversation, and
he is outraged.)

DAMIS: No. There should be no hushing up of this and there shall
not be, either!

ELMIRE: Damis!

TARTUFFE: My—my dear young friend. You have mistaken an innocent phrase for—!

(The attack was too sudden for Tartuffe's comfort. For a moment he lost his bearing.)

DAMIS: Mistaken! I have heard every word that was spoken, and so shall my father. Thank heaven I am at last able to open his eyes and make him see how vile a traitor and hypocrite he has been harboring!

TARTUFFE: You do me wrong, dear young friend, you do indeed!

(It seems he is in his stride again. He withdraws into his piousness once more.)

ELMIRE: Now, Damis, listen to me. There must be no noise about this—I do not wish it talked of. I have promised him my forgiveness on condition that he behaves himself for the future, as I am sure he will. I cannot take back my promise. Indeed the matter is too absurd and trifling to make a fuss about—to your father of all people.

DAMIS: That may be your view, it is not mine. I've borne too much from that canting square-toes there—that schemer who has gained complete control over father, set him against both my marriage and Valère's, and sought to turn this house into a conventicle. Now when I may never have so good a chance again!

ELMIRE: But, Damis, I assure you—

DAMIS: No. I shall do as I said, make an end once and for all of this domineering. The whip has been put in my hand, and I shall take great joy in applying it!

ELMIRE: Damis dear, if you will only be advised by me—

DAMIS: I am sorry, but I can take no advice. Father must know all.

(Orgon enters from doors at left.)

ORGON: [As he enters] What is this that I must know?

There is subtle conflict in this transition, which slowly accumulates tension as it goes along and arrives to a breaking point, in even tempo. The first high point is when Tartuffe openly declares his love; the second, Damis' accusation of his treachery.

After Orgon's arrival, we can witness once more the transition in Tartuffe. The insidious acceptance of guilt seemingly in true Christian spirit lifts him in the esteem of Orgon, and makes him disown his son.

The conflict rises higher and higher, and between one conflict and the next conflict, there is perpetual transition, which makes dynamic conflict possible.

Years ago, the father of one of our friends passed away. We went to our friend's home after the funeral and found the family sitting about in great gloom. The women wept, the men stared at the floor stonily. The atmosphere was so depressing that we went out for a walk. We opened the door a half-hour later, on our return, and found the mourners in an uproar. They were laughing merrily—but stopped abruptly at our entrance. They were ashamed. What had happened? How had they come to laughter from such genuine sorrow?

We have met like situations since, and found the transition fascinating. Here is a scene from *Dinner at Eight*, by Kaufman and Ferber. We will try to trace transition in it. They start with "irritation" and go to "rage." This is Act Three, the last part of Scene One:

PACKARD: [*Striding into the room*] You've been acting damn funny lately, my fine lady, and I'm getting good and sick of it.

KITTY: [*Ruffled, not angry yet, but transition has started toward anger*] Yeah? And so what?

PACKARD: [*Doesn't mean any harm. Reads the riot act as a matter of form*] I'll tell you what. I'm the works around here. I pay the bills. And you take orders from me.

KITTY: [*Considers this a challenge and counterattacks. Rising, brush in hand hanging idly*] Who do you think you're talking to? That first wife of yours in Montana?

PACKARD: [*Considers this a foul and doesn't like it*] You leave her out of this!

KITTY: [*She smells blood. This is his weak point, and an old resent-*

ment kills all her caution] That poor mealy-faced thing, with her flat chest, that never had the guts to talk up to you!

PACKARD: [*Still willing to call it quits. His transition toward anger is sluggish, has to be fed*] Shut up, I tell you!

KITTY: [*Doing the feeding*] Washing your greasy overalls, cooking and slaving for you in some lousy mining shack! No wonder she died!

PACKARD: [*Becomes violently angry—a jump*] God damn you!

KITTY: [*Gesticulating with the hairbrush*] Well, you're not going to get me that way! You're not going to step on my face to get where you want to go—you big windbag! [*Turns away from him, drops her hairbrush among the bottles and jars on the dressing table.*]

PACKARD: Why you cheap little piece of scum! I've got a good notion to drop you right back where I picked you up, in the checkroom of the Hottentot Club, or whatever the dirty joint was.

KITTY: Oh, no you won't! [*The upward movement is swift. Shortly the transition will be complete.*]

PACKARD: And then you can go home and live with your sweet-smelling family, back of the railroad tracks in Passaic. That drunken bum father and your jail-bird brother that I'm always coming through for. The next time he can go to the pen, and I'll see that he gets there.

KITTY: You'll be there ahead of him—you big crook!

PACKARD: And get this! If that sniveling, money-grubbing mother of yours comes whining around my office once more, I'm going to give orders to have her thrown the hell out of there and right down sixty flights of stairs, so help me God! [*Tina has entered as Dan is almost at the end of this speech. In her hand is Kitty's evening bag, jeweled and metallic, and containing Kitty's powder compact, lipstick, cigarette case, and so forth. Finding herself in the midst of a storm, she hesitates briefly. Dan, on his last word, and coincident with Tina's entrance, snatches the bag from Tina's hand, dashes it to the floor, gives Tina a shove that sends her spinning out of the room.*]

KITTY: [*The transition is complete. Her first real resentment. From here she must move more quickly, her transition reaching a still higher note.*] You pick that up! [*For answer, Dan gives the bag*

a violent kick, sending it to a corner of the room. Beside herself.]
Bracelets, eh? [*She takes off a three-inch jeweled band; drops it
onto the floor, and kicks it viciously across the room.*] That
shows you what you know about women! You think if you give
me a bracelet— Why do you give 'em to me! Because you've
put over one of your dirty deals and want me to lug these around
to show what a big guy you are! You don't do it to make me feel
good; it's for you! [*She does not know in what direction her anger
will take her, but she hits into the dark.*]

PACKARD: Oh, it is, is it! What about this place and all these clothes
and fur-coats and automobiles! Go any place you want to, money
to throw away! There ain't a wife in the world got it softer than
you have! I picked you up out of the gutter, and this is the
thanks I get!

KITTY: [*Like a good hunting dog, gets the scent at last. Now she
knows where she's going*] Thanks for what? Dressing me up like
a plush horse and leaving me to sit alone, day after day and night
after night! You never take me anywheres! Always playing poker
and eating dinner with your men friends—or say you are. [*She
is moving toward a new goal—watch her.*]

PACKARD: That's a nice crack. [*Still unsuspecting, he is ready to be
conciliatory.*]

KITTY: You're always either coming in or going out, blowing what
a big guy you've just been, or going to be. You never think about
me, or do any of the nice little things that women like—you
never sent me a flower in your life! When I want to wear flowers
I got to go out and buy 'em! [*With a gesture to the door where
Tina has lately stood with the orchids.*] What woman wants to
buy theirself flowers! You never sit and talk to me, or ask me
what I've been doing, or how I am, or anything!

PACKARD: Well, go and find yourself something to do! I ain't stopping you!

KITTY: You bet you ain't! You think I sit home all day looking at
bracelets! Hah! Of all the dumb bunnies! What do you think
I'm doing while you're pulling your crooked deals! Just waiting
for Daddy to come home! [*Now the conflict reaches its crisis.*]

PACKARD: What're you driving at, you little—

KITTY: You think you're the only man I know—you great big noise.

Well, you aren't! See! There's somebody that just knowing him has made me realize what a stuffed shirt you are! [*Transition completed again—climax.*]

PACKARD: [*In an upward swing—counterattacks*] Why you—you—

KITTY: [*Helping him—she wants to see him furious. They are moving toward new transition and new conflict on a higher plane*] You don't like that, do you, Mr. Cabinet Member!

PACKARD: [*Still dazed. Transition from the impact to realization not yet completed*] Do you mean to tell me that you've been putting it over on me with some other man!

KITTY: [*She is in for it now. Means to go through with it*] Yes! And what're you going to do about it! You big gasbag!

PACKARD: [*Drawing the full breath of the outraged male*] Who is it?

KITTY: [*A purr of malice*] Don't you wish you knew!

PACKARD: [*Seizes her wrist. Kitty screams*] Tell me who it is!

KITTY: I won't.

PACKARD: Tell me or I'll break every bone in your body!

KITTY: I won't! You can kill me and I won't!

PACKARD: I'll find out, I'll— [*Drops her wrist.*] Tina! Tina!

KITTY: She don't know. [*There is a moment during which the two stand silent, waiting for the appearance of Tina. There comes slowly into the door, and a step or two into the room, a Tina, who, in spite of the expression of wondering innocence on her face, has clearly been eavesdropping. She comes forward so that she stands between the two silent figures.*]

PACKARD: Who's been coming to this house?

TINA: Huh? [*In the following, transition runs smoothly to form.*]

KITTY: You don't know, do you, Tina?

PACKARD: Shut your face, you slut! [*Turns again to Tina.*] You know, and you're going to tell. What man's been coming to this house?

TINA: [*A frantic shake of the head*] I ain't seen nobody.

PACKARD: [*Grasps her shoulder. Gives her a little shake*] Yes you have. Come on, who's been here? Who was here last week? Who was here when I went to Washington?

TINA: Nobody—nobody—only the doctor.

PACKARD: No, no, I don't mean that. What man's been coming here behind my back?

TINA: I ain't seen a soul.

KITTY: [*Kills two birds with one stone—he is jealous, but he does not suspect the doctor, the man Kitty loves*] Hah! What did I tell you!

PACKARD: [*Looks at her as though trying to find a way of worming the truth out of her. Decides it is hopeless. Gives her a push toward the door*] Get the hell out of here. [*Kitty stands waiting to see what turn events will take. Packard paces a step this way and that. Wheels suddenly.*] I'll divorce you. That's what I'll do. I'll divorce you, and you won't get a cent. That's the law for what you've done.

KITTY: You can't prove anything. You've got to prove it first.

PACKARD: I'll prove it. I'll get detectives to prove it. They'll track him down. I'd like to get hold of the guy just once. How I'd like to get my fingers around his neck. And I will too. I'll get him. I'll kill him and I'll throw you out like an alley cat.

KITTY: Yeah? You'll throw me out. Well, before you throw me out you'd better think twice. Because me, I don't have to get detectives to prove what I've got on you.

PACKARD: You've got nothing on me.

KITTY: No? So you want to go to Washington, do you? And be a big shot, and tell the president where to get off. You want to go in politics? [*Her tone becomes savage.*] Well, I know about politics. And I know all about the crooked deals you bragged about. God knows I was bored stiff—the Thompson business, and gypping old man Clarke, and now this Jordan thing. Skinning him out of his eyeteeth. When I tell about those it'll raise a pretty stink. Politics! You couldn't get into politics. You couldn't get in anywhere. You couldn't get into the men's room at the Astor.

PACKARD: You snake, you. You poisonous little rattlesnake. I'm through with you. I've got to go to this Ferncliffe dinner, but after tonight we're through. And I wouldn't go there with you except that meeting Ferncliffe is more important to me than you are. I'm clearing out tonight, get me? Tomorrow I send for my clothes. And you can set here and get flowers from your soulmate. We're through. [*Packard stalks off to his own room and slams the door. The transition is complete.*]

This scene starts with *irritation* and ends with *rage*. In between the steps lead up from the first to the last.

An almost universal fault of mediocre writers is ignoring transition, but believing that their portrayals are true to life. It is true that transition can take place in a very short time, and in a character's mind, without the character being aware of it. But it is there, and the author must show it to be there. Melodramas and stock characters have no transition which is the lifeblood of real drama.

Eugene O'Neill invented many devices with which to convey his characters' thought to the audience. Yet none of them was as successful as the simple, transitional method employed by Ibsen and others of the great.

In *The Bear*, Chekhov's fine one-acter, there is a fine visible transition. Popova, the lady, has agreed to "shoot it out" with Smirnov, since she has insulted him.

SMIRNOV: It's about time we got rid of the theory that only men need pay for their insults. Devil take it, if you want equality of rights you can have it. We're going to fight it out!

POPOVA: With pistols? Very well!

SMIRNOV: This very minute.

POPOVA: This very minute! My husband had some pistols. I'll bring them here. [*Is going, but turns back.*] What pleasure it will give me to put a bullet into your thick head! Devil take you! [*Exit.*]

SMIRNOV: I'll bring her down like a chicken! I'm not a little boy or a sentimental puppy; I don't care about this "softer sex." [*A movement toward weakening has started.*]

LUKA: [*The servant*] Gracious little fathers! [*Kneels*] Have pity on a poor old man and go away from here. You've frightened her to death, and now you want to shoot her!

SMIRNOV: [*Not hearing him*] If she fights, well, that's equality of rights, emancipation, and all that! But what a woman! [*The visible transition starts.*] [*Parodying her.*] "Devil take you! I'll put a bullet into your thick head." Eh? How she reddened, how her cheeks shone! . . . She accepted my challenge! My word, it's the first time in my life that I've seen—

LUKA: Go away, sir, and I'll always pray to God for you!

SMIRNOV: She is a woman! That's the sort I can understand! A real woman! Not a sour-faced jelly-bag, but fire, gunpowder, a rocket! I am even sorry to have to kill her!

LUKA: [*Weeps*] Dear—dear sir, do go away!

SMIRNOV: I absolutely like her! Absolutely! Even though her cheeks are dimpled, I like her. I am almost ready to let the debt go— and I'm not angry any longer—wonderful woman!

The transition is too obvious at the end. It lacks the subtlety which makes the transition in *A Doll's House* an integral part of the play.

Without transition there cannot be development or growth. T. A. Jackson writes in his book, *Dialectics:*

Considered qualitatively, it is . . . self-evident that the universe is never for any two successive moments the same.

To paraphrase this for our own uses, it is self-evident that a play is never for any two successive moments the same.

A character who travels from one pole to the opposite one, as from religion to atheism or vice versa, has to be on the move constantly to traverse this immense space in the allotted two hours in the theater.

Every tissue, every muscle and bone in our bodies, is rejuvenated every seven years. Our attitude and outlook on life, our hopes and dreams are also constantly changing. This transformation is so imperceptible that usually we are not even aware that it is taking place in our bodies and in our minds. *This is transition: we are never, for any two successive moments, the same.* And transition is the element which keeps the play moving without any breaks, jumps, or gaps. Transition connects seemingly unconnected elements, such as winter and summer, love and hate.

2

One, two, three, four, five, six, seven, eight, nine, ten. This is the perfect rising conflict. The jumping conflict is erratic: one, two—five, six—nine, ten.

In life there is no such thing as a jumping conflict. "Jumping to a conclusion" indicates an acceleration rather than a break in the mental processes.

Here is the opening scene from *Stevedore*, by Peters and Sklar. It is a short scene, but there is a jump in it. Try to find it.

FLORRIE: Gee, Bill, what's happened to us? Why do we have to fight all the time? We never used to be like this. [*She puts her hand on his arm.*]

BILL: [*Throwing her hand off*] Aw lay off, lay off!

FLORRIE: You pig! [*She begins to weep.*]

BILL: You're all alike, you little married sluts; you never know when to quit.

FLORRIE: [*She slaps his face.*] Don't you talk to me like that.

BILL: All right. All right. That suits me. Only we're through now and don't you forget it. I don't want to see you any more and I don't want you to come down to the office any more. Go back to that sap husband of yours and try loving him for a change. He sure needs it. [*He turns to go.*]

FLORRIE: Now you wait a minute, Bill Larkin.

BILL: Oh, shut up! And don't you go calling me up with this line of yours about something important to tell me, either.

FLORRIE: I've got something important to tell you right now. I wrote those letters to Helen, if you want to know. And that isn't all, either. I'm going to fix you. Just you wait and see. I'll go to Helen and tell her just what kind of a pig she's going to marry. You can't treat me like that and get away with it. Maybe that stuff worked with your other women, but you picked the wrong number this time, dearie. You're not through with me; oh, no, you're not. Not by a hell of a ways.

BILL: You God damned— [*The man seizes her by the throat in rage. She bangs his face and shrieks. Now he beats her up in a*

blind fury. She shrieks louder and falls to the ground. Doors slam, voices are heard. Bill runs away.]
FREDDIE: [*Offstage*] Florrie, was that you? Florrie! Where are you?

Now go back to where Bill said, "Oh, shut up!" and read Florrie's speech. She announces that she has written certain letters to the girl Bill wishes to marry, and we expect him to be enraged. But she continues with a fairly long speech, and he does nothing. This is static. The only vital line in the speech is the opening sentence, and it arouses no reaction. What does arouse him is so trivial that his reaction is a jumping conflict.

The authors subconsciously felt the need for transition, but, not understanding the principle, they reversed the process. Thereby they created a static conflict, followed by a jumping one—signs of character trouble. From his warning, "Oh, shut up!" to the end of Florrie's speech, Bill's mental processes are blank, so far as the audience is concerned. If she had begun: "You can't treat me like that and get away with it," Bill would have had a chance to react with some counterthreat. Then she would continue: "Maybe that stuff worked with your other women, but you picked the wrong number this time, dearie!" Bill's impatience and rising temper would have caused her to hurry on to: "I'll go to Helen and tell her just what kind of a pig she's going to marry." This is Bill's chance to threaten to beat her if she approaches Helen, and the attack which causes her to speak her big line: "I wrote those letters to Helen, if you want to know." In a completely comprehensible rage, he gives her a beating.

In this way we could have witnessed the transition from *irritation* to *rage*. As the scene stands now, the strongest line ushers in a long-winded tirade. Bill is forced to stand there, glaring at her—static—then start to choke her suddenly—jump—after a pale and inconsequential line.

Now read a scene from *Black Pit*, by Maltz, and try to discover another jumping conflict—lack of transition. This is a much more serious defect than the one just discussed, because here the foundation is laid for the future conduct of the character.

PRESCOTT: [*He wishes Joe to turn stool pigeon.*] . . . An' all I know is if you gonna be wantin' your gravy you better stay friends with the cook. Yessir! Of course, maybe you don't care. But I'm telling you my woman ain't going hungry an' my boy ain't gonna work in the mines, neither. Well, think it over, boy. [*He stands up.*] I reckon it's kinda hard on you, Iola. Well— [*He shrugs and goes to the door.*] Let me know when your kid comes. If anything should change your mind, boy, I don't think the job'll be filled before tomorrow. [*He goes out. Silence.*]

IOLA: Joe— [*Joe doesn't answer. She gets up and goes over to him, putting her hand on his arm.*] Joe—ah don't care. Don't feel bad, ah don't want a doctor. Ah'm not afraid. [*She starts to cry.*] Ah won't be afraid, Joe— [*She is shaken by her weeping.*]

JOE: [*Trying to control himself.*] No cry, Iola! No cry! I no want you cry!—

IOLA: [*Choking back her tears.*] Ah won't, Joe—ah won't. [*She sits with clenched hands. Her whole body is trembling. Joe walks the room—looks at her—walks again.*]

JOE: [*Suddenly turns around and yells*] What you wan' me be stool pigeon?

IOLA: No—ah don't—ah don't.

JOE: You t'ink I no wan' job—no wan' eat—no wan' have doctor? You t'ink I wan' you have baby, maybe die?

IOLA: No, Joe—no—

JOE: Christus! What I'm gone do! [*Silence. He walks, then sits down. He starts to beat his clenched fist on the table with increasing force. Finally he brings his hand down with all his strength, and then again there is silence.*] Man got to be man. Man got to live like man. Man got have eat, got have woman, got have house— [*He jumps up.*] Man no can live in hole lak animal . . .

MARY: [*Opens the door from the other room. Sleepily.*] What be matt'r? I hear yell.

JOE: [*In control of himself*] No yell, Mary. Outside. We be talk.

MARY: Go sleep now.

JOE: We go sleep.

MARY: No worry. Everyt'ing's gone be okay. [*She hesitates.*] I pray for you. [*She goes out. Silence.*]

JOE: [*With a little laugh*] She pray for us. [*A pause.*] Company boss here, Iola! Man got help self li'l bit, hah? Iola, no can let Tony live in coke oven—live in hill. [*In a whisper.*] No can let you have li'l feller, maybe—you all time wear shawl, Iola. [*He goes over to her.*] You wan' hide belly? You be shame—shame for li'l feller? *I no be shame.* I lak li'l feller—you t'ink he be wake now? [*He puts his ear to her belly.*] No, he sleep. He go sleep early. He go sleep when whistle blow. [*He gives a little chuckle, then he puts both hands out and strokes her face.*] You lak me, Iola?

IOLA: Joe, couldn't you fool him? Mistah Prescott?—Couldn't you take the job and then just not tell him anythin'? [*A pause. Joe's hands come away from her face.*]

JOE: [*Slowly, quietly, as though stating something they both know.*] Yah. Sure, sure, Iola. I can fool heem. Take'm job. Tal heem li'l t'ing no matt'r anybody. Sure.

IOLA: [*Passionately*] Nobody'll know. We don't hafta tell 'em—and it'll only be for a little while. We don't hafta tell Tony.

JOE: [*In the same slow way*] Sure! Sure, I fool heem. Take'm job. Get doctor. Make li'l bit money. After while—say g'bye go away —sure. [*A pause. He presses his head to her breast. Then, fearfully, as though trying to persuade her.*] Man got live lak man, Iola. [*He raises his head. With increasing pain and determination.*] Man no can live in hole, lak animal!

Curtain

Now go back to the end of Joe's speech, where he says, "You lak me, Iola?" Her answer is the suggestion that he fool Mr. Prescott. She may have been thinking about this all along, but the audience is not made aware of it. When Prescott departs she tells Joe that she does not expect the sacrifice from him—and then, two pages later, she reverses her decision. The reversal is legitimate, but we must know how the change occurred.

Joe tops this apparent jump with a greater one—he agrees
with her immediately. The decision is so swift as to be incredible. Doesn't Joe know what the step entails? Doesn't he know
that he'll certainly be an outcast and perhaps lose his life as
well? Or does he feel that he can outsmart both the company
and his friends? We don't know what he thinks.

If we could see what goes on in Joe's mind—see what he sees
when he thinks of the bosses, the watchmen, the blacklists, the
ostracism—his downfall would be that much more tragic to us.

With this jumping conflict, with this lack of transition, the
fate of the play was sealed. Joe never was a tridimensional
character. The author never gave him a fighting chance—he
determined Joe's fate, instead of letting Joe figure it out for
himself.

Joe's decision would have come after much more ponder-
ing, much more struggle between Joe and Iola, much more
procrastination, and it would have resulted in a rising conflict.

Look at Nora. The transition from despair to the decision
to leave is short, but it is logical. Maltz attempts transition
once or twice, but his handling of it is clumsy. When Joe says:
"Man got help self li'l bit," we get the idea that he's bending
toward the stool-pigeon career. But a few lines later he says
that he wouldn't be ashamed if Iola had no shawl to cover her
belly—and both Iola and the audience understand that he is
not going to take the job—else why should she make the coun-
tersuggestion that he take it and fool the boss?

This jumping back and forth between negative and positive
retards Joe's growth, thus garbling the message of the play.
There is no doubt that Joe is a weak character, never sure of
what he wants. And, should the author say that this is just why
he became a stool pigeon, we would refer him to the chapter:
"Strength of Will in a Character."

QUESTION: You've taught me that it's of prime importance for
a play to move. But do we see every turn of the wheel when

a car drives by? No, because that's not important to us as long as the car is moving. We know that the wheels are turning, because we feel the motion of the car.

ANSWER: A car may jump, stop, jump, stop, endlessly. It is in motion, all right, but such motion would shake the life out of you in a half-hour. A gearshift in a car is comparable to a transition in a play, because it is the transition between two speeds. Just as the bucking car shakes you, physically, a series of jumping conflicts shakes you emotionally. Your question was an interesting one: shall we observe every turn of the wheel? Shall we record every movement of a transition? The answer is no. It is not necessary. If you suggest a movement in transition, and this suggestion throws a light on the working of the character's mind, we think it is sufficient. It depends upon the dramatist's ability, how successfully he can compress his material in transition, giving—or suggesting—the whole movement.

10. Crisis, Climax, Resolution

In birth pains, there is crisis, and the birth itself, which is the climax. The outcome, whether it is death or life, will be the resolution.

In *Romeo and Juliet,* Romeo goes to the hated Capulets' home disguised with a mask, to catch a glimpse of Rosalind, his love. There he discovers another young girl so beautiful, so enchanting, that he falls madly in love with her (crisis). With dismay he finds that Juliet is the heiress of the Capulets (climax), the bitterest enemy of his family. Tybalt, nephew of Lady Capulet, discovering Romeo, attempts to kill him (resolution).

Meanwhile Juliet also learns Romeo's identity and tells her sorrows to the moon and stars. Romeo, driven by his incomparable love for Juliet, returns and hears her (crisis). They decide to get married (climax). The next day, in the cell of Friar Lawrence, a friend of Romeo, they do get married (resolution).

In every act, crisis, climax, and resolution follow each other as day follows night. Let us look into this matter more closely in another play.

Krogstad's threat against Nora, in *A Doll's House,* is a crisis:

Let me tell you this—if I lose my position a second time, you shall lose yours with me.

Krogstad means to expose her as a forger if she does not persuade Helmer to allow him to keep his job.

This threat—whatever the outcome—will be a turning point in the life of Nora; a crisis. If she can influence Helmer to keep Krogstad in the bank, it will be the culmination of all that went before; the climax. But it will also be a climax for this scene if Helmer refuses to keep him.

I assure you it would be quite impossible for me to work with him; I literally feel physically ill when I am in the company of such people,

declares Helmer, and with this statement we have arrived at the highest point of this scene: the climax. He is adamant. Krogstad will expose her—and Helmer had said that a person who forges signatures is not fit to be a mother. Besides the scandal, she will lose Helmer, whom she loves, and her children. The resolution is: terror.

In the next scene she tries again, but Helmer once more is immovable. She accuses him of being narrow-minded. He is hurt to the quick. Crisis. It seems Helmer is determined now. He says:

Very well—I must put an end to this.

He calls the maid, and gives her a letter to mail immediately. She goes.

NORA: [*Breathlessly*] Torvald—what was that letter?

HELMER: Krogstad's dismissal.

NORA: Call her back, Torvald! There is still time. Oh, Torvald, call her back. Do it for my sake—for your own sake—for the children's sake! Do you hear me, Torvald? Call her back! You don't know what that letter can bring upon us.

HELMER: It's too late.

Climax. The resolution is Nora's resignation. This crisis, and climax, are on a higher plane than the previous one. Before, Helmer only threatened, but now he has fulfilled his threat. Krogstad is dismissed.

Here is the next scene, where crisis, climax, and resolution appear again on a still higher plane. Note also the perfect transition between the last crisis and the coming one.

Krogstad comes stealthily through the kitchen. He has received his dismissal. Helmer is in the other room. Nora is in terror that he may find this man here. She bolts the door and asks Krogstad to "speak low—my husband is at home."

KROGSTAD: No matter about that.

NORA: What do you want of me?

KROGSTAD: An explanation of something.

NORA: Make haste then. What is it?

KROGSTAD: You know, I suppose, that I have got my dismissal.

NORA: I couldn't prevent it, Mr. Krogstad. I fought as hard as I could on your side, but it was no good.

KROGSTAD: Does your husband love you so little, then? He knows what I can expose you to, and yet he ventures—

NORA: How can you suppose that he has any knowledge of the sort?

KROGSTAD: I didn't suppose so at all. It would not be the least like our dear Torvald Helmer to show so much courage—

NORA: Mr. Krogstad, a little respect for my husband, please.

KROGSTAD: Certainly—all the respect he deserves. But since you have kept the matter so carefully to yourself, I make bold to suppose that you have a little clearer idea than you had yesterday of what it actually is that you have done?

NORA: More than you could ever teach me.

KROGSTAD: Yes, such a bad lawyer as I am.

NORA: What is it you want of me?

KROGSTAD: Only to see how you were, Mrs. Helmer. I have been thinking about you all day long. A mere cashier, a quill-driver, a—well, a man like me—even he has a little of what is called feeling, you know.

NORA: Show it, then; think of my children.

KROGSTAD: Have you and your husband thought of mine? But never mind about that. I only wanted to tell you that you need not take this matter too seriously. In the first place there will be no accusation made on my part.

NORA: No, of course not; I was sure of that.

KROGSTAD: The whole thing can be arranged amicably; there is no reason why anyone should know anything about it. It will remain a secret between us three.

NORA: My husband must never get to know anything about it.

KROGSTAD: How will you be able to prevent it? Am I to understand that you can pay the balance that is owing?

NORA: No, not just at present.

KROGSTAD: Or perhaps that you have some expedient for raising the money soon?

NORA: No expedient that I mean to make use of.

KROGSTAD: Well, in any case, it would have been of no use to you now. If you stood there with ever so much money in your hand, I would never part with your bond.

NORA: Tell me what purpose you mean to put it to.

KROGSTAD: I shall only preserve it—keep it in my possession. No one who is not concerned in the matter shall have the slightest hint of it. So that if the thought of it has driven you to any desperate resolution—

NORA: It has.

KROGSTAD: If you had it in your mind to run away from your home—

NORA: I had.

KROGSTAD: Or even something worse—

NORA: How could you know that?

KROGSTAD: Give up the idea.

NORA: How did you know I had thought of *that?*

KROGSTAD: Most of us think of that at first. I did, too—but I hadn't the courage.

NORA: [*Faintly*] No more had I.

KROGSTAD: [*In a tone of relief*] No, that's it, isn't it—you hadn't the courage either?

NORA: No, I haven't—I haven't.

KROGSTAD: Besides, it would have been a great piece of folly. Once the first storm at home is over—I have a letter for your husband in my pocket. [*The crisis begins.*]

NORA: Telling him everything?

KROGSTAD: In as lenient a manner as I possibly could.

NORA: [*Quickly*] He mustn't get the letter. Tear it up. I will find some means of getting money.

KROGSTAD: Excuse me, Mrs. Helmer, but I think I told you just now—

NORA: I am not speaking of what I owe you. Tell me what sum you are asking my husband for, and I will get the money.

KROGSTAD: I am not asking your husband for a penny.

NORA: What do you want, then?

KROGSTAD: I will tell you. I want to rehabilitate myself, Mrs. Helmer; I want to get on; and in that your husband must help me. For the last year and a half I have not had a hand in anything dishonorable, and all that time I have been struggling in most restricted circumstances. I was content to work my way up step by step. Now I am turned out, and I am not going to be satisfied with merely being taken into favor again. I want to get on, I tell you. I want to get into the Bank again, in a higher position. Your husband will make a place for me—

NORA: That he will never do!

KROGSTAD: He will; I know him; he dare not protest. And as soon as I am in there again with him, then you will see! Within a year I shall be the manager's right hand. It will be Nils Krogstad and not Torvald Helmer who manages the Bank. [*Crisis. Now they move toward climax.*]

NORA: That's a thing you will never see!

KROGSTAD: Do you mean that you will—?

NORA: I have courage enough for it now.

KROGSTAD: Oh, you can't frighten me. A fine, spoilt lady like you—
NORA: You will see; you will see.
KROGSTAD: Under the ice, perhaps? Down into the cold, black water? And then, in the spring, to float up to the surface, all horrible and unrecognizable, with your hair fallen out—
NORA: You can't frighten me.
KROGSTAD: Nor you me. People don't do such things, Mrs. Helmer. Besides, what use would it be? I should have him completely in my power all the same.
NORA: Afterwards? When I am no longer—
KROGSTAD: Have you forgotten that it is I who have the keeping of your reputation? [*Nora stands speechlessly looking at him.*] Well, now, I have warned you. Do not do anything foolish. When Helmer has had my letter, I shall expect a message from him. And be sure you remember that it is your husband himself who has forced me into such ways as this again. I will never forgive him for that. Good-by, Mrs. Helmer. [*Exit through the hall.*]
NORA: [*Goes to the hall door, opens it slightly, and listens.*] He is going. He is not putting the letter in the box. Oh, no, no! that's impossible! [*Opens the door by degrees.*] What is that? He is standing outside. He is not going downstairs. Is he hesitating? Can he—? [*A letter drops into the box, then Krogstad's footsteps are heard, till they die away as he goes downstairs. Nora utters a stifled cry, and runs across the room to the table by the sofa. A short pause.*]
[*Climax.*]
NORA: In the letterbox. [*Steals across to the hall door.*] There it lies—Torvald, Torvald, there is no hope for us now! [*Resolution. Resignation—but since there is no absolute resignation while there is life, she will try again.*]

The precise moment of climax came when Krogstad dropped the letter into the mailbox.

Death is a climax. Before death is crisis, when there is hope —however slim it is. Between these two poles, transition. A turn for the worse in the patient's condition or an improvement will fill that space.

If you desire to depict how a man burns himself to death in bed through carelessness, first show him smoking, falling asleep, and the cigarette igniting a curtain. At this moment you've arrived at crisis. Why? Because the careless man might awaken and put out the fire, or someone might smell the burning material; and if neither of these happens, he'll burn to death. It is a matter of moments in this case, but crisis can be longer.

Crisis: a state of things in which a decisive change one way or the other is impending.

Now let us examine what causes a crisis and climax. We'll take *A Doll's House*, which the reader by now knows quite well. The climax was inherent in the premise: "Inequality in marriage breeds unhappiness." In the very beginning of the play, the author knew the end, so he could consciously select his characters to fulfill this premise. We have dealt with "plot" in the chapter, "Characters Plotting Their Own Play." We have shown how Nora was forced by necessity to forge her father's name and borrow from Krogstad to save Helmer's life. If Krogstad were simply a money-lender, the drama would have missed fire. But as it was, Krogstad was a thwarted individual; he had forged a signature, as Nora did, to save his family. The thing had been hushed up somehow, but he was stigmatized. He became a shady character, but he moved heaven and earth to clear his name for the sake of his family. He worked hard to rehabilitate himself in the eyes of the world. To be employed in a bank meant to Krogstad the road back to respectability.

This is how affairs stood with Krogstad when Nora approached him for money. He was lending money to others, so there was no reason why he should not lend to Nora. Besides, Helmer had been his schoolmate, although no love was lost between the two. Helmer snubbed Krogstad and was almost ashamed to know him, largely because of the rumor about his alleged forgery. It was a sweet revenge to Krogstad to see the wife of this scrupulously respectable man in the same predicament as he had been in. When Helmer got the managership in the bank and fired Krogstad, chiefly through principle, but also because Nora dared to think that she or anyone else could influence his sound judgment, Krogstad was aroused to fighting fury. Now he wanted more than money. Now he wanted to humiliate or destroy Helmer and get on in the world himself. He has the weapon in his hand and he will use it.

As you notice, the unity of opposites is perfect in this case. Nora is by now aware of the implications of her deed, but too horror-stricken to tell Helmer, because she knows now what Helmer thinks of such a serious breach of ethics. On the other hand, there is Krogstad who, besides being humiliated, sees the good name of his children jeopardized again and is ready to fight it out even if someone has to perish as a result.

This conflict cannot be bridged by compromise. Nora offers money, as much as Krogstad is willing to name, but Krogstad is by now thoroughly aroused, and no money will suffice. He will have to be vindicated. Helmer wanted to destroy him, so he will destroy Helmer.

This unbreakable bond between the parties will ensure rising conflict, crisis, and climax. The crisis was inherent from the very beginning of the play; the choosing of these particular characters predicated it. But—the climax can still be ruined if any character weakens for some reason or other. If Helmer's love would have been greater than his responsibility, he would have listened to Nora's pleading and let Krogstad keep his job in the bank. But Helmer is Helmer, and he runs true to form.

As we see, crisis and climax follow each other, the last one always on a higher plane than the one before.

A single scene contains the exposition of premise for that particular scene, exposition of character, conflict, transition, crisis, climax, and conclusion. This procedure should be repeated as many times as there are scenes in your play, in an ascending scale. Let us examine the first scene of *Ghosts,* to see whether this is so.

After the curtain rises, we find Engstrand standing near the garden door, with Regina blocking his way.

REGINA: [*Below her breath*] What is it you want? Stay where you are. The rain is dripping off you.
ENGSTRAND: God's good rain, my girl.
REGINA: The devil's own rain, that's what it is.

The first three lines establish the antagonism between these two. Every line thereafter lets us know the relationship between them, as well as their physical, sociological, and psychological make-up. We learn that Regina is healthy, good-looking, and that Engstrand is crippled, with a flair for exaggeration and a taste for liquor. We learn that he has had many schemes for bettering his position—all of which had failed. We learn that his current premise is to open a lodging for sailors, with Regina to serve as a lure, making the dubious patrons pay for her favors. We discover that Engstrand almost killed his wife with his temper. We learn further that Regina's education has been improved in the service of the Alvings; that she and Oswald have some attachment; that she is supposed to be teaching at the orphanage for which Engstrand works.

In these first five pages one can see the perfect co-ordination of the elements we listed earlier. Engstrand's *premise* is to take Regina home with him, regardless of consequences. Regina's premise is to stay. His motivation is to use her in his business, hers is to marry Oswald. The characters are made known to us (*exposition*) through conflict. Every line spoken throws light on their traits and relationships. The very first line starts the *conflict* which culminates when Regina wins.

Transition is perfect in the small conflict between Regina's desire to stay and Engstrand's determination that she shall leave. Watch closely the lines from the opening until he divulges his desire to take her home. From there, trace the movement until Regina becomes indignant, remembering the names he used to call her; from there until he tells her his plan for a "high-class eating place"; and from there, to the point where he advises her to take money from the sailors as her mother did. *Crisis* sets in right after his advice, and the *climax* follows rapidly.

REGINA: [*Advancing toward him*] Get out!
ENGSTRAND: [*Stepping back*] Here! Here!— You're not going to hit me, I suppose?
REGINA: Yes! If you talk like that of Mother, I will hit you. Get out, I tell you! [*Rushes him up to the garden door.*]

The climax has come about naturally, and the resolution is apparent before Engstrand leaves. He reminds her that she is his daughter, according to the Register, implying that he can force her to go home with him. Yes, here again are all the elements we were discussing before.

The next scene, between Manders and Regina, immediately follows the first scene and also contains all that is necessary. The climax comes when she offers herself to him, and poor timid Manders, in a panic, says: "Perhaps you will be so kind as to let Mrs. Alving know I am here?"

You will discover sharply defined climaxes throughout *Ghosts*.

Nature works dialectically; she never jumps. In nature all the dramatis personae are well orchestrated. The unity of opposites is ironbound, and the crisis and climax come in waves.

The human body is swarming with bacteria, which are kept by the white corpuscles from doing harm. The healthy body is the scene of many crises and climaxes. But if the resistance of the body is lowered, and the number of white corpuscles diminished, the bacteria multiply alarmingly and make themselves felt. There is constantly rising conflict between the germs and the defensive corpuscles. The crisis comes when the defensive forces are in full retreat, and it seems that the body is doomed. Just as in a play, there is the great question of whether or not the protagonist (the body) will be destroyed. The white corpuscles, although weakened, go into an offensive drive, and the body girds itself for a final decisive battle. The deadliest of all bacteria fighters steps into the fight—fever. The bacteria created the fever, and it now steps in on the side of the body. This last crisis has led to the climax, in which the body is willing to die fighting. If the body does die, we have the conclusion—burial. If the body recovers, we have the conclusion just the same—recovery.

A man steals: conflict. He is pursued: rising conflict. He is caught: crisis. He is condemned by the court: climax. Transferring him to prison is the conclusion.

It is interesting to note that "a man steals" is a climax in itself, as is "courtship" or "conception." Even a minor climax can lead up to the major climax of a play or a life.

There is no beginning and no end. Everything in nature goes on and on. And so, in a play, the opening is not the beginning of a conflict, but the culmination of one. A decision was made, and the character experienced an inner climax. He acts upon his decision, starting a conflict which rises, changing as it goes, becoming a crisis and a climax.

We are quite certain that the universe is homogeneous in its composition. The stars, the sun, even other suns millions of miles away, are composed of the same elements as our earth. All the ninety-two elements found in our insignificant globe can be found in the light rays which travel three thousand light-years to reach us. A man contains these same elements. So does a protozoon—and everything else in nature.

The difference between star and star is the same as that between man and man: age, abundance of light, heat, and so on, depending upon the proportion of these various elements in them. The knowledge of one star brings us closer to the knowledge of all stars. Take a drop from the ocean and you will find that it contains the same elements that constitute all oceans.

The same principle holds true for human beings—and for the drama. The shortest scene contains all the elements of a three-act play. It has its own premise which is exposed through conflict between the characters. The conflict grows through transition to crisis and climax. Crisis and climax are as periodical in a play as exposition is constant.

Let us ask the question once more: what is crisis? And we answer, "Turning point; also a state of things in which a decisive change one way or the other is impending."

In *A Doll's House* the main crisis occurs when Helmer finds the letter from Krogstad and learns the truth. What will he do? Help Nora in her predicament? Will he understand the motivation of her act? Or, true to his character, will he condemn her? We don't know. Although we know Helmer's attitude toward such things, we also know that he loves Nora a great deal. This uncertainty will then be the crisis.

The climax, the culminating point, comes when Helmer, instead of understanding, bursts into an uncontrollable fury. The conclusion will be Nora's decision to leave Helmer.

The resolutions in *Hamlet, Macbeth,* and *Othello* are short. Almost immediately after the climax, the promise of punishment and a just future brings down the curtain. In *A Doll's House,* the resolution takes the better half of the last act. Which is better? There can be no set rule on this point, if the playwright can maintain the conflict, as Ibsen did in *A Doll's House.*

IV

GENERAL

◇◇◇

1. Obligatory Scene

A SCIENTIST died the other day—a man who added to the world's knowledge. Let me tell you about his life, and then I want you to tell me which phase of his history was most important.

He was conceived. He was born healthy, but when he was four years old, he became ill of typhoid fever. As a result, his heart was weakened. When the boy was seven, his father died, and his mother was forced to work in a factory. The neighbors cared for him, but he suffered from malnutrition.

Wandering alone through the streets one day he ran in front of a car. Both his legs were broken, and he was confined to bed, first at the hospital, then at home. He whiled away the hours by reading more than the average boy of his age. At ten he read philosophy; at fourteen he decided to be a chemist. His mother worked hard, but could not afford to send him to school.

He was well now, and he ran errands so that he might attend night school. At seventeen he won twenty-five dollars for an essay on biochemistry. When he was eighteen he met a man who recognized his potentialities and sent him to college.

He progressed rapidly, but his benefactor was angry when the young man fell in love and married. With financial support withdrawn, the boy managed to obtain work as a laborer in a chemical factory. At twenty he was a father, with a salary

far too small to support his family. He undertook additional
work and broke down. His wife left him with the child and
went back to her family. He was bitter, contemplated suicide,
but by twenty-five we find him back at night school, complet-
ing his studies. His wife had divorced him, and his weak heart
was troubling him.

At thirty he remarried. The woman, five years his senior,
was a teacher who understood his ambitions. He built a small
laboratory at home and went to work on his theories. Success
came almost immediately. A big company encouraged him in
his inventions, and when he died at sixty, he was acknowl-
edged the most prolific inventor of his time.

Now, which was the most important phase of his life?

YOUNG LADY: Meeting the schoolteacher, of course. This gave
him the chance to experiment—and succeed.

I: What about the accident which broke his legs? He might
have been killed.

YOUNG LADY: True. If he had died, there wouldn't have been
any success story. This is an important phase too.

I: How about his wife's divorcing him?

YOUNG LADY: I see. If she hadn't divorced him, he couldn't
have remarried.

I: He had a breakdown, remember. If he hadn't, she might
have never thought of divorce. If his heart hadn't been
weakened by typhoid, he might have been able to hold several jobs at once, and his wife would not have left him. He
might have had more children and remained a laborer. Now
which phase was most important?

YOUNG LADY: His birth.

I: What about the conception of the child?

YOUNG LADY: I see. Of course, that was the most important
phase.

I: Just a second: suppose his mother had died carrying him in
her womb?

YOUNG LADY: What are you driving at?

I: I am trying to find the most important phase of this man's life.

YOUNG LADY: It seems to me that there is no such thing as a most important phase, since each phase grows out of the one before it. Every phase is equally important.

I: Isn't it true, then, that each phase is the result of many events at a specific time?

YOUNG LADY: Yes.

I: Each phase, then, is dependent on the one before it?

YOUNG LADY: It seems so.

I: Then we can safely say that there is no phase which is more important than the others?

YOUNG LADY: Yes—but why are you taking this roundabout way to our discussion of the obligatory scene?

I: Because all textbook writers seem to agree that the obligatory scene is the scene which a play must have. It is expected. It is the scene for which everyone is waiting, the scene which has been promised throughout and which cannot be eliminated. In other words, the play builds to an inevitable scene which will tower over all the others. There is such a scene in *A Doll's House* when Helmer takes the letter out of the mailbox.

YOUNG LADY: Don't you approve of it?

I: I don't approve of the concept, because every scene in a play is obligatory. Do you understand why?

YOUNG LADY: Why?

I: Because if Helmer hadn't been ill, Nora wouldn't have forged the signature, Krogstad would have had no excuse to come to the house demanding money, there would have been no complications, Krogstad never would have written the letter, Helmer would never have opened it, and—

YOUNG LADY: What you say is true, but I agree with Lawson when he says: "No play can fail to provide a point of concentration toward which the maximum expectation is aroused."

1: True, but misleading. If a play has a premise, only the proving of the premise should create a "point of concentration
toward which the maximum expectation is aroused." What
are we interested in, anyway—an obligatory scene or the
proving of the premise? Since the play grew from the premise, naturally the proving of the premise will be the "obligatory scene." Many obligatory scenes misfired because there
was an ambiguous premise or no premise at all, and the
audience had nothing to wait for.

"Ruthless ambition destroys itself" is the premise of *Macbeth. The proving of this premise will provide a "point of
concentration toward which the maximum expectation is
aroused."* Every action brings forth a reaction. Ruthlessness
carries in itself its own destruction—to prove this is obligatory. If for any reason this natural sequence is delayed or
omitted, the play will suffer.

There is no moment in a play which does not grow from
the one before it. Any scene should be supreme in its moment. Only an integrated scene has the vitality to make us
eager for the next. The difference between scenes is that the
vehemence of each should mount over that of the last. If we
consider only the obligatory scene, we might be likely to concentrate on just one tense scene in a play, forgetting that the
scenes before it need equal attention. Each scene contains the
same elements as the whole.

The play as a whole will rise continuously, reaching a pitch
which will be the culmination of the entire drama. This scene
will be more tense than any other, but not to the detriment
of any previous scene, or the play will suffer.

The success of the scientist we were talking about can be
measured only by the steps leading up to it. Any phase of his
life might have been the last one, culminating in failure or
death. Lawson writes: "The obligatory scene is the immediate goal toward which the play is driving." Not true. The im-

mediate goal is the proving of the premise, and nothing else. Statements like Lawson's will obscure the issue.

The scientist wished to succeed, just as a play must prove its premise, but there are issues at hand which must be dealt with first, and as well as possible. The obligatory scene must not be treated as an independent issue. Character and its determinants must be taken into account. "The climax has its roots in the social conception. The obligatory scene is rooted in activity, it is the physical outgrowth of the conflict," says Lawson.

All activity, physical or otherwise, must have its roots in social conception. A flower is not buried in the soil, but it would not exist if it had not grown on a stem with roots in the soil. Not one but many obligatory scenes created the final clash, the main crisis—the proving of the premise—which Lawson and others mistakenly call the obligatory scene.

2. *Exposition*

There is a mistaken idea that exposition is another name for the beginning of a play. Textbook writers tell us that we must establish mood, atmosphere, background, before our action begins. They tell us how characters should make their entrances, what they should say, how they should behave to impress and hold the audience. And while all this seems very helpful at first, it leads to confusion.

What does *Webster's* say?

Exposition: a setting forth of the meaning or purpose of a writing; designed to carry information.

And March's *Thesaurus?*

Exposition: the act of exposing.

Now then, what do we want to expose? The premise? The atmosphere? The character's background? The plot? The scenery? The mood? The answer is, we must expose all these at once.

If we choose only "atmosphere," the question arises almost immediately: who lives in this atmosphere? If we answer: a lawyer from New York, we are a step nearer to establishing the atmosphere.

If we pursue the question further, and ask what kind of man this lawyer is, we shall learn that he is a man of integrity, uncompromising, and a failure. We shall learn that his father was a tailor who lived in poverty so that his son might become a professional man. Without once mentioning "atmosphere" in the questions we ask ourselves, and the answers we give, we shall be on the way to establishing it. If we become still more inquisitive about this lawyer, we shall find out everything about him: his friends, ambitions, station in life, immediate premise, and mood at the time.

The more we know about the man, the more we shall know about the mood, locale, atmosphere, background, and plot.

It would seem, then, that what we want to expose is the character of whom we are writing. We want the audience to know *his goal*, since through knowing what he wants they will know a lot about what he is. We need not expose the mood, or any of the other stock subjects. They are an integral part of the whole play; they are established when the character tries to prove his premise.

"Exposition" itself is part of the whole play, and not simply a fixture to be used at the beginning and then discarded. Yet textbooks on writing deal with exposition as if it were a separate element in dramatic construction.

Moreover, "exposition" should proceed constantly, without interruption, to the very end of the play.

In the beginning of *A Doll's House* Nora exposes herself through conflict as a naïve, spoiled child who doesn't know much about the outside world. Ibsen achieves this without having a servant tell the new butler who their masters are while instructing him how to behave. There are no telephone conversations informing the audience that Mr. X has such a fiery temper that heaven knows what he will do if he hears what is happening.

Reading aloud a letter to expose the background of a character is also a poor device. All these makeshift tricks are not only bad but unnecessary.

When Krogstad enters to demand money from Nora, the ensuing threat, her reaction to this threat, reveal unmistakably who Krogstad and Nora are. They expose themselves through conflict—and will expose themselves throughout the play.

Says George Pierce Baker:

First we arouse emotion in an audience by mere physical action; by physical action which also develops the story, or illustrates character, or does both.

In a good play physical action must do both of those things and many, many more.

Percival Wilde, in his *Craftsmanship*, writes of "Exposition":

Closely akin to the establishment of mood is the creation of atmosphere.

Make this advice specific and you have something like this: "In your play about starving share-croppers, be sure not to have them wear full-dress. It is better to put them in rags and show them in their tumbledown shacks to establish atmosphere. Insist that the costume designer avoid the use of diamonds, lest it give the impression of wealth and thus confuse the audience."

Mr. Wilde continues with this crowning piece of advice:

Action may always be interrupted by exposition when the latter is of the same or of a greater degree of interest.

But if you read any good play, you will notice that the *exposition is uninterrupted, continuous to the drop of the last curtain.* Moreover, by action he means conflict.

Whatever a character does, or does not do, whatever he says or does not say, reveals him. If he decides to conceal his identity, if he lies or tells the truth, if he steals or does not steal, he is forever revealing himself. The moment you stop exposition in any part of a play, the character stops growing, and, with it, the play.

"Exposition," as the word is generally used, is misleading. If our great writers had taken the advice of the "authorities," and confined exposition to the opening of the play, or to odd spots between action, the greatest characters would have died stillborn. Helmer's big exposition scene comes at the end of the play—and could not have come anywhere else. Mrs. Alving kills her son at the end of *Ghosts* because we have seen her growth through uninterrupted exposition. Nor does it end there. Mrs. Alving could go on for the rest of her life, exposing herself constantly, as everyone does.

What most teachers call exposition, we prefer to call "point of attack."

QUESTION: I, for my part, accept your suggestion. But I see no harm in using "atmosphere, mood, and setting," if those terms clarify things for the beginner.

ANSWER: But they clarify nothing. They confuse. If you worry about mood, you will neglect character study. William Archer says, in his *Playmaking:*

. . . The art of so unfolding the drama of the past as to make the gradual revelation no mere preface or prologue to the drama of the present, but an integral part of its action.

If you follow this advice, you cannot stop here, there, anywhere, because your character is always involved in vital action, and action, any kind of action (conflict), is exposition of a character. If for any reason a character is not in conflict, the exposition—as everything else in the play—stops right then and there. In other words, conflict is really "exposition."

3. Dialogue

Students of my playwriting class submitted papers on "Dialogue." Miss Jeanne Michael wrote one which was so clear cut, terse, and to the point that we feel we must quote from it. Here it is:

In a play, dialogue is the chief means by which the premise is proved, the characters revealed, and the conflict carried. It is vital that the dialogue be good, since it is the part of the play which is most apparent to the audience.

But the playwright, acknowledging that a play is not good with poor dialogue, must also acknowledge that really fine dialogue is impossible unless it follows clearly and validly from the character that uses it; unless it serves to show, naturally and without strain, what has happened to the characters that is important to the action of the play.

Only a rising conflict will produce healthy dialogue. We have all experienced the long, dull period when characters sit about on a stage, talking endlessly, trying to fill the space between one conflict and the next. If the author had provided the necessary transition, there would have been no need for this bridge of chitchat. And no matter how clever connective dialogue is, it is always very shaky because it has no solid foundation.

On the other hand, we have the shallow dialogue which results from static conflict. Neither of the opponents is going to win this motionless battle, and their dialogue has no place to go. One witty thrust immediately capped by another throws neither of the combatants over, and the characters—although it is a rare "witty" play that has living characters—freeze into standard types that never grow. The characters and dialogue in high comedy are often of this nature, which is why so few society dramas are lasting plays.

Dialogue must reveal character. Every speech should be the product of the speaker's three dimensions, telling us what he is, hinting at what he will be. Shakespeare's characters grow throughout, but they do not startle us, since their first speeches suggest the stuff of which the last will be made. So, when Shylock shows himself avaricious in his first appearance, we are justified in suspecting that his behavior at the end will be the result of his avariciousness in conflict with the forces around it.

We have no notebooks left by Shakespeare or Sophocles, describing their protagonists. We have no diary written by the Prince of Denmark or the King of Thebes. But we have pages of dynamic dialogue telling most clearly how Hamlet thought, what Oedipus' problem was.

Dialogue must reveal background. The first lines spoken by Sophocles' Antigone are:

> Sister, mine own dear sister! O Ismene!
> Of all the ills bequeathed by Oedipus
> What is there Zeus yet faileth to fulfill
> On us twain while we live?

conveying immediately the relationship between the characters, their ancestry, their religious beliefs, and their mood at the moment.

Clifford Odets handles this function of dialogue expertly in the opening scene of *Awake and Sing*, when Ralphie says: "All my life I wanted a pair of black and white shoes and I can't get them. It's crazy." There you have economic background, as well as something of his personality. Dialogue must give this, and it must begin to give it from the moment the curtain goes up.

Dialogue must foreshadow coming events. In the murder

play there must be motivation and often preparatory information as to the actual crime. For instance:

The sweet young thing kills the villain with a bill file. Simple enough? Not unless you show logically that the girl in some way knew of the existence of the file and knew that it was sharp—else it might not occur to her to use it as a weapon. And her original discovery of the file and its potentialities must be dialectically valid, not casual. It must be within her character to handle the weapon—and to comment if she sticks herself with it. The audience likes to know what is going on, and dialogue is one of the best ways of giving information.

Dialogue, then, grows from the character and the conflict, and, in its turn, reveals the character and carries the action. These are its basic functions, but they merely open the subject. There are many things the playwright must know to keep his dialogue from falling flat.

Save words. Art is selective, not photographic, and your point will carry further if unhampered by unnecessary verbiage. A "talky" play is the sign of internal trouble—trouble coming from poor preliminary work. A play is talky because the characters have ceased to grow and the conflict has stopped moving. Hence the dialogue can only mill around and around, boring the audience and forcing the director to devise business for the actors, in the vain hope of diverting the unfortunate playgoers.

Sacrifice "brilliance" for character, if need be, rather than character for brilliance. Dialogue must come from the character, and no bon mot is worth the death of a character you have created. It is possible to have lively, clever, moving dialogue without the loss of a single growing character.

Let the man speak in the language of his own world. Let the mechanic speak in terms of machines, and the race-track tout of bets and horses. Don't carry occupational imagery to ridiculous lengths, but don't try to do without it, or any dialogue you achieve will be shallow and worthless. Mixing imagery is a device which may be successfully employed in burlesque. It is rib-tickling for prim Aunt Miranda to use the underworld idiom in low comedy, but it would be painful in serious drama.

Don't be pedantic. Never use your play as a soapbox. Have a message, by all means, but have it naturally and subtly. Don't let your protagonist break out of character and make a speech. The audience will quiver in embarrassed empathy and take refuge in laughter.

The plea for reform of social injustice and class tyranny has been voiced from Elizabeth's day to ours—and well voiced. The cry must be in keeping with the character who makes it and the provocation of the moment. In *Bury the Dead*, the command to rise against war comes from a poverty-created shrew, Martha Webster. It is not incongruous, but fitting and heartbreaking.

And in Paul Green's *Hymn to the Rising Sun* we see how competent exposition removes completely the need for sermons. Mr. Green's simple, tense dialogue is the vehicle for cutting satire of character and situation.

The action occurs in the hour before sunrise on the fourth day of July, in a chain-gang camp. One of the convicts, a newcomer, cannot work or sleep in his horror over the fate of the Runt, who has been imprisoned in the sweatbox for eleven days on bread and water rations, for masturbation. The climax of action and irony comes when the new prisoner, upon the captain's orders, turns his voice from the shrieks of the beating just administered to "harden him up" to the strains of *America*. The Runt is taken from the box, dead, and the report is made: "Dead of natural causes." The gang shuffles off to work while the impassive, elderly cook croaks *America*. That is all. There is no word of condemnation for the law that advocates such inhumanity. Rather, there is the captain's oration, given in his blunt, straightforward manner, explaining the rigors of the chain gang. Yet the play is a most fierce indictment of this portion of the United States' penal code.

You need not make a speech to make a protest.

Make clever language truly part of the play. Remember that your drama is not a vaudeville skit. "Gags" for their own sake ruin continuity. Only complete compatibility with the speaker can justify them, and they must fulfill some function besides "getting a laugh." The Shakespeare of *The Comedy of Errors* has the Dromios speak mainly in very bad puns, adding nothing to the play. But in *Othello* he has learned to use wordplay as an integral part of the whole. "Put out the light, and then put out the light," Othello says before the murder, thus suggesting both the events and his reaction to them.

Kids Learn Fast is dotted with applied humor. Mr. Shifrin has certain things to say which he says in his own words, put into the mouths of babes. "The sheriff always comes the day after the lynching"; "Mississippi, Tennessee, Georgia, Florida, it makes no difference, it's always the nigger what's chased and everything." These are not the natural language of the children he has sketched.

We have discussed so far the dialectics of dialogue in that it grows from character and conflict which must be dialectical to exist. But dialogue must also be dialectical in itself, in the small degree to which it can be divorced from its mates. It must work within itself on the principle of slowly rising conflict. When you name several things you save the most impressive for last. "The Mayor," you say, "was there, and the Governor—and the President!" Even the voice recognizes growth: one, *two*, THREE, we say; not ONE, *two*, three. There is that classic reversal which warns against murder since it may lead to drinking, which in turn may lead to smoking, which may lead to nonobservance of the Sabbath, etc. This is good humor, but bad drama.

One of the finest examples of dialectical growth in dialogue can be found in an otherwise poor play, *Idiot's Delight* (Act II, Scene II).

IRENE: [*Talking to the munitions magnate*] . . . I have to run away from the terror of my own thoughts. So I amuse myself by studying the faces of the people I see. Just ordinary, casual, dull people. [*She is speaking in a tone that is sweetly sadistic.*] That young English couple, for instance. I was watching them during dinner, sitting there, close together, holding hands, and rubbing their knees together under the table. And I saw him in his nice, smart, British uniform, shooting a little pistol at a huge tank. And the tank rolls over him. And his fine, strong body, that was so full of the capacity for ecstasy, is a mass of mashed flesh and bones—a smear of purple blood—like a stepped-on snail. But before the moment of death he consoles himself by thinking, "Thank God *she* is safe! She is bearing the child I gave her, and he will live to see a better world." . . . But I know where she is. She is lying in a cellar that has been wrecked by an air raid, and her firm young breasts are all mixed up with the bowels of a dismembered policeman, and the embryo from her womb is splattered against the face of a dead bishop. That is the kind of thought with which I amuse myself, Achille. And it makes me so proud to think that I am so close to you—who make all this possible.

Mr. Sherwood builds from "A tone that is sweetly sadistic" to a tragedy. He tops that by a hope quickly made more tragic by its irony. That irony is a description more terrible than the one before. And then the final peak of self-loathing, conscious degradation, conscious participation in the horror. No other arrangement could have been as effective. Anticlimax would have been inevitable and disastrous.

Just as conflict must come from character, and the sense of the speech from both, so must the sound of the speech come from all the others. The sentences must build up as the play builds up, conveying the rhythm and meaning of each scene by sound as well as sense. Here again, Shakespeare is our best

example. The sentences in his philosophical passages are
weighty and measured; in his love scenes lines are lyrical and
flow easily. Then, with the mounting of action, sentences become shorter and simpler, so that not only the sentence content, but the word and syllable content, vary with the development of the play.

The dialectical method does not rob the playwright of his
creative privilege. Once your characters have been set in motion, their path and their speech are determined, to a great
extent; but the choice of character is completely your own.
Consider, therefore, the idiom your people will employ, and
their voices, and methods of delivery. Think of their personalities, and backgrounds, and the influence of these on their
speech. Orchestrate your characters, and their dialogue will
take care of itself. When you laugh at *The Bear,* remember
that Chekhov gained his bombast and ridiculous dignity from
a bombastic character played against a ridiculously dignified
one. And in *Riders to the Sea,* John Millington Synge sways
us to the tragic yet lovely rhythm of people who employ
harmonious rhythms which are not identical. Maurya, Nora,
Cathleen, and Bartley all use the accent of the Aran Islanders.
But Bartley is swaggering, Cathleen patient, Nora quick with
youth, and Maurya slow with age. The combination is one of
the most beautiful in English.

One thing more. Do not overemphasize dialogue. Remember that it is the medium of the play, but not greater than
the whole. It must fit into the play without jarring. In the
production of *Iron Men,* Norman Bel Geddes was criticized
for his excellent set, showing the actual building of a sky-
scraper on the stage. It was too good a set for the play, and
distracted any attention that might have been directed to the
characters. Dialogue often does this, breaking away from the
character and diverting attention to itself. *Paradise Lost,* for
instance, disappointed many of Odets' admirers by its wordi-

ness. There are gratuitous speeches throughout, departures
from the true idiom of the characters, inserted so that the
dialogue might be accented. Both characters and dialogue
suffered.

In summary, then: good dialogue is the product of characters carefully chosen and permitted to grow dialectically,
until the slowly rising conflict has proved the premise.

4. Experimentation

QUESTION: I don't see how anyone can experiment, with the
rigid rules you lay down. According to your warning, if
an unfortunate playwright omits any one of the ingredients you say a play must contain, the consequences will be
dire. Don't you know that man makes rules just to break
them—and that he often gets away with it?

ANSWER: Yes, we know. You can do almost anything with
this approach—experiment to your heart's content; just
as a man can go under water, fly, live in the arctics or the
tropics. But he cannot live without his heart or lungs, and
you cannot write a good play without the basic ingredients.
Shakespeare was one of the most daring experimenters of
his day. To break any one of Aristotle's three unities was
a major crime, yet Shakespeare broke all three: the unities
of time, place, and action. Every great writer, painter, musician, has broken some ironclad rule which was held sacred.

QUESTION: You are strengthening my argument.

ANSWER: Then examine the work of these men. You'll find
character development through conflict. They broke all
rules—save the fundamental ones. They built on character.
A three-dimensional character is the foundation of all good
plays. You'll see perpetual transition in their work. And
above all, you'll find direction: a clear-cut premise. Further-

more, if you know what to look for, you'll find sharp orchestration as well. They were dialectical, without knowing it.

There are no two men who talk alike, think alike, speak alike. And there are no two men who write alike. You are very wrong if you imagine that the dialectical approach tries to force every man's play into the same mold. On the contrary, we ask you not to confuse originality with trickery. *Do not look for special effects, surprises, atmosphere, mood, without knowing that all of them, and more, are in the character.* Experiment as you choose—but within the laws of nature. Anything can be created within these laws. It is interesting to know that stars are born as men are: the attraction of opposites brings forth a nebulous form of matter which will evolve if conditions are favorable. Transition is prevalent there, too. Every nebula, every star, every sun, is different, but their composition of elements is the same. Stars are as dependent upon each other as humans. If their relationship were not fixed, they would collide almost instantaneously, destroying each other. The stars have vagabonds, too—comets, but they are controlled by the same laws. Now, since everything is dependent upon everything else, characters are also dependent upon each other. They must have certain basic elements in common —the three dimensions. Beyond that, you can experiment as you choose. You can emphasize one trait above another; you can enlarge details; you can deal with the subconscious; you can try a variety of effects in form. You can do anything conceivable, as long as you represent character.

QUESTION: How would you classify William Saroyan's *My Heart's in the Highlands?*

ANSWER: As an experiment, of course.

QUESTION: Do you think it is a good play?

ANSWER: No. It is divorced from life. The characters live in a vacuum.

QUESTION: Then you disapprove of it?

ANSWER: Emphatically no. Every experiment, no matter how
bad the results, is worth the labor put into it in the long
view. Nature, too, is experimenting constantly. If the ex-
perimental creation miscarries, it is done away with, but
not before all the possibilities of improvement have been
exhausted. If you know anything about natural history, you
will have been struck by the way in which nature tries
every conceivable method of expressing herself.

When Matisse, Gauguin, Picasso, experimented with
painting, they did not throw away the basic principles of
composition. Rather, they reaffirmed them. One empha-
sized color, another form, the third design, but each built
on the rock bottom of composition, which is contradiction
in lines and in color.

In a bad play, people live as if they were self-sufficient,
alone in the world. A comet is not self-sufficient, nor is a
vagabond, who must beg, steal, or borrow to live. Everything in nature and in society is dependent on other things,
whether it be an actor, the sun, or an insect.

Here is an experiment that nature performed with a tree.
As you know, a tree grows toward the sun, despite obstacles.
But it happened, once, that an acorn dropped into a crevice
of a perpendicular rock. The seed sprouted, became a sapling, and was normal except that it grew horizontally instead of toward the sun. The rocky bed gave it no chance
to straighten out. After a while it managed to turn upward,
having grown out from under its rocky roof, but it became
top-heavy and seemed sure to crash. Then a miraculous
thing happened. One of the top branches turned back
toward the hillside, dug into another crevice, and secured
a foothold. Another branch followed the first, and still another, until the tree was well supported. *This so-called experiment by nature is no experiment at all, because it happened under the inescapable force of necessity.* Necessity

makes characters do things they would never think of doing under normal circumstances.

Artists and writers experiment because they feel that it is necessary for them to do so if they are fully to express their characters. Their experimentation, even if we refuse to accept it, is good, because we learn from it.

We want to emphasize over and over again that nature is invariably dialectical in all her manifestations. Even that tree we spoke of before had a premise. There was orchestration between the tree and gravity. There was conflict between gravity and the tree's will to live. There was transition in the growth of the tree, the action of the branches. There was crisis and climax, and resolution in the tree's victory. What nature did with a tree a playwright can do with characters. He can experiment if he follows the fundamental principles of dialectics.

5. *The Timeliness of a Play*

QUESTION: I agree with most of the things you've told me about playwriting. But what about the selection of a timely subject? We may find a clean-cut, legitimate premise, which promises plenty of conflict, and yet have a manager turn it down because it is not timely.

ANSWER: The moment you start to worry about the opinion the managers will have of your play, you are lost. If you have a deep-rooted conviction, write it, regardless of what the public and the managers think. The moment you try to think with another man's head, you might as well stop writing. If your play is good, the public will like it.

QUESTION: Isn't it true that there are subjects which are timely while others are not?

ANSWER: Everything is timely if it is well written. Human values remain the same if they grow naturally out of the

forces around them. Human lives have always been precious, and always will be. A man of Aristotle's day, portrayed honestly, and in his environment, can be as exciting
as any man of today. We are given the chance to contrast
his day with ours. We can see the progress which has been
made since then, and guess the road ahead of us. Haven't
you ever seen an up-to-the-minute play which was as dull
as two mothers reciting the virtues of their offspring? But
Abe Lincoln in Illinois, by Robert E. Sherwood, is important for today; *The Little Foxes,* by Lillian Hellman,
which takes place in the early nineteen hundreds, is superior to the crop of that year for the simple reason that
the characters have been given a chance to grow. *Family
Portrait* concerns Jesus' family and is not exactly spot news,
but it is exciting. On the other hand, there is *The American Way* by Kaufman and Hart, and *No Time for Comedy,*
by S. N. Behrman. Both deal with actual and burning issues
of the day, yet neither is new nor alive. Plays which are
valid and well written, like *A Doll's House,* will reflect
their time forever.

QUESTION: I still feel some topics are more timely than others.
For instance, the plays of Noel Coward are about useless
people who neither add to nor subtract from the main
stream of progress. Is it worth while to write of such people?

ANSWER: Yes—but in better plays, of course. Coward hasn't
a single real character in his plays. If he had created tridimensional characters; if he had penetrated their backgrounds, their motivations, their relationship with society,
their premises, their disappointments, the plays would have
been worth seeing.

Although literature has been dealing with man for hundreds of years, we only began to understand character in
the nineteenth century. Shakespeare, Molière, Lessing,
even Ibsen, knew character instinctively rather than sci-
entifically. Aristotle declared that character was second-

ary to action. Archer said that it must be in an author to penetrate character. Still other authorities admit that character is a mystery to them. It is pleasant to know that science provides a precedent for our disagreement with Aristotle and his interpreters. Millikan, one of the greatest American scientists, Nobel prize winner, stated a few years ago that the conversion of atomic energy to use was a pipe dream, never to be realized, because we are forced to use more energy in breaking down the atom than we can ever hope to get out of it. But now another Nobel prize winner, Arthur H. Compton, declares that actino-uranium, if completely converted into energy, would yield two hundred and thirty-five billion volts per atom. Actino-uranium breaks up into two gigantic atomic bullets of one hundred million volts each upon bombardment with a neutron carrying an energy of only about one fortieth of a volt, thus releasing eight billion times more energy than was originally put in. Character possesses limitless energy, too, but many playwrights have yet to learn how to release it and use it for their purposes. Wherever there is a man, whether it be in the past, present, or future, there can be an important play—provided the character is portrayed in all its three dimensions.

QUESTION: Then there is no difference what era I tackle, if I realize tridimensional characters?

ANSWER: When you say tridimensional, we hope you understand that environment is included, and that that means a thorough knowledge, on your part, of the customs, morals, philosophy, art, and language of that time. If you write, for instance, of the fifth century B.C., you must know that era as you are supposed to know your own. Personally, we suggest that you stay here, in the twentieth century, perhaps in your own town or city, and write about people whom you know. Your task will be much easier. The timeliness of your play will be timeless if you realize your characters in their physical, sociological, and psychological dimensions.

6. Entrances and Exits

QUESTION: I have a friend, a playwright, who has a great deal of difficulty with entrances and exits. Can you give a few pointers on this?

ANSWER: Tell him to integrate his characters more thoroughly than he has done.

QUESTION: How do you know he didn't integrate them?

ANSWER: When you find the floor near the windows wet after a rainstorm, it is logical to suppose that the windows were open during the downpour. Trouble with entrances and exits indicates that the playwright doesn't know his characters well enough. When the curtain rises in *Ghosts*, we find Engstrand and his daughter, who serves at the Alving house, on the stage. Almost at once she warns him not to talk loud enough to wake Oswald, who has arrived home from Paris tired. Besides, she feels that it is not Engstrand's business how long Oswald sleeps, when the old man comments. He suggests, slyly, that she may have designs on Oswald. Regina is furious, indicating the truth of the thrust. This conversation, besides its other virtues, prepares us for Oswald's entrance later. We learn from Engstrand that Manders is in the city, and from Regina that he is expected at any moment. Manders' entrance is well grounded, but it is not a device. There is every reason, in the play, for Manders' appearance at this time. Regina pushes Engstrand out, and Manders enters. She has much to say to him—none of it idle chatter. The talk is deeply integrated and grows from the previous scene. Manders is forced to call Mrs. Alving, in order to escape from Regina's insinuations. In the pause before she enters he picks up a book—a gesture which motivates an important scene to come. Mrs. Alving enters, in answer to Manders' call. We have had two entrances and two exits thus far, each a necessary part of the play. Before Oswald actually enters, there is much more talk of him, so that we look forward to his entrance.

QUESTION: I see the point. But not everyone is an Ibsen. We write differently today. The tempo of our plays is more swift. We have no time for such elaborate preparation.

ANSWER: In Ibsen's time there were almost as many playwrights as there are today. How many of them can you name? What happened to the others, who wrote popular but bad plays? They've been forgotten, as will all those who think as you do. Yes, times have changed, customs have changed, but man still has a heart and lungs. Your tempo may change, *should change, but motivation must remain.* The cause and the effect may be different from the cause and effect of a century ago, but they must be present, clearly and logically. Environment, for instance, was a vital influence. It still is. It was bad to send a character out of the room for a glass of water merely so that two other characters could talk privately and then have him return when they finish their chat. It is still inexcusable.

People can't wander in and out without rhyme or reason, as they did in *Idiot's Delight*. Entrances and exits are as much a part of a play's framework as are windows and doors in a house. When someone comes in or goes out he must do so *of necessity. His action must help the development of the conflict and be part of the character in the process of revealing himself.*

7. Why Are Some Bad Plays Successful?

Would-be playwrights often wonder whether it pays to study, to go out of their way to write a good play, when plays which aren't worth the paper they're written on make millions. What is behind these "successes"?

Let's look at one of these phenomenal successes: *Abie's Irish Rose*. The play, despite its obvious shortcomings, had a premise, conflict, and orchestration. The author dealt with people whom the audience knew very well from life and from vaudeville. The weak characterization was balanced by this knowledge. The audience thought the characters were real, although they were only familiar. Then, too, the audience was familiar with the religious problem involved and felt the superiority which comes from being "in the know." This was intensified by the climax. The audience was fascinated by the problem of which religion would claim the child. They took sides, mentally. When the climax—and the twins—came, both sides were satisfied. Everyone was happy: parents, grandparents, audience. We think the play succeeded because the audience took an active part in making the characters live.

Tobacco Road is a different case entirely. No doubt *Tobacco Road* is a very bad play—but it has characters. We not only see them—we smell them. Their sexual depravity, their animal existence, capture the imagination. The audience looks at them as it would at the man in the moon, if he were displayed on the stage. The most poverty-stricken New York audience feels that its fate is incomparably better than that of the Lesters. Here again is the feeling of superiority. The emphasis on the distortion of the characters obscures the vital issue: social readjustment. *The play has characters, but no growth, which is why it is static, making its chief purpose the exposition of these brutal, demoralized creatures.* The audience, mesmerized, flocked to see these animals who some-how resembled human beings.

Noel Coward's extraordinary success arises from the fact that *his* horrors are much more pleasant: who will sleep with whom? Will he get her, will she get him? Remember that Coward came after the World War, with his wealthy English sophisticates, oh so eager to get everything they could from life. A war-weary audience, surfeited with blood and death, gobbled up his farces. The lines seemed witty because they helped the audience to forget the battering the world had taken. Coward, and many like him, came and lulled the shocked audience into numbed relaxation. His reception to-day would be tepid.

Kaufman and Hart's *You Can't Take It with You* wasn't a bad play; it wasn't a play at all. It was a cleverly con-structed vaudeville piece, with a premise. The characters were amusing caricatures, no one of them related to the other. Each had his own hobbies, needs, peculiarities. The authors had a task in fitting them all into one scheme. It succeeded because it presented a moral lesson which every-one could approve without following; and it made the au-dience laugh, which was its purpose.

Do not forget that most plays which become successful are *not* terrible. Plays like Sherwood's *Abe Lincoln in Illinois,* Kingsley's *Dead End,* Housman's *Victoria Regina,* Bein's *Let Freedom Ring,* Carroll's *Shadow and Substance, The White Steed,* and Lillian Hellman's *Watch on the Rhine* merit seri-ous consideration, despite their obvious shortcomings. And they are based on character. The really bad plays had some-thing strange about them, something outlandish which put them over *despite* their flaws. Tridimensional characters would have made them even more successful.

If you are interested not in writing good plays, but in making money quickly, there's no hope for you. Not only won't you write a good play; you won't make any money.

We've seen hundreds of young playwrights work feverishly at half-digested plays, under the impression that producers were waiting in line to snatch them away. And we've seen them disheartened when their manuscripts finished the rounds. Even in business, those men go ahead who give the customer more than he expected. If a play is written for the sole purpose of making money, it will lack sincerity. Sincerity cannot be manufactured, cannot be injected into a play when you do not feel it.

We suggest that you write something you really believe in. And, for heaven's sake, don't hurry. Play with your manuscript, enjoy yourself. Watch your characters grow. Draw characters who live in society, whose actions are forced by necessity, and you will find that you've bettered your chances of selling the play. Don't write for the producers or for the public. Write for yourself.

8. Melodrama

Now for a word about the difference between drama and melodrama. In a melodrama the transition is faulty or entirely lacking. Conflict is overemphasized. The characters move with lightning speed from one emotional peak to another—the result of their one-dimensionality. The ruthless killer, pursued by the police, suddenly stops to help a blind man cross the street. This is phony on the surface. It is unlikely that a man running for his life would even see the blind man, let alone help him. And, certainly, a ruthless killer would be more likely to shoot the blind man for getting in his way than to make kindly gestures toward him. Transition must be present to make even a three-dimensional character believable. The lack of transition produces melodrama.

9. On Genius

Let us examine the definition of genius:

Genius is a transcendent capacity for taking trouble first of all.
                                —*Frederick the Great* by THOMAS CARLYLE

We agree.

From a maximum of observations the talented man draws a minimum of conclusions, whereas the genius draws a maximum of conclusions from a minimum of observations.
                                —*General Types of Superior Men* by OSIAS L. SCHWARZ

We still agree.

Genius is the happy result of a combination of many circumstances.
                                —*The Study of British Genius* by HAVELOCK ELLIS

We shall come back to this later.

Genius: the mental endowment peculiar to an individual; that disposition or aptitude of mind which qualifies a person for a certain kind of action or special success in a given pursuit; extraordinary mental superiority; unusual power of invention or origination of any kind.
                                —*Webster's International Dictionary.*

The "genius" can learn more rapidly than the average man. He is inventive, he does things which do not occur to the ordinary person. He is mentally superior. But none of this means that a "genius" can be truly a genius without serious study. We have seen mediocre men outstrip geniuses who were too lazy to learn and to work. Call these latter "half-talented," the fact remains that the world is littered with them. Why do these mental giants remain obscure? Why do so many of them die in misery? Look at their background, at their physiology, and you will see the answer.

Many never have the chance to go to school (poverty). Others fall in with bad company and their extraordinary talent is wasted on useless or evil ventures (environment). There are others who study, but have a false picture of the subject under consideration (education). You may claim that a real genius always finds a way to succeed, but that is not so. Every man who has succeeded, despite adversity, has been given the chance to do so.

The extraordinary mental power of a genius is not necessarily strong enough to create his success. First, one must have a start, an opportunity to deepen one's knowledge in a chosen profession. A genius has the ability to work at something longer and with more patience than any other man.

The implication here is that geniuses are not rare. *Webster's* says that genius is the "disposition or aptitude of mind which qualifies a person for a certain kind of action." This "certain kind of action" is denied to many who have the aptitude. What is this type of man supposed to do if he is forced by circumstance to engage in action which is exactly opposite to the "certain kind" for which he is qualified? In this case the word "certain" possesses the utmost importance. A genius is a genius in only one thing, "a certain kind of action." There are exceptions, of course: Leonardo da Vinci, Goethe—perhaps a dozen rare men in the history of mankind who excelled in more than one field. But we are speaking of the others: men like Shakespeare, Darwin, Socrates, Jesus—each a genius in one field. Shakespeare had the good fortune to be connected with the theater, though that connection was lowly at first. Darwin came from a well-to-do family which considered him a failure despite his college degree. And then he was taken on an expedition to the tropics, and the mind which was "qualified for a certain kind of action" had a chance to display its aptitude. And so with the others.

No one is born to be great. We love one certain subject

more than any other. Given all we need to further our knowledge, we are likely to make great strides; forced to do something else, we become disgruntled, discouraged, and end in
failure.

We call an apple tree an apple tree before it bears fruit.
But isn't it different with genius? May it not be said that a
genius is a man who has accomplished something, and not
a man who has almost accomplished something, or who
wanted to accomplish something and has been thwarted in
some way?

Not if the quotations above make sense. Not one speaks
of accomplishment. They merely try to analyze the material
of which genius is made. Success is a happy combination of
circumstances which help a genius to expand, to produce the
thing for which he has infinite capacity. That is the meaning
of the quotation from Havelock Ellis. Nor is there anything
wrong with Osias L. Schwarz' observation that "a genius
draws a maximum of conclusions from a minimum of observations." But does this hold true only if the genius happens
to succeed? Does an apple seed cease to be an apple seed if
it is carried to the heart of the city and deposited on hard
asphalt, to be crushed by heavy wheels? No, it remains an
apple seed anywhere, although it is denied the chance to
fulfill its destiny.

A fish lays millions of eggs, of which only one in a thousand
live. Out of those hatched, only a few reach maturity. Yet
every single egg was a bona fide fish egg, having all the attributes necessary for the development of a fish. They were
eaten by other fishes, and those eggs which survived owe
nothing to their clever insight. Ellis is right: "Genius is the
happy result of a combination of *many* circumstances." Sur-
vival is one of these, inheritance another. Freedom from poverty is a third, although ninety-nine per cent of the known
geniuses mankind has produced came from the lower depths,
fighting every inch of the way toward the sun. Poverty could

not keep down these few but it does keep down thousands of others who would have succeeded had "the happy result of a combination of many circumstances" favored them.

As for all the braggarts who run around, beating their collective chests and claiming to be geniuses, we cannot dismiss them out of hand. They are offensive, but some of them may be the genuine article.

It is said that all murderers claim innocence, insist that they were railroaded. Criminal history teaches us that some of them really were innocent, despite the derisive laughter of those who "knew better."

Yet we must not forget one important attribute of the genius: an infinite capacity for taking pains in the field where his interest lies. The majority of braggarts spend too much time boasting to have much left for painstaking work.

We cannot emphasize too strongly the fact that, although geniuses are equipped with uncommon powers of mental absorption in their particular field, many of them are *never given the chance* to approach the thing in which they are interested. Remember that most geniuses are one-sided, and you will see that in an alien atmosphere they have no chance to develop.

A fish out of water is a dead fish, and a genius kept from his art is often a simpleton.

10. What Is Art?—A Dialogue

QUESTION: Would you say that one individual embodies within himself good and bad, noble and depraved thoughts? Is it in every character to be a martyr or a betrayer?

ANSWER: Yes. A man not only represents himself and his race, but mankind. His physical development is, on a small scale, the same as that of mankind as a whole. Starting in his mother's womb, he goes through all the metamorphoses man underwent from the time he started his long journey from the protoplasm. And the same laws apply to man and to nations. Man fumbles through mist, over unchartered roads, as the tribes, groups, and races once did. In his childhood, in his adolescence, in his manhood, he experiences the same tribulations, the same battle for happiness that nations experience. One man is the replica of all. His weakness is our weakness, his greatness our greatness.

QUESTION: Must I be my brother's keeper? I don't want to be responsible for his actions. I am an individual.

ANSWER: So is a cat, or a rat, or a lion, or an insect. Take termites. They have females who do nothing but lay eggs. They have workers, guards, soldiers, and other individuals whose sole function is to be stomach for the community. They chew the fibrous raw food, digest it, and only then is it fit to eat. All the members of this insect society flock to this individual, this living stomach, and suck the prepared food to sustain life. Each has a specific function, each is indispensable. Destroy any branch of this well-organized society and all of it will perish. Separately, they cannot live, any more than a nerve, a lung, or a liver can live without the rest of the body. Put together, these individual insects make an individual—society. It is the same with your body. Every part functions separately; co-ordinated all these separate parts make one man. And a man, too, is only part of the whole: mankind. Every individual in a termite family has its own personality, just as every leg, arm, or lung has its own characteristics, but it is still only part of the whole. It is for this reason that you had best be your brother's keeper; he and you are parts of the same whole, and his misfortune necessarily affects you.

QUESTION: If one man is the possessor of all the attributes of mankind, what chance have I of depicting him in totality?

ANSWER: It isn't an easy task, by any means, but your character drawing is good only to the extent that you approach this "totality." Only by aiming for perfection in art can you succeed, even if you never reach your goal.

QUESTION: What is art, anyway?

ANSWER: Art is, in a microscopic form, the perfection not only of mankind but of the universe.

QUESTION: Universe? Aren't you going a little bit too far?

ANSWER: The protozoon is composed of the same elements as the human body cells. The conglomeration of millions of these cells, the body, contains the same elements as each individual cell. Each cell has its specific function in the society of cells which is the body, just as each man has his function in the society of men which is the world. And just as the cell represents the man, and the man the society, so does the society represent the universe. The universe is governed by the same general laws that govern human society. The compound, the mechanism, the action and reaction are the same.

When a dramatist creates one perfect human being he reproduces not only the man but the society to which he belongs, and that society is only an atom of the universe. So the art which created the man reflects the universe.

QUESTION: The "perfection" you speak of might become a slavish imitation of nature, or an enumeration of the contents of a human being.

ANSWER: Are you afraid of knowledge? Does it hurt an engineer to know the science of mathematics, the law of gravity, the tension of the material with which he is working? He must know everything that pertains to his profession, before we can ask whether he possesses the talent to produce a bridge which will be a joy to look at, as well as a useful construction. *His knowledge of the exact sciences does not exclude imagination, taste, grace in actual execution.* The same holds true of playwrights. Some men may obey all the laws of technique, yet their work is lifeless. Others—

and there have been such men—utilize all the available
data, obey the rules which they find valid, and fuse this
information with their emotions. They lift their knowledge
on the wings of their imagination, and create a masterwork.

11. When You Write a Play

Be sure to formulate a *premise*.

Your next step will be to choose the *pivotal character*,
who will force the conflict. If your premise happens to be
"Jealousy destroys itself and the object of its love," the man
or the woman who will be jealous should be inherent in
your premise. The pivotal character must be a person who
will go all the way to avenge his injury, whether it be real
or imaginary.

The next step will be to line up the other characters. But
these characters have to be *orchestrated*.

The *unity of opposites* must be binding.

Be careful to select the correct *point of attack*. It must be
the turning point in the life of one or more of your characters.

Every point of attack starts with *conflict*. But don't forget
that there are four kinds of conflict: static, jumping, foreshadowing and slowly rising. You want only rising and foreshadowing conflict.

No conflict can rise without *perpetual exposition,* which is
transition.

Rising conflict, the product of exposition and transition,
will ensure *growth*.

Characters who are in conflict will go from one pole to
another—like *hate* to *love*—which will create *crisis*.

If growth continues in a steady rise, *climax* will follow
crisis.

The aftermath of climax is the *conclusion*.

Be sure that the unity of opposites is so strong that the

characters will not weaken or quit the play in the middle. Every character has to have something at stake, as, for example, property, health, future, honor, life. The stronger the unity of opposites, the more certain you can be that your characters will prove your premise.

Dialogue is as important as any other part of a play. Every word uttered should stem from the characters involved.

Brander Matthews and his pupil, Clayton Hamilton (in his *The Theory of the Theatre*), insist that a play can be judged only in a theater, before an audience.

Why? We grant that it is easier to see life in a flesh-and-blood actor than on a printed page, but why should that be the *only* way of recognizing it? What a waste of material there would be if builders used the same method of judgment. Houses would be built in actual size and material before the prospective owners decided whether or not they wanted that kind of house at all; bridges would span rivers before the government could tell the engineer whether or not his bridge was acceptable.

A play can be judged before it reaches actual production. First, the premise must be discernible from the beginning. We have a right to know in what direction the author is leading us. The characters, growing out of the premise, necessarily identify themselves with the aim of the play. They will prove the premise through conflict. The play must start with conflict, which rises steadily until it reaches the climax. The characters must be so well drawn that, whether or not the author has declared their individual backgrounds, we can make out accurate case histories for each of them.

If we know the composition of character and conflict, we should know what to expect from any play we read.

Between attack and counterattack, between conflict and conflict, is transition, holding them together as mortar holds bricks. We will look for transition as we look for characters, and if we do not find it we will know why the play progresses by leaps and bounds, instead of growing naturally. And if we find too much exposition, we know that the play will be static.

If we read a play in which the author discusses his characters in minute detail without starting his conflict, we know he is ignorant of the ABC of dramatic technique. When the characters are obscure, the dialogue rambling and confused, we need no production to determine whether the play is good or bad. It must be bad.

A play should start at a turning point in the life of one of the characters. We can see, after the first few pages, whether or not this is the case in the play. Similarly, we can learn, in our first few minutes of reading, whether or not the characters are orchestrated. No production is necessary to tell us these things.

The dialogue must stem from the character, not the author. It must indicate the character's background, personality, and occupation.

If we read a play which is cluttered up with people who do nothing to further the ultimate aim, who are there simply for comic relief or variety, we know that the play is fundamentally bad.

To say that we must have a production to judge a play is, to say the least, begging the question. It shows an ignorance of the fundamentals of playwriting and the need of an outside stimulus to make a vital decision.

True, many a good play has been ruined by bad casting or an inadequate production. By the same token, many a good actor has been thrown out of gear by a bad play. Give Fritz Kreisler, the great fiddler, a Woolworth violin to play on and see what happens to his artistry. Reverse this and give a person who is ignorant of music, a Stradivarius. The results will be disastrous.

We are not unaware of the answers we may expect. "Art," certain men have said—and will say—"is not an exact science, such as bridge building or architecture. Art is governed by moods, emotions, personal approach. It is subjective. You cannot tell a creator what formula to use when he is inspired. He uses what his spark of inspiration points out. There is no set rule."

Every man writes as he pleases, of course, but there are certain rules he must follow. He is forced, for instance, to use a writing instrument and something on which to write. These may be ancient or modern, but you cannot do without them. There are rules of grammar, and even those writers who employ the stream-of-consciousness technique are observing certain rules of construction. As a matter of fact, a writer like James Joyce sets up rules far more rigid than the average writer is able to follow. So, in playwriting, there is no conflict between personal approach and basic rules. If you know the principles, you will be a better craftsman and artist.

It wasn't a simple task to learn the alphabet. Do you remember when a "B" looked dangerously like a "D," the "W" like a drunken "M"? It was difficult to make sense of what you read when you were so occupied in watching the letters themselves. Did you imagine there would be a time when you could write without stopping to think that there was such a thing as "A" or "W"?

12. *How to Get Ideas*

Whenever you have a fully rounded character who wants something very badly, you have a play. You don't need to think about situations. This militant character creates his own situations.

On page 130 of "The Art of Dramatic Writing" is a list of abstract nouns. Read it.

You must first remember that *art is not the mirror of life, but the essence of life.* When you take a basic emotion, you might as well emphasize that emotion or trait.

If you write about *love,* you should write about *great love.* If you write about *ambition,* it should be *ruthless ambition.* If you choose *affection,* it should be *possessive affection.* They generate conflict.

Let us take the simple noun "affection." Affection was the motivating emotion in *The Silver Cord.* This is not an ordinary affection or love. It is a selfish, over-possessive love of a mother for her sons.

It is not enough, of course, to know that a person is possessive; you must know *why.* Generally, *insecurity* and the desire to be *important* are the fundamental reasons for all exaggerated traits. The mother wanted to be the center of interest, instead of permitting the women her sons brought home to have their natural importance.

Affection is a basic human need, but affection, overdone, can be crushing. If you wish to escape from excessive affection, you find it almost impossible. After all, what can you do about a person who loves you? If you are a decent fellow you are bound hand and foot to the one who loves you, although you may wish to be a million miles away.

Drama must not only entertain but teach as well. The dramatist interprets man to man. When you see a character on the stage causing unhappiness, you might recognize yourself in the same act.

Let us go back to page 130 and take the word *abusive.*

Abusive: An abusive character suggests one who doesn't realize his own shortcomings. He is shortsighted, narrow-minded, lacks imagination. He tries to do the right thing but can't. He doesn't know how. This man will inevitably force you into conflict.

Accuracy: Can you imagine living with a man who is accurate twenty-four hours a day? Such a person must be abhorrent; his perfection demands perfection from everyone else. You must note that it is impossible for a human being to be one hundred per cent perfect, but of course the perfectionist is not aware that he is an ordinary human being too, who also has faults and weaknesses. And so, such an individual *must create conflict* with the people around him.

Conceit: A conceited person (not one with the ordinary amount of vanity, but an ego-maniac) must necessarily be hypersensitive. He is quick to take offense at any real or imaginary criticism. He is so terribly insecure that he must bloat his own ego constantly to reassure himself of his own importance. Such a person must always have things done his own way, and it takes adroit handling and diplomacy on the part of others to accomplish anything with him. Such a person must inevitably lose the love, affection, and respect of those around him—and therein lies your play.

Dignity: An overdignified person (remember we must exaggerate this trait) should be good material for a comedy. Your character would be pompous, a stuffed shirt, mortally afraid of stepping out of line the least bit. Put him in conflict with a person who is just his opposite, make sure to create a *unity of opposites* between them so that they cannot separate, and you have a hilarious play.

Wisdom: Too much of anything, even a good thing, can be very irritating. Your wise person who is always right, who never makes a mistake, can make the ordinary mortals around him feel very stupid and unimportant. Even though they admire and respect him, the fact that he makes them feel inferior instead of making them love him, which he desires most, makes them rebellious, resentful, and angry.

There are people who start things and never finish them. There are the eternal procrastinators, who will always do the thing *tomorrow*. There are the impulsive, who act first and think later. There are, in fact, thousands of human traits, emotions, qualities which can create characters for a play, a novel, or a story.

You can take an honest-to-goodness person, a real individual, but with one of these traits exaggerated. You will have so many characters for plays or novels that it would take more than a lifetime to write half of them.

Every word on page 130 represents a character. Let us see again: *Clumsy:* You needn't take a stock character, a "dolt." Take a woman who is beautiful and clever, but clumsy.

Anybody who overdoes something is good material for a story. Remember: Your characters must be militant. A militant person is bound to expose himself through conflict. The secret of happiness is the understanding that no one is perfect; we must always realize that there is room for improvement for all of us.

You must feel your story deeply—in fact, it should be a conviction of yours. You must never be afraid of conflict in your writing, because if you do, you will have a dull and static piece of work in whatever form you happen to use.

Even a good idea at best is only an idea. What is an idea anyway? A seed. Nothing more, nothing less. It's up to you to do something with it. Any idea without three-dimensional characters isn't worth a plugged nickel.

Allegory or any imaginative conceptions are good only if they represent human aspirations.

To get an idea for any type of writing is the easiest thing. Look around you and be observant. Be observant and you will be forced to admit that the world is an inexhaustible pastry shop and you are permitted to choose from the delicacies the tastiest bits for yourself.

Here are a few characters you might try your strength on. I

tried to find out what goes into a character. The following are types. You should make living people out of them.

What Makes a Ruthless Character?
   (A ruthless character is not necessarily bad.)

Something vital at stake
Can't turn back
Determination
Ambition
Desperation
Cornered—trapped
Fear of failure
Truthfulness (Militant)
Great Passion (Love, Hate, Greediness, Jealousy, etc.)
Fixation on goal
Self-centeredness
One-track mind
Farsightedness
Revengefulness
Opportunism
Greediness
Vindictiveness

   This is a composite of many ruthless characters. Pick your own.

A Shiftless Man suggests:

Day-dreaming
Lack of initiative
Laziness
One who has no objective in life
Devil-may-care

A Clever Man suggests:

Shrewdness
Quick-wittedness

Persuasiveness
Observation
Intellect
Talent
A good psychologist

A Bored Person suggests:

Slow-wittedness
Egotist
Self-centeredness
Worry or fear
Lacking in insight, observation or intelligence
Blasé

Ill-Temper suggests:

Inconsiderate
Irascible
Nervous
Lacking in understanding
Impatient
Frustrated
Hating
Sick
Self-willed
Spoiled
Quick-witted

Anti-Social suggests:

Cruel
Rapacious
Inhibited
Inhuman
Ruthless
Anything which hurts mankind
Bigoted
Perverse

Love of Luxury suggests:

Self-indulgent
Sensuousness
Self-expression
Great hunger for beauty
Decadence
Over-indulgence

Self-Righteousness suggests:

Hypercritical
Bigoted
Fearful
Insecure
Inferiority complex
Domineering
Egotistical
Selfishness
Gossipy
Fighter

Mistrustfulness suggests

Insecurity
Guilt complex
Skepticism
Sneakiness
Vanity
Cowardly
Unhappy
No power of evaluation
Inferiority complex

Bigotry suggests:

Narrow, judging others according to a single set of standards
Conformist, righteous, unimaginative
Cold anger

Propriety
Inflexibility
Reactionary
Formal
Courteous
Polite
Zealot (A zealot is bigoted, but a bigot is not necessarily a zealot
   yet.)
Guilt complex

A Cad suggests:

Egotist
Unscrupulous
Selfishness
Envy
Insecurity
Vanity
Fickle
Loneliness
Inferiority complex
Lacks ability to do something creative

Ambition suggests:

Rebellion against the status quo
Desire for recognition
Desire to justify existence
Dissatisfaction
Craving for change
Craving for fame
Escape from frustration
Craving for power
Jealousy
Control
Desire to entertain
Self-fulfillment

Ruthlessness
Desire to be secure

You can go on from here, finding new, exciting ideas *ad
infinitum,* with only old age or lack of imagination to stop
you.

QUESTION: I suppose all these examples will help me get ideas,
    but . . . I don't understand why people, characters, must
    be the epitome of their type. People in real life are not
    necessarily mad, or as extreme as the characters you say we
    should look for. Following your suggestions, I am afraid,
    our stories or plays will be more exaggerated than normal.
ANSWER: Were you ever so angry that people thought you were
    losing your mind? No? Other people were. Were you ever
    so jealous that you thought you couldn't bear it any longer?
    If your answer happens to be "no," you are a rare one, and
    you'll never understand the motivation of a mere human.

There are times when the most normal people feel that the
most dreadful revenge is an absolute necessity. A writer is
supposed to catch people in crisis. Unfortunately, in crisis,
no-one behaves normally. If you ever went through a cataclysm,
you will understand not only the mental state of your
characters in crisis, but the motivation, the tortuous road
your people wandered through to their sad or triumphant
destination.

When we read in a story or see on the stage, cruelty, vio-
lence, abuse, and all the passion that will transform men into
beasts, we really see ourselves as we were, perhaps only for
moments, sometime in our lives.

No doubt about it, there were ruthless characters throughout history, and they were the ones who influenced, for better
or for worse, the destiny of man.

Let me emphasize it once more—it is worth your while to

write about people only when they have arrived at a turning point in their lives. Their example will become a warning or an inspiration for us.

13. Conclusion

If you cannot differentiate between fragrances, you cannot be a perfume maker; if you have no legs, you cannot be a runner. If you are tone-deaf, you cannot be a musician.

To become a playwright you should be a man with imagination and common sense, to begin with. You must be observant. You must never be satisfied with superficial knowledge. You must have patience to search for causes. You must have a sense of balance and good taste. You should know economy, psychology, physiology, sociology. You can learn these things with patience and hard work—and if you do not learn them, no approach will make a good playwright of you. We are often astonished at how glibly people decide to be writers or playwrights. It takes about three years of apprenticeship to make a good shoemaker; the same is true of carpentry or any other skill. Why should playwriting—one of the hardest professions in the world—be acquired overnight, without serious study? The dialectical approach will help those who have prepared for this work. It will also help the beginner by giving him a clear picture of the obstacles in his path and of the road he must travel if he is to achieve his ambitions.

APPENDICES

A

PLAYS ANALYZED

◇◇

1. Tartuffe

A Comedy in Three Acts
by
Molière

SYNOPSIS

TARTUFFE is a penniless scoundrel who, under the guise of fervent religiousness, endears himself to Orgon, a wealthy ex-officer of the King's Guard.

Once established in Orgon's home, Tartuffe proceeds to reshape the family, endeavoring to lead them from their social life to a puritan one. His designs are really on Orgon's lovely young wife. He induces Orgon to make his daughter Mariane break her engagement with her beloved Valère, saying she needs a pious man to lead her on to a pure life. This infuriates Damis, Orgon's son, who is in love with Valère's sister.

Damis catches Tartuffe making advances to his stepmother. He tells his father in front of Tartuffe, but his father does not believe him. Orgon insists that Damis apologize to Tartuffe. Damis refuses, and his father, enraged, disowns him.

In the midst of this family turmoil, Orgon entrusts Tartuffe with a box containing important information given him by an exiled friend. The revealing of this information means treason for Orgon and probably death to his friend.

Orgon believes so implicitly in Tartuffe's honesty and

piousness that he deeds his whole estate to his care to manage for him. To make the bond even closer, he wishes Tartuffe to marry his daughter.

Orgon's wife, Elmire, embittered by these goings-on, entices Tartuffe to make love to her while Orgon is hidden, but within hearing. Disillusioned and outraged, Orgon orders Tartuffe from his house, forgetting he has placed his estate in Tartuffe's power.

The next day, Tartuffe uses his legal right to force Orgon and his family from their house and is ready to take possession himself. He has also brought to the king the box containing the secrets of Orgon's friend. The king recognizes Tartuffe as a scoundrel who has committed crimes in another city. Tartuffe is imprisoned. In view of Orgon's loyal services in the army, the king returns the box unopened.

ANALYSIS

Premise

He who digs a pit for others falls into it himself.

Pivotal Character

Tartuffe forces the conflict.

Characters

Orgon is wealthy, an ex-officer, dominating, stupid, blindly trusting, religious—but why? We never find out.

Tartuffe is a finely drawn character, suave, soft-spoken, a clever psychologist. Yet we see only two sides of him—physical and psychological. His background remains a blank. We would like to know how he came to pursue a life of chicanery, possessing, as he does, many abilities. Not knowing his background, we see the results, but not the causes which make him what he is.

Elmire is a good stepmother and wife. She is much younger

than her husband. Did she marry him for love, money, or both? What makes her such a model wife when she is sadly neglected by Orgon whose every thought is for Tartuffe?

Damis, the son, is lively and headstrong. We look to him to help the situation. He succeeds only in angering his father and being ordered from the house. He goes, leaving behind a man who he knows will play havoc with his family. He returns when bidden, and all is forgiven. He does not grow.

Mariane, the daughter, is a weak young girl, too spineless even to fight for the man she loves. Although in that era, strict obedience to parental wishes was the rule, at least she could have put up a violent protest for her love. When confronted with her father's wishes, she remains dumb and remonstrates but weakly. She has to be pushed by her servant, first to make up with her sweetheart, second, to defy her father quietly; and we have little confidence in her. She is completely static, prompted by her maid.

Cléante, Elmire's brother, contributes nothing to the play. He merely tries to dissuade Orgon from his blind trust, as everyone does. He goes out in the first act, having accomplished nothing, returns to persuade Tartuffe to make Orgon forgive his son. He does not succeed, and we see him again in the third act, for some additional dialogue. He does not help the conflict.

Mme Pernelle, Orgon's mother, is used for exposition at the opening of the play, returns at the end for a bit of comedy; contributes nothing.

Valère, we see as Mariane's sweetheart, and he, at least, is determined that she will marry no one but himself. He would not be needed had Mariane the strength of character to fight for her love. She has not, so Valère is necessary to the play to fight for her. As an extra bit to prove how blind Orgon's trust was, he shows he is a true friend when he offers to help Orgon escape the police. By this time, however, Orgon realizes his mistake fully, and this act of friendship proves what he already knows.

Dorine is the saucy, outspoken, sharp servant who is necessary to the play because, without her, some of the characters would hardly move. In spite of her wit, she is a stale character, for we like to see human beings move of their own accord —which they do, when they are tridimensional and in the proper conflict.

Orchestration

Orgon and Tartuffe are well matched, the one simple and trusting, and the other crafty. Elmire, who is no match for her husband, is yet able to outwit Tartuffe. Damis and Valère are similar in type and hardly able to stand up against the pivotal character. Mariane is colorless, ready to be blown down by the slightest wind. Dorine, the maid, alone stands out fearless and shrewd. She is best orchestrated with Tartuffe, and we should have liked to see them in dual conflict.

Unity of Opposites

This is the strong bond which keeps the play together. The love affairs of Mariane and Damis are vital to them. The wish of the whole family to continue life undisturbed by Tartuffe's interference keeps each from leaving the scene. Of course, Elmire can leave her husband, and we don't see why she doesn't because we know so little about her, but possibly love or money holds her. We assume that one or both are the reason.

Point of Attack

The crisis comes in the middle of the first act when Orgon decides to break his daughter's engagement to Valère and marry her to Tartuffe. The first half of the act is pure exposition, therefore the proper point of attack should have been Orgon's decision, when something would have been at stake.

Conflict

The first half of the first act is static. After that, the play moves toward the crisis and climax, coming in waves, but the conflicts are not powerful enough, because the opposition to Orgon by his family is in protest, rather than open defiance.

Transition

In the case of Orgon and Tartuffe, the transitions are good. In Act Two, Tartuffe deftly goes from piousness to an open declaration of his love and desire for Elmire, still attempting to cloak his passion in the light of a heavenly emotion.

Orgon gradually goes deeper and deeper in his blindness regarding Tartuffe.

Throughout the play, barring a few exceptions, transitions are excellently handled.

Growth

Tartuffe goes from deception to humiliation. Orgon, from trust to disillusionment.

The rest of the family do not grow. They start by hating Tartuffe and end still hating him. The only growth is in Elmire, the young wife. She goes from passiveness to the actual action of tricking Tartuffe. Yet in emotion she remains the same. We would expect her to grow in stature in the eyes of her husband, or else to change from an obedient to an independent wife. She does not.

Crisis

When Elmire induces Orgon to hide while she plans to expose Tartuffe.

Climax

Tartuffe is exposed. He orders Orgon and family to move.

Resolution

At the end, Tartuffe, on the verge of a perfect triumph, is recognized by the king as a rogue who, under an assumed name, had committed a series of crimes in Lyons, and Tartuffe is arrested.

The premise is: "He who digs a pit for others falls into it himself." The king's interference was a weak device to prove the premise.

Dialogue

Good, especially in the case of Tartuffe and Orgon. Both of the men's speeches can be identified with the characters.

2. Ghosts

by

Henrik Ibsen

SYNOPSIS

Mrs. Alving has built an orphanage which is to be dedicated to her late husband. Mr. Manders, the priest, comes to consult her on whether they should insure the building. To do so would be to imply that they have no faith in God; to fail to insure it would be a risk. Mrs. Alving agrees to do without the insurance, but says she will not make good the loss should the building burn.

Mrs. Alving's son Oswald has been home from abroad for two days. He is an artist who has lived away from his parents since he was seven. He holds, from experience, the same ideas his mother has arrived at from books—ideas Mr. Manders finds dreadful, since they deal with truth rather than with duty.

Engstrand, a disreputable old man, is the father of Regina, a servant in the Alving home who has been educated by Mrs. Alving. Engstrand wishes to open an inn for sailors and wants Regina to work in it. But she has other ideas, having to do with Oswald. He has appealed to the priest to force Regina to do her duty. Mrs. Alving refuses to let Regina go.

Mr. Manders feels it is his duty to talk to Mrs. Alving about her behavior. He reminds her that she was a bad wife, that after only one year of marriage she left her husband and ran to him for love and protection. And he is proud that he sent her back. And now, he says, he finds her agreeing with her son's wicked belief that there can be decency outside of the church's sanction. Mrs. Alving lets him in on the secret of her married life. She reveals to him that her husband never mended his ways, that his good reputation was her doing. He had been syphilitic when they married and he became more profligate as the years passed. The culmination was his seduction of the housemaid—Regina's mother. Captain Alving, not Engstrand, is the girl's father. It is on the heels of this revelation that Oswald and Regina are heard in the dining room, ghosts of their parents.

Oswald tells his mother that he is ill. He went to a doctor who revealed the nature of his illness and remarked that "the sins of the fathers are visited upon the children." Oswald, knowing only the glorious picture of his father that his mother's letters have given him, is furious. He believes that his own mild pleasures are to blame and is tortured by the thought that he has brought about his own disaster. He wants to marry Regina and make what is left of his life happy.

Mrs. Alving decides to tell both the young people the truth, but is interrupted by the news that the orphanage is on fire. When the place is in ruins, we learn that Manders and Engstrand have been praying in the carpentry shop near by. Engstrand insists that the priest dropped a burning wick into some shavings. Manders is terrified at what this will do to his position in the community, and Engstrand seizes the opportunity for blackmail. He will take the blame for the fire if Manders will see that the money remaining from the Captain's private fortune helps him build his inn. Manders agrees gladly.

Mrs. Alving tells her story, and Regina is angry. She feels she should have been educated and raised as Alving's daughter. She is glad that she did not marry Oswald, now that she knows he is ill, and she decides to cast her lot with Engstrand. Alone with his mother, Oswald reveals the final horror. He is not merely ill. He is suffering from softening of the brain, and as time goes by, he will be more and more helpless. He knew that Regina would kill him if that were the case, and he wants his mother to promise to do the same. She refuses, horrified, as he shows her the morphia tablets. But with the coming of dawn he has another attack and sits blindly asking for the sun. She realizes that death would be merciful and searches for the tablets.

ANALYSIS

Premise

The sins of the fathers are visited on the children.

Pivotal Character

Manders.

Characters

Mrs. Alving is a well-rounded character. We are able to trace her life from the dutiful daughter she was to the frightened young wife, who in spite of great misery, forsook freedom to follow her "duty." From then on her one purpose in life was to save her husband's reputation for the sake of her son. In the intervening years her mind developed so alarmingly that she easily cast aside the flimsy fabric of her earlier beliefs. She is a strong, determined woman.

Mr. Manders is revealed in his piousness and refusal to let truth touch him. He has been guided by his conscience all his life, but when his reputation is threatened, he, the torch-bearer of truth, allows himself to be corrupted by necessity.

Oswald is intelligent, artistic, a believer in reality. He has lived his life as he saw fit and judged it from what he had seen, not from what he had heard.

Regina is a robust, coarse, shrewd girl.

Engstrand is a clever liar with innate shrewdness. He is not malicious, however—in fact, he has a certain charm.

All characters are tridimensional.

Orchestration

They are well orchestrated: Mrs. Alving's clear mind against Manders' blind piousness, Engstrand's wiliness in opposition with Manders' great trust, Regina's independence and shrewdness matched with Engstrand's shrewdness. Oswald is intelligent and determined.

Unity of Opposites

Mrs. Alving and Mr. Manders are united to keep alive the legend of Captain Alving's nobleness of character and at all costs to prevent a marriage between Regina and Oswald, as they are half sister and brother.

Point of Attack

The first act is a splendid example of exposition through conflicts, rising in a steady crescendo.

Conflict

The conflicts are on a low plane at the beginning, but rise in an ascending scale. The main issue is foreshadowed temporarily in the scene between Manders and Engstrand, then rises to a tense pitch at the end of Act Two. Act Three starts on a low plane again, though still tense, and then rises with full strength until the resolution.

Transition

There are superb transitions between the conflicts, from the very beginning—at first leading up to Mrs. Alving's revelation that her husband never mended his ways, and that Regina is his illegitimate child, then in the scene between Manders and Engstrand, and again Oswald's decision to marry Regina. Finally Manders is persuaded to let Engstrand take the blame for the orphanage fire; persuaded in a manner which would ordinarily be revolting to his standards. Transition in Act Three rises steadily to the very climax.

Growth

Mrs. Alving perceives her folly in hiding her husband's true nature all those years.

Mr. Manders grows from strict morality to saving his reputation with a lie.

Oswald goes from normality to insanity.

Regina from a dutiful girl, who has regard for Mrs. Alving and Oswald, to one who deserts them.

Engstrand succeeds in getting the money for his sailors' home.

Crisis

Oswald's decision to marry Regina.

Climax

Oswald's mental breakdown.

Resolution

Mrs. Alving's search for the morphia tablets.

Dialogue

Good; all lines come from the personality of the characters.

3. *Brass Ankle*

A Play in Three Acts

by

Du Bose Heyward

SYNOPSIS

Act 1

Larry is the leading citizen of Rivertown, a growing town in the deep South.

As the play opens, Larry, his wife Ruth, and a neighbor are discussing the Jackson case, a family of white people who have Negro blood. Larry is the leading antagonist in the case. He believes one drop of Negro blood makes a person black and unfit to associate with white people.

Ruth is in the last hours of her pregnancy, and Larry is debating whether or not to go to the school-board meeting that night. They are discussing the Jacksons there. He goes.

Later, Larry is waiting for his child to be born. His friends and neighbors are keeping him company. They drink and talk about the Jacksons. They, and the town reverend, are determined to oust these people. They discuss liquor and other things. Larry is determined that his daughter June will have a fine education and become a lady like her mother. At last the doctor comes out to talk to Larry, and the men leave.

The doctor tells him the story of the Brass Ankles, white people with Negro blood, and how tragic it is to segregate them. Most white people who have Negro blood do not know they have it. They think themselves white. Once in a while there is a throwback, to the horror of the parents.

He reveals that Ruth's mother was a mulatto. Ruth did not know this, and always thought she was a pure white. Now she has given birth to a child who has Negro blood.

Act 2

Larry has refused to come into Ruth's room during her recovery. She is frightened.

The doctor tries to penetrate Larry's dazed condition, forcing him to make plans, to send Ruth and the child away to a large city or deep country, where their affairs will be private.

Larry reacts sharply, saying he has no intention of keeping the baby. Later he gets a grip on himself and explains he would leave immediately with his family, but if he does, the neighbors will be suspicious. The main tragedy is his daughter, June. Now she will be considered a Negro. Larry is desperate.

The doctor leaves and Ruth comes out. At first Larry shrinks back. Then they cling to each other desperately. They start to make plans. Larry wants to leave town quietly. Then they can leave the baby in somebody else's care, come back, and tell the townsfolk the baby fell ill and died.

Ruth will not give up her baby whom she loves and who needs her more than June and Larry do.

She makes plans to return to her own people. Larry and June must remain where they are. She goes into her room to pack.

Two of Larry's friends come in, drunk. In a nervous frenzy, Larry tries to get rid of them with a gun. Just then the reverend and a neighbor come in. Larry is wary and suspicious.

The talk again turns to the Jackson case. A society of Negro helpers in the North have taken an interest in the case and sent an investigator down. The case will probably go to court.

Larry is desperate. This means lawyers and detectives coming down, and his secret will be exposed.

He tries to convince them to drop the case.

Mr. Jackson comes in and pleads with Larry to be left alone. Larry tries to make the others vote his way. They insist that the fight to rid the community of mixed blood must go on.

Since Larry has pleaded Jackson's case, the others become suspicious. They taunt him, and Larry, in a rage, shows them his son. They shun him immediately.

Act 3

Ruth, dressed for traveling, awakens Larry from a drunken slumber. She is leaving. Later, Larry can divorce her.

Then Larry makes her understand for the first time what she, in her excitement, had overlooked—that now June is also a Negro.

Ruth cannot have her daughter go through life with a stigma upon her. Calling the neighbors, she tells them the doctor was lying. She is really white, but had had an affair with a Negro servant who had died a short time ago.

In a frenzy, Larry kills her and the baby, as she had expected.

4. Mourning Becomes Electra

Home-coming, The First Part of a Trilogy

by

Eugene O'Neill

SYNOPSIS

Through the conversation of a group of people who are looking at the Mannon home in New England, we learn that the Mannons are a wealthy family and that the father and son of the family are away fighting in the Civil War while the mother and daughter are at home. We learn that the towns-folk dislike Christine, the mother, because of her foreign descent. We hear about the family skeleton: the marriage of Ezra Mannon's uncle David to a French-Canuck nurse girl he had "gotten into trouble."

The action reveals that Lavinia, the daughter, hates her mother as much as she loves her father and brother. She has followed Christine on a trip into New York, and verified her suspicion that Christine and Adam Brant are lovers. Brant is a sea captain who has been coming to the house, ostensibly to court Lavinia. Lavinia suspects further that Brant is the son of the once-betrayed nurse girl. She tricks him into admitting this, and they quarrel. She then turns upon her mother, telling her that unless she gives up Brant and becomes a dutiful wife to Ezra, Lavinia will let her father know of the affair and have Brant blacklisted on all sailing vessels. Christine consents, having revealed to Lavinia her loathing of her husband.

Christine forces Brant into a plan for poisoning Ezra. He is to buy the poison and she will administer it.

Ezra returns and is petted by his daughter. She does not wish to leave her parents alone together, but is forced to. Ezra tells Christine of his love for her, and of his desire to begin a better life. She tries to keep him quiet by denying any coldness on her part or obstacle between them.

Later that night they are talking in their room. Ezra is hurt because Christine's attitude to him is dutiful but cold. She is deliberately cruel, revealing her affair with Brant. Ezra has a heart attack, and Christine forces the poison on him. He calls Lavinia, who bursts into the room. Ezra says, "She's guilty—not medicine!" before he dies in her arms.

Lavinia questions Christine, who collapses. The daughter finds the pellets of poison on the floor, and her suspicions turn into certainty. She cries to her dead father for guidance as the curtain falls.

5. *Dinner at Eight*

A Drama in Three Acts
by
George S. Kaufman and Edna Ferber

SYNOPSIS

Millicent Jordan, a society woman, plans a dinner for Lord and Lady Ferncliffe, social lions. She invites Dr. and Mrs. Talbot, Dan and Kitty Packard, Carlotta Vance, and Larry Renault. Her daughter, Paula, is not included.

The play deals with the individual tragedies of the guests, the host, Paula, and the domestic staff of the Jordan home. We discover that Oliver Jordan's business is shaky and that Dan Packard, whom he hopes will help him, intends to cheat him. We learn too that Oliver has a heart condition which leaves him a short while to live.

Dan Packard, in his turn, is being betrayed by his cheap little wife. He gives her luxuries, but neglects her, and she busies herself with Dr. Talbot. In a quarrel, she lets Dan know she is unfaithful, but does not disclose Talbot's name. Dan cannot divorce her without her letting the world in on his crooked deals. Kitty's maid, Tina, begins to blackmail her in return for not revealing the lover's identity.

Dr. Talbot is tired of Kitty. He is a man who has had many affairs, despite his love for his wife. Lucy Talbot is aware of his infidelity, but still hopes for his regeneration.

Carlotta Vance, a once-famous actress, owns stock in Jordan's company and promises not to sell it. She does, however, to one of Packard's stooge representatives.

Larry Renault, invited as extra man for Carlotta, is a motion-picture actor on the road down. He and Paula Jordan have been lovers, although neither her parents nor her fiancé are aware that they are even acquainted. His arrogance and drunkenness lead him into a quarrel with his agent, Max

Kane, who has been trying to get him a stage role. Kane reveals what his pity has led him to hide all along: that Renault is a has-been, a laughingstock to producers. Realizing that he now has neither fame nor money, Larry commits suicide.

Ricci, the Jordan chauffeur, and Gustave, the butler, both desire Dora, the maid. Dora prefers Gustave, but insists on marriage. They are married the day before the dinner. When Ricci learns of this he assaults Gustave, and the men fight. Both are bruised. Then, on the afternoon of the party, Carlotta Vance mentions in the presence of both butler and maid that she knows Gustave's wife and three children.

During the battle between the servants, the lobster aspic has been spoiled. Millicent learns of this and of the fact that both men have had "accidents" just before the dinner. The Ferncliffes go off to Florida, leaving Millicent hysterical. At this point Paula attempts to tell her mother of her love for Renault (she does not know of his death), and Oliver tries to beg off from the after-dinner party because he does not feel well. Millicent turns on them in rage because they dare disturb her with their petty problems when she has only eight for dinner. She invites her sister and brother-in-law to fill in, and, promptly at eight, the group adjourns for dinner.

6. Idiot's Delight

by

Robert Sherwood

SYNOPSIS

A group of people are in a hotel in what used to be the Austrian Alps but is now part of Italy. There is threat of war in the air, and Italian officers are constantly in evidence. Those at the hotel include Dr. Waldersee, a German scientist who is eager to get to Zurich where he can continue his experiments to find a cure for cancer; Mr. and Mrs. Cherry, English honeymooners; Quillery, a French radical-socialist; Harry Van, a vaudevillian, and Les Blondes, his troupe of six girls; Achille Weber, a munitions magnate; and his traveling companion, Irene.

Harry Van is sure that Irene is a girl he once slept with in Omaha. She denies it. Quillery rushes about shouting against war as practiced by England, France, Italy—any country. Then, when war between France and Italy is declared, Quillery turns violently patriotic and anti-Italian. He is shot. The passports arrive in the morning, and everyone but Irene is able to leave. The Doctor is going back to Germany, bitter about his own humanitarian work and the world. Mr. Cherry is going back to enlist in the war. Weber is going to further his militaristic moneymaking enterprises. But because Irene has finally told him how much she despises his activities, he has arranged for her to be left behind.

Irene admits to Harry that she is the girl he knew, and he returns to the hotel when the others have gone. The whole world has gone to war "against the little people," as Irene says. She and Harry sing and play *Onward, Christian Soldiers* while the battle rages above and around them.

7. Black Pit

by

Albert Maltz

SYNOPSIS

Joe Kovarsky, a miner who has been railroaded to jail for union activity on charges of dynamiting a tipple, returns home to find his wife, Iola, being supported by his sister, Mary, and his brother-in-law, Tony Lakavitch. Tony has been crippled in a mine accident and receives hardly enough compensation to support even himself and his family. Joe, though blacklisted, tries to find jobs under a different name, but is always exposed and fired. He returns to his sister's home and is offered a stool pigeon's job by Prescott, his wife's brother who is superintendent of the mine. Terrified by his wife's pregnancy, he accepts.

Joe's buddy, Anetsky, is injured by a flareup of gas in a "hot" room in the mine, and Joe is ordered to spread a rumor that Anetsky was injured in a condemned room where he had no right to be. When the men meet to discuss calling a strike, Joe lies about Anetsky's injury and delays the action.

Then Prescott forces Joe to reveal the name of the organizer. He threatens Joe with eviction, and exposure as a stool pigeon, and the miner accedes to his demands.

When the baby is born, Joe throws a party and is flatly accused of being a stoolie, since he is known to be on good terms with the mine superintendent—and because the organizer was beaten up and fired the day before.

Tony, his brother-in-law, now sees only one solution for Joe. He must leave the mine and make a new life for himself. His wife and baby will remain until he can support them. Just as Joe leaves we hear the sounds of the men going out on strike.

B

HOW TO MARKET YOUR PLAY

PLAYWRITING is not confined to a select group. Is there an intelligent person who, sometime in his life, did not feel the urge to write a poem, short story, novel, or play? Playwriting lures thousands yearly. They recognize it as a veritable gold mine.

Dwight Deere Wiman, the well-known Broadway theatrical producer, wrote an informative article in the *New York Herald Tribune* on Sunday, April 6, 1941, called "Advice: Producer to Playwright." He tells some interesting facts, important and encouraging to the young playwright.

"Each year," Mr. Wiman writes, "thousands of tired businessmen and work-weary housewives find sublimation for their restlessness and frustration in playwriting. Next to watching professional baseball it's America's greatest pastime, indoors or out. And please don't get me wrong. I have no intention of making any belittling remarks or sounds of derision. It's a healthy sign, I think, and ever so often it actually turns up someone who, by all the rules and regulations, should know nothing at all about the snide intricacies of the theater.

"*Three-cornered Moon* and *Another Language* were written by housewives, and *Journey's End*, which was penned by a humble insurance broker, are samples of the inherent democracy of dramaturgical endeavor. Even for those less skillful scribblers whose works never pass our first line of defense, the Broadway play broker, the very act of putting their dreams into words, sentences, and scenes is an inexpensive and harmless way of escaping reality and must have an indeterminable value as occupational therapy."

Producers are constantly on the lookout for plays, writes Mr. Wiman, contrary to the popular misconception that managers do not read the play of an unknown. Plays are needed, and your play will be read if it is presented in the proper physical form. This means no gaudy cover, no illustrations of characters, costumes, or stage settings, no lengthy description of characters. See that your play leaves your hands in this condition or have it groomed by a professional theatrical stenographer.

Use plain white regulation typewriter paper, faultless single-space typing on one side of the page, and wide margins all around. The play should run from about ninety to one hundred twenty pages in length, and the whole thing should be bound simply and neatly by three removable fasteners in a durable manuscript cover. The first page next to the cover is left blank, the next page carries only the title and your name, and perhaps at the lower right-hand corner the author's copyright. The next page lists the characters in the order of their appearance.

You list only the names of your characters, give no lengthy descriptions as to marital status, how many times divorced, in love with whom at the present time, and the like. This extra writing is the mark of the novice and creates a negative impression upon whoever reads it. On this page list only name and number of characters. Everything else about them should be exposed in the course of your play.

The synopsis of scenes follows, the play's divisions into acts and scenes, and a brief statement of time and place of each scene. Then one blank page (you might give the title again, but that is all), and then Act I, Scene I. Make a brief word picture of the setting, writing it on the right-hand half of the page. Tell who is on stage at the rise of the curtain and begin the dialogue. All speeches are written underneath the character's name, never beside it. Have as few stage instructions as possible, and make them brief.

Now you are ready to send it out.

It is impractical to mail copies of your script to producers individually, not because it will not be read, but because you won't know when they will get around to it. Sometimes they take three weeks, three months, sometimes even more. You therefore need an agent. Ninety-five per cent of the plays produced have been sold, controlled, and managed by play brokers. Your agent knows the theater and knows who wants what. His fee is ten per cent of the playwright's royalties.

If the agent is a member of the group known as the Incorporated Society of Authors' Representatives, you must send ten dollars with your manuscript. This is a reading fee. You can be assured that your play will be carefully read by a competent person who knows the current market. You will get a complete criticism and analysis of your script and suggestions to make it more salable.

Now, if the agent thinks your work has a chance, you will be invited to sign a contract, appointing him as your exclusive representative for several years. If he doesn't take your play, you will receive the criticism and an explanation as to why he isn't taking it. If he feels you have future possibilities, he might not charge for further readings.

If your agent has taken your play and found a producer, you should enroll in the Dramatists' Guild. This is an affiliate of the Authors' League of America and performs a real service for the playwright. The dues are ten dollars a year, and the dramatist is assured of legal advice and protection against "negligent" managers. The Guild has an effective closed shop, and every producer is obliged to meet its requirements. The Guild contract demands the following: at the signing of the contracts, the author must receive one hundred dollars a month until the play is produced. If, after six months, the production is not ready, the author receives one hundred and fifty dollars a month. If, at the end of a year, there is still no production, the contract is null and void, and the author retains the money advanced to him. After the *première* the author cannot accept less than a minimum of five per cent on the first five-thousand-dollar box-office gross, seven and one-half per cent of the next two thousand dollars, and ten per cent on all over seven thousand dollars. The average weekly return is about five hundred dollars for the author, and occasionally a smash hit pays fifteen hundred weekly.

Good luck to you.

C

PLAYS THAT HAVE MADE MONEY

◇◇◇

(DERIVED from *Billboard Index, Variety,* and the Burns Mantle *Year Book.*)

Royalties are on a sliding scale. As already stated, the first $5000 gross pays five per cent to the author, the next $2000 pays seven and one-half per cent, and after that, straight ten per cent. Not all weekly earnings were recorded; we were therefore forced to choose between the highest and the lowest figures, and we chose the lowest. The gross might have been somewhat higher or lower. The earnings on the road and the motion-picture prices are not included.

PLAY	NUMBER OF PERFORMANCES	APPROXIMATE GROSS
Life with Father	2718	$8,850,221
Tobacco Road	3200	4,500,000
Abie's Irish Rose	2532	3,500,000
Sailor Beware	500	562,000
Personal Appearance	501	1,500,000
Children's Hour	691	700,000
Bury the Dead	97	60,000
Victoria Regina	517	1,500,000
Pride and Prejudice	219	300,000
Moon Over Mulberry Street	300	130,000
Idiot's Delight	299	750,000
Boy Meets Girl	669	1,600,000
Dead End	687	1,500,000
Three Men on a Horse	835	1,125,000

PLAY	NUMBER OF PERFORMANCES	APPROXIMATE GROSS
Tovarich	356	$500,000
Brother Rat	577	1,200,000
The Women	654	1,630,000
Yes, My Darling Daughter	404	700,000
Having Wonderful Time	370	500,000
Room Service	500	875,000
Louisiana Purchase	651	1,686,000
You Can't Take It with You	837	1,300,000
The Green Pastures	640	1,625,000
Strictly Dishonorable	557	975,000
Street Scene	601	1,500,000
Bird in Hand	500	675,000
The New Moon	508	2,000,000
Show Boat	572	2,750,000
Good News	551	2,000,000
Sunny	517	2,500,000
Broadway	603	1,800,000
Is Zat So?	618	1,160,000
The Student Prince	608	1,350,000
The Vagabond King	511	1,625,000
The Show-off	571	1,000,000
Seventh Heaven	704	1,312,000
First Year	760	790,000
Shuffle Along	504	625,000
Blossom Time	592	1,425,000
Kiki	600	1,275,000
The Bat	867	1,083,000
Sally	570	2,076,000
Peg o' My Heart	692	1,115,000
Irene	670	1,260,000
East Is West	680	1,470,000
Lightnin'	1291	1,800,000

Several seasons ago Congressional Copyright Committee hearings at Washington disclosed actual figures on playwrights' royalties:

The Trial of Mary Dugan	$312,650
The Green Hat	236,411
Beggar on Horseback	79,760
Potash and Perlmutter	378,285
The Shanghai Gesture	128,000
The Constant Wife	122,226
The Cardboard Lover	43,722
Road to Rome	133,365
Command to Love	86,678
Little Jessie James	118,067
The Spider	114,922
Funny Face	135,000
Animal Crackers	109,070
Follow Thru	251,167
Hold Everything	135,000
My Maryland	182,445
Friendly Enemies	232,331
Let Us Be Gay	52,180
Green Pastures	296,563

D

HOLLYWOOD BUYS

◇◇◇

Warner Bros.

The Voice of the Turtle	$500,000
(plus 15 per cent of film's box-office receipts)	
Life With Father	500,000
(plus film royalties)	
Chicken Every Sunday	250,000
The Visitor	150,000
The Two Mrs. Carrolls	200,000
A Connecticut Yankee	100,000
Three Men on a Horse	75,000
Big-Hearted Herbert	35,000
Heat Lightening	20,000

Paramount

Dear Ruth	$450,000
Feature for June	50,000
(unproduced play)	
Oh, Brother	75,000
(plus percentage of box-office receipts until $200,000 is reached)	
The Odds on Mrs. Oakley	15,000
Claudia	187,000
Lady in the Dark	285,000
Accent on Youth	60,000
Louisiana Purchase	150,000
Anything Goes	85,000
Sailor Beware	75,000

She Loves Me Not	60,000
Double Door	55,000
Her Master's Voice	37,500
Murder at the Vanities	35,000
Pursuit of Happiness	30,000

Metro-Goldwyn-Mayer

On the Town	$100,000
(against ceiling price of $250,000)	
Violet	100,000
Soldier's Wife	75,000
(plus 15 per cent of weekly receipts from stage presentation until $200,000 is reached)	
But Not Goodbye	20,000
Merrily We Roll Along	76,000
Ah, Wilderness!	75,000
No More Ladies	50,000
Men in White	45,000
The Shining Hour	45,000
All Good Americans	18,000

R-K-O

I Remember Mama	$150,000
The Fabulous Invalid	35,000
Sex Is Out	10,000
(unproduced play)	
The American Way	250,000
Roberta	65,000
Wednesday's Child	25,000
By Your Leave	20,000

United Artists

One Touch of Venus	$150,000
(against 10 per cent of distributor's gross)	
Decision	25,000

Twentieth Century-Fox
Junior Miss $400,000

Samuel Bronston
Ten Little Indians $150,000
   (plus percentage)

Hal Wallis
The Searching Wind $200,000
   (plus royalties)
The Perfect Marriage   35,000

Columbia
My Sister Eileen $225,000

Sam Goldwyn
The Little Foxes $100,000

Fox
The Farmer Takes a Wife $ 65,000

According to the Dramatists' Guild, the authors receive sixty per cent of the movie sale.

INDEX

◇◇◇

Leeuwenhoek, Anton van, 87
Lessing, Gotthold Ephraim, xxi, 61,
  91, 249
Let Freedom Ring (Bein), 254
Let Us Be Gay (Coward), 301
Life with Father (Lindsay and
  Crouse), 299, 302
Lightnin', 300
Liliom (Molnar), 148, 184
Lion Is in the Street, A (Langley), 28
Little Foxes, The (Hellman), 13, 249,
  304
Little Jesse James, 301
Louisiana Purchase, 300, 302

Macbeth (Shakespeare), 3-4, 20, 35,
  62, 109, 152, 184, 233
Madach, Imre, 184
Made for Each Other (Swerling), 59
Maginn, 72
Malevinsky, Moses L., 6, 7
Maltz, Albert, 28, 115, 214, 217, 293
Mamba's Daughters (Heyward), 62
March's *Thesaurus*, 234
Marlowe, Christopher, 184
Matisse, Henri, 247
Matthews, Brander, 2, 263
Maupassant, Guy de, xvii, 27
Medea (Euripides), 36, 61, 95, 96
Men in White (Kingsley), 303
Merchant of Venice (Shakespeare), 61
Merrily We Roll Along (Kaufman and
  Hart), 303
Michael, Jeanne, 238
Millikan, Robert, 250
Molière (Jean Baptiste Poquelin), 15,
  23, 25, 27, 61, 99, 166, 168, 249, 277
Molnar, Ferenc, 148
Moon Over Mulberry Street, 299
Mourning Becomes Electra (O'Neill),
  72-73, 77-78, 109, 152, 169-170, 289-
  290
Murder at the Vanities, 303
My Heart's in the Highlands (Sa-
  royan), 246-247
My Maryland, 301
My Sister Eileen (Fields and Chodo-
  rov), 304

Nathan the Wise (Lessing), 61
New Moon, The, 300
New York Herald Tribune, 295
New York Times, The, 13, 59, 83
Night Music (Odets), 12
No More Ladies (Thomas), 303
No Time for Comedy (Behrman), 249

Notebooks (Leonardo), 193
Nugent, Frank S., 59

O'Casey, Sean, 5
Odds on Mrs. Oakley, The, 302
Odets, Clifford, 12, 181, 239, 244
Oedipus Rex (Sophocles), 95-96, 97-98,
  108, 164, 183
Oh, Brother, 302
O. Henry, xvii
On the Town, 303
Once in a Lifetime (Kaufman and
  Hart), 184
One Touch of Venus, 303
O'Neill, Eugene, 72, 76, 77-78, 169, 170,
  211, 289
Othello (Shakespeare), 4, 35, 61, 106,
  113, 152, 154, 186, 242

Paradise Lost (Odets), 244-245
Peg o' My Heart, 300
Perfect Marriage, The, 304
Personal Appearance, 299
Peters, 213
Philadelphia Story, The (Barry), 11-
  12
Picasso, Pablo, 247
Plato, 50
*Playmaking, a Manual of Craftsman-
  ship* (Archer), 87, 88, 93, 237
Poetics (Aristotle), 92-93
Potash and Perlmutter, 301
Pride and Prejudice (Jerome), 299
Pride of the Marines (Maltz), 28-29
Professor Mamlock, 62, 75
Prologue to Glory (Conkle), 62
Pursuit of Happiness (Langner), 303
Pygmalion (Shaw), 118

Raphaelson, Samson, 12
Riders to the Sea (Synge, 244
Road to Rome (Sherwood), 301
Roberta, 303
Rodin, François Auguste, 30-31
Romeo and Juliet (Shakespeare), 2-3,
  11, 12, 15, 70-72, 94, 99, 109, 190,
  218-219
Room Service (Boretz and Murray),
  184, 300
Roughead, William, 13

Sailor Beware, 299, 302
Sally, 300
Sardou, Victorien, 92
Saroyan, William, 12, 73, 246
Savory, Gerald, 182

ABOUT THE AUTHOR

On the wall of one of Hollywood's major studios there is a placard that reads: "It isn't enough to be a Hungarian; you must have talent, too." Lajos Egri has both these requirements for success in the theater. He was born fifty years ago in the city of Eger in Hungary and he wrote his first three-act play at the age of ten. Since then he has worked as a newspaperman, as the editor of an illustrated Hungarian weekly and, for more than twenty-five years, he has written and directed plays in Hungary and the United States. Mr. Egri is an advanced student of biology, bio-chemistry, and human nature. He is the director of the Egri School of Writing, in New York.

CPSIA information can be obtained at www.ICGtesting.com
Printed in the USA
LVOW06*0008290715

447972LV00013B/131/P